Home
#ITS COMPLICATED

LIBERTY
Publishing

Published by Liberty Publishing
C-16, Sector 31-A Mehran Town Extension,
Korangi Industrial Area, Karachi – Pakistan

1 2 3 4 5 6 7 8 9 10

This book is a work of non-fiction. The views and opinions expressed in this book are the authors' own and the facts are as reported by them, and the publishers are not in any way liable for the same.

ISBN **978-627-7626-49-5**

Printed and bound in Pakistan

For Ammi, my lynchpin and biggest cheerleader

You taught us so much, except how to go on without you ...

But as you would always say ...

Que sera, sera, whatever will be, will be

Forever missed

Table of Contents

Table of Contents

Introduction

Home
#itscomplicated

The local saying goes that everyone from Pakistan has a story.

But Pakistan is deeply misunderstood, not least of all because people are experiencing, absorbing and judging it from mostly behind breaking news screens. Other times, we are viewed through the lens of storytellers from the West—which can be legitimate—but also makes me wonder when we will start telling some of our own stories. As a country steeped in storytelling, narrative-building is not new to us. Nonetheless, the growth of Pakistani literary voices appears to have stagnated over the last few decades. Reading culture among Pakistanis has spiralled downwards and young writers receive little institutional support. In the wake of this, the vibrant legacy of storytellers our country has produced over the decades also seems to have been written off.

The Home #itscomplicated anthology is an attempt to get Pakistanis to read and tell stories again. That, along with an attempt to address the undiminished, nagging question, "But where are you really from?" which Pakistanis tackle at almost every juncture: at immigration, from strangers next to you on airplanes, at job interviews, for pre-school applications, in classrooms and boardrooms, you name it. I usually respond with, "I'm from Pakistan." But what about my daughters, born and residing in Abu Dhabi, not fluent in Urdu or any other Pakistani regional language, yet holding Pakistani passports?

Which brings me to the title of this anthology, inspired in part by Omar Shahid Hamid's poignant letter to his son in this collection:

Home

#itscomplicated

The underlying sentiment emerging from the essays in this anthology can be distilled into a contemporary hashtag which Hamid astutely conveys towards the end of his essay: #itscomplicated. For most of our contributors, that's precisely what home is—a complex web, messy, evolving, evocative; profoundly emotional but simultaneously instilling a sense of stoicism, from time to time.

As someone who has been living outside Pakistan for over a decade, the romanticised notion of a physical home prevailed in my mind for the longest time. Home was a neatly bounded, clearly recallable, fleshed-out entity offering me a passport, even if that came with few other rights. The obsession with academic notions of belonging and intransience, and the assumed stability they're supposed to bring, obstructed my ability to find harmony in the idea of home as defined by family, a space in the mind, wandering and changing contours, but whose nucleus remains the same. It has taken me time, courage and tenacity to acknowledge the possibility of a liminal home and life; of the fluid spaces between here and there and sometimes nowhere, and to realise that within those, too, you can begin to forge familiarity, alliances and attachments. Several pieces in this anthology remain nestled in these "in-between" crevices and are open to hybridity's abundance without undermining the heightened fears accompanying such impermanence.

The politics of home and identity is fraught with debates about who gets to write about what and where. This can become dreadfully limiting. It also makes curation for an anthology such as this fairly tricky. What goes in? What gets filtered? How do you broaden your reach beyond those we see as authors or book writers? Who is Pakistani enough to be part of the collection? Are those living outside Pakistan equally entitled to speak it and call it home? Do names of places matter?

But stories are everywhere and waiting to be told. With that in mind, we have intentionally aimed for a collection where the essence of people's voices, lives, stories and backstories take centre-stage, instead of the other boxes of identity that require ticking. We have included writers within and beyond Pakistan's borders and no one was required to pass a litmus test for how Pakistani they are to write about their relationship with Pakistan!

One of the most rewarding aspects of curating this anthology is the time and effort dedicated to including such a versatile range of voices. Writers across ages are included and we attempted to go beyond those we see as "book writers." We've prioritised "voice" and the urgency of a story that needs to be heard. We have contributors from medicine, arts, acting, screenwriting and theatre, scientists, security and intelligence personnel, academics, entrepreneurs, home-makers, and students among others. This anthology is a rich stew of influences and ingredients.

How we received contributions is equally thrilling. An "all-encompassing" collection of voices would be a myth; however, we mindfully employed a two-pronged approach in gathering submissions for this anthology. We invited specific individuals whose voices we deemed a compelling fit, asking them to contribute to the anthology. Simultaneously—and this is the part I am particularly enthusiastic about—we put out a public call for submissions to those who might be interested in writing about home. I am delighted to report that multiple entries made it to our final anthology through the latter route. In fact, we unearthed some extraordinary voices we might have completely missed had our curation process been invite-only. I find this a significant step towards nurturing fresh voices, especially young Pakistani writers, who hold a novel perspective and write dynamically. It also strips away at the bureaucracy, barriers and enigma surrounding the publishing industry. I firmly believe that in order to elevate Pakistani writing communities, we must make room and let others in. For our stories to be heard around the world, for those stories to go beyond a singular elite or privileged lens, and for a culture of reading to be revived, we cannot be territorial and stay trapped in a literary clique. The echo chamber must break open.

I hope our readers, too, are a versatile bunch; those with visceral and raw connections to Pakistan as well as those who want to discover this place and its people beyond the headlines. These essays encapsulate the writers' embodied and jugular experiences—in a sense, they pull you backstage and show you the BTS life of a Pakistani. There is rage and violence, loss and pathos, everyday contention, intimacy and frustrations, wounded attachments, frolicking, festivities and growth, comic relief, spiritedness and tiny moments of redemption. There is no underplaying the giant, combustible, often seething place that is Pakistan, but equally, these stories are not devoid of love, longing and hope.

A lot is said in this anthology, but a lot also remains unsaid—this book, therefore, aims to be an act of co-creation. As Mohsin Hamid and Arundhati Roy put it, this is an invitation for a dance or a walk, welcoming readers to solve the pieces of the puzzle alongside us. The words on the page, lifted by imagination, should do the trick. The hope is that each of these pieces entertains you and moves you to reflect, feel, creatively imagine and interpret Pakistan.

If reigniting a reading culture among Pakistanis is the quest, access is crucial. Despite working in academia, I always struggle with texts that limit their readership due to the inaccessibility of their writing style. As I have mentioned in multiple book talks and interviews, for any stories I tell—be they fiction, journalistic writing or personal non-fiction—my rule of thumb is always that my mother should be able to understand it. Ever since she passed away in April 2024, I've slightly altered that mantra to imagine whether she would have made sense of it. It's not as accurate as when she would actually read it, but it comes close. I don't subscribe to the view that writing which remains within ivory towers is richer than more lucid and reachable forms of storytelling. This anthology has been curated to be accessible, inclusive and inspiring.

With the internet, diverse Pakistani voices are telling their stories in different formats, languages and tonalities. This is helping to popularise and preserve narratives that might have otherwise been lost. Social media, despite much destruction, is helping to build reading communities. Book clubs, bookstagram, online bookstores and libraries, virtual book talks and festivals are all aiding in the revival of a reading culture among Pakistanis. However, there is still a long way to go, not least because we are simultaneously battling the instant gratification of technology. To try and raise a reader today seems much harder than when my parents were bringing us up, but we must persist. I hope this anthology moves the needle on revitalising readership in Pakistan.

Whilst curating this anthology, I was also acutely aware that as Pakistanis, we have inherited a stellar legacy of stories that don't always get their due. As a girl growing up in Pakistan, I was surrounded by ideas of the "saving mission." Cinema and literature seemed to suggest that our species required redemption by the West. The white woman must bear the burden of enlightenment, speaking and writing on behalf of her less informed counterparts. Brands of feminism emerged in the country which sought to copy-paste Western forms of women's empowerment without reflecting on local syntax and necessities. Anyone who critiqued this type of feminism was instantly chastised and cancelled. We seem to have forgotten the pioneering feminists and storytellers born out of Pakistan itself, men and women trailblazing issues of gender and sexuality, body politics, identity and the state through their stories. They were writing with tremendous bravery, well before we needed the West to save us.

This "firebrand feminism first" approach has also neglected the stories of our mothers, grandmothers and great-grandmothers, all feminists in their own rights—resilient, if not rebellious.

Unfortunately, we only clock and relate to stories of a "strong woman" which are offering a caricature of some Western ideal. Much is lost in this desire to mirror the West, ignoring forms of agency that may be quieter, yet equally compelling.

The bottom-line is: we don't need saving; what we do need is to start telling our own stories. This will allow us to showcase what home looks and feels like without incessantly apologising for it or becoming the pastiche of another place or people. This anthology was ideated, curated, and is now sent into the world with these hopes in mind. I hope you find it a complex, witty and thought-provoking read.

Over to you, reader!

A Letter To My Son
Omar Shahid Hamid

I have often thought about how I would explain my relationship with Pakistan to my son. He has already spent almost half of his young life abroad and is likely, if current indicators continue heading the way they are for the country, to spend just a handful more years here until he departs for good. Therefore, the country and its myriad issues will never grip him the same way they grip me. He will never live or die on the successes and failures of this nation. It will be an abstract concept for him, a place where he spent some time, an ethnicity he identifies with, a memory bank of images: parents, grandmothers, dogs, school, friends, various chachas and bajis who helped him. At least, that's what I think. Children have a unique way of confounding their parents. Perhaps my father thought I would be the same. I doubt he would have imagined in a million years that I would end up doing the things I have done. But whatever my son chooses to do in his life, it struck me that I had never given him a context for the strange bond that ties me to this place. He will never understand me fully without that context. So, this is for him.

To say my relationship with Pakistan is a complex one, would be an understatement. I hate it. I love it. I can't stand being here anymore. I can't bear to be away. It is where my heart has been broken. It is where I found love. It is where I have witnessed the power of humanity; it is where I have seen the heart of evil.

Pakistan is a series of snapshots in my head. Standing in my father's office in the City courts, banging on his desk like a ten-year-old brat, thinking that my banging, like that of a judge's gavel, would silence the arguing maulvis sitting in front, forgetting that Pops was the District Magistrate and not I. The searing heat of April, sweating through the cheap material of the Ghani Sons school uniform, standing under the old school bell, covered in *rang*, saying goodbye to friends on the last day of school as if we were going off to war. Eating Karachi Broast and Mezban's toxic chicken corn soup at 2 a.m. on a chilly December night, discussing relationships that never were, pining over unrequited love and loss, and imagining that we would never face greater tragedy than this—how wrong we were! Silly boys pretending to play gangsters, angered over some imagined slight (a friend's girlfriend had dumped him and moved on to someone else; hardly a *Casus belli*, but at the time, grounds for the high school equivalent of the Russian invasion of Ukraine), driven to fistfighting ridiculously dressed in silk shirts. Who the fuck goes to a fistfight dressed in a baggy silk shirt? There was no fight, there never was, and the end result was the inevitable 'compro' conducted by some older, more menacing individual with shady connections. I have often wondered since, what those 'compro' specialists must have thought of us, a bunch of 'burger boys' pretending to be tough guys in a city that was already beginning to descend into its long night.

Shards of glass, shining like diamonds on the asphalt road on a July morning when the humidity was already making Karachi an outdoor sauna at 8:30 in the morning; and a white 1992 Honda Civic standing at the corner of the road at an odd angle, shredded with bullet holes like a piece of Swiss cheese. My father's body, lying inert on the back seat and me peering in, not quite understanding that he was gone forever. The Karachi police chief, a Deputy Inspector General and a commander of a police force of twenty thousand men, sitting in our dining room that evening and informing my mother that she should not register a case against the city's most powerful political party or the head of that party, who sat thousands of miles away in suburban Edgware and controlled the city via satellite phone. The DIG's argument was that he would not be able to guarantee our security, and my mother replying to him by saying she was going to do exactly that, and it was his job to protect us. Throngs of people coming to our house in the days and months that followed, many, including close family members and lifelong friends, admonishing us for having taken such a 'position', and distancing themselves. A much smaller number, people I will never forget, standing by us and commending our bravery.

Almost two years later, a strange man, dressed in a starched white shalwar kameez, plops his Glock pistol on to a glass tabletop in my grandfather's house, twirls his handlebar moustache, and starts explaining to my mother and I how he arrested my father's killer. Mistaking the shock on our faces for disbelief, he offers to take me to his police station to interrogate the suspect myself. And I, having never come across anyone as unique as this odd policeman called Chaudhry Aslam, slowly shake my head, mortified at the thought of having to go to a police station. To partake in an *interrogation*. Who does that? A thousand interrogations and hundreds of police stations later, I look back and laugh at the stupidity of my twenty-year-old self.

It is hard to imagine at that moment, in the winter of 1998-99, but that odd policeman with the handlebar moustache will become one of my closest friends. In a strange way, he will inspire me to become a cop. Not a civil servant, fretting over summaries and memoranda, not a policeman, with the whiff of social order enforced by a Constable Carthorse-like figure implicit in that term, but a cop, with all the gritty and hard edges that implies.

For those of us born in the last quarter of the 20th century, we have become used to drawing arbitrary lines to divide history. Perhaps the seminal events of the last century were so monumental that all that came after them seemed irrevocably altered. Thus, we have the world before the Great War to end all Wars, and the world after; the world before the first brick was dislodged from the Berlin Wall, and everything after; the world before the planes hit the Twin Towers on September 11th, and the one after; the world before Covid and post-Covid. On a winter's day in December 1998, a chance encounter, will become my inflection point. It will divide my life into the world before and the world after. It will lead me down a path that I could never have imagined travelling, and it will take me to people and places that were once so far removed from my life that they would not only be unrecognisable but unfathomable to the me that existed before the crossroads in my personal history.

It will create a thread that will lead, first of all, to an examination that nobody thinks I will be able to pass. It will take me out of the cocoon of Pakistan in which I had existed for the first two decades of my life, and immerse me in a much more real version of Pakistan. Ultimately, for good or bad, it will bind me more tightly to this country than ever before.

But it is a journey that will begin with tragedy. An August day in 2001, and my first day on the job as a trainee police officer. In the sweltering heat is a smell I will never forget. Cartons of orange juice concentrate gone bad and a rotting corpse in an abandoned house, and the faint whiff of bitter almonds which I will later learn to recognise as a sign of cyanide. At the centre of it is a young man. He's my contemporary, he is someone with whom I share common friends. He had been in England at the same time as me, studied law as I had, and returned home, flying in the face of compelling arguments not to do so, just as I had. It's a strange sensation, staring at the decomposing body of someone so young, so full of life—so like me—and thinking: *there*, but for the grace of God, *was me*.

It's also the first time I find myself on the other side. As I stand outside this young man's house, I watch his friends and relatives grieve. I see them trying to absorb the shock not only of a life brutally cut short well before its time, but also at the gruesome and fantastic details of the crime. The victim, kidnapped and killed by his next door neighbour, who continued to demand a ransom even after murdering the young man. A murder so bizarre it belongs in the pages of the

Old Testament, and certainly not at the turn of the 21st century. I look at them—many of them friends and acquaintances of mine as well crying and wringing their hands at the injustice of this country. Just as I had done with many of them when my father was murdered, just four years prior. But I realise that something has changed. I will never wring my hands again. Instead of helplessly cursing the injustice of this world and those that perpetrate it, I will become someone who hunts those perpetrators. I will not always succeed. It wouldn't be life if I did. But I will never feel powerless again.

Life cannot only be about conflict. It has to be about love as well. It is a late summer evening in 2003. In a truly sad Bollywood cliché, at my best friend's wedding, I see a girl wearing a green ... sari or a shalwar kameez, or something. All I remember is that it is green and her eyes are hazel and I know that if I don't meet her, my life will never be complete. In the years to come, she will tell me about her faint disgust at my oily, gelled-back hair—despite the turn of the century, my fashion sense at the time remained firmly rooted in the 1980s—and the fact that I seemed to think that being a cop was actually a *good* thing. But despite her reservations about me, she will save me. She will keep on saving me every day for the following twenty years, and may just continue to do so for another twenty if I'm lucky.

Pakistan will also teach me, repeatedly and bitterly, about betrayal. It is another summer's day in 2005, cool and crisp because I am in Hub, Balochistan, and it is dawn. I am on my way to arrest one of the most notorious criminals of Karachi, and my thoughts turn to nothing more significant than the coolness of the morning. Little do I realise that within twenty minutes, I will be fighting for my life, ambushed and abandoned, my closest friends wounded, watching a friend and colleague bleed to death ten feet from where I am taking cover. Those ten feet feel like ten thousand because I am unable to reach him as we draw heavy and ceaseless fire. Wounded by shrapnel myself, I think, this is it. By some miracle, I manage to survive for the three hours that it takes reinforcements to make their way to our location. In the months to come, as I recuperate, I seethe silently, and vow retribution against whoever set us up, thinking that no betrayal will ever be greater. And then fate says, "hold my beer."

It's a year later, and another deadlier and more diabolical betrayal strikes. It's perpetrated by predatory colleagues taking advantage of my extraordinary naïveté, and it turns me into a fugitive overnight. It teaches me one of life's most important lessons: just because you believe that you are just and good, it doesn't mean shit to a world full of sharks. To survive and indeed, to thrive in this country, I will have to sacrifice a portion of my innocence. I will have to become a shark too.

A friend once told me I have survivor's guilt. Every few years, I get this feeling, and I ask myself why I survive while others around me are struck down. Starting with my father's murder, to the day in Hub in 2005 when I see Arshad Butt die in front of my eyes, but I live on, defying all logic; to a few months later when I flee the country mere hours before my colleagues are arrested in a false case; to the conversation with one of my dearest friends from the police academy—a man who started his career with me on the mean streets of Karachi—just a day before he commits suicide in the District Police Officer's bungalow in Nankana Sahib. It is the most normal conversation I have ever had, and I curse myself for my obliviousness to his pain. And then, of course, there is Aslam. The same policeman from that fateful day in 1998, who becomes a colleague, a mentor and a friend over the years. We survive the ordeal of Hub together, both wounded but functional. In 2010, I tell him to sacrifice a black goat, light a candle in a church, give alms in every Sufi shrine from Karachi to Kathmandu—anything we can do to thank the Almighty for the stroke of luck that made us shift our joint offices a week before a Taliban suicide team blew up our old offices, shattering the lives of twenty families. Our office furniture is still in the old premises. As far as close shaves go, it doesn't get any closer.

In 2011, Aslam and his family miraculously survive a ruthless attack on his house, an attack that appears even more ruthless in retrospect years later, when I arrest the perpetrators and discover that they were given the address by Aslam's own bodyguard, the man who took his children to school. Again, it seems to me as if the angel of death has passed close enough to whisper in my ear, but has gone on to strike down someone else. Three months before the attack on his house, I have left for England, taking heed of various intelligence reports that indicate that both Aslam and I are on a Taliban hitlist. That attack causes Aslam to enter into a death spiral with the terrorists which will only end one way.

For the remaining two and a half years of his life, I will remain in London, giving counsel but no longer an active player in the game. I convince myself that I am out for good. But my wife doesn't believe me. She keeps saying Pakistan still calls to me, still pulls at my heartstrings. Irony of ironies, the day Aslam is martyred, I am actually in Karachi, promoting the release of my first book. As I reach the scene of the crime and turn my eyes to the still-burning remains of his SUV, I cannot believe he is gone, and I have survived yet again.

In 2016, I will prove my wife correct and return home. Friends in London will ask why I am putting my head in the lion's mouth again. Friends in Pakistan will say, why the fuck did you come back? But it doesn't feel like entering the lion's den. It just feels ... normal. I return to my old office and the orderly greets me as if I had left last Tuesday, instead of five years ago. This place, this city, has a weird familiarity even as its fundamental nature changes. I travel around various cantons like a macabre tourist, recalling the crimes that have occurred on each street corner.

There's the Village Restaurant—great chicken tikkas and also, incidentally from where the American journalist, Daniel Pearl, was kidnapped. And here we have the Lyari Expressway, a modern marvel that means you can travel from the affluent southern suburbs to the Super Highway in 30 minutes flat. Oh and Chaudhry Aslam's vehicle was blown up by suicide bombers just opposite Exit 6. Nice to see that someone's grown a bougainvillea to cover the dumpster into which my father's car crashed when his murderers opened fire.

Briefly, I consider becoming a tour guide through the madness of this city. A colleague in London informs me that ex-IRA gunmen do something similar in Belfast, giving guided tours of the Falls and Shankill roads, and getting tourists discounts in the same pubs where terrorists sipped pints of Guinness and planned unthinkable atrocities. I even come up with a catchy name for the business: 'Omar's Terrorism Tours'. FML, as my son would say.

And then, around the same time, two things happen that change my perspective. In the months after Aslam's death, for reasons that remain unfathomable to me, my first book, that had started as a random personal attempt at catharsis, is read by more and more people. It acquires commercial and critical acclaim and is soon followed by another. And then another. And another. It transforms me into something I had never imagined becoming: a chronicler of this mad, dystopian, Alice-in-Wonderland place called Pakistan. And, further stretching the bounds of credulity, my mother and I finally get justice. After an interlude of 17 years, involving so many political machinations that they would have prompted Machiavelli to write a sequel to *The Prince*, and despite the best efforts of a sociopath who lived in London and controlled Karachi via satellite phone for three decades, my father's murderer finally hangs for his crimes.

Centuries of evolution in religion, philosophy and the construct of society have established this belief that it is wrong to desire a man's death. But I have developed a slightly different philosophy after 17 years of simultaneously being a victim and a law enforcer. I believe that at heart, despite what we say, we are still a tribal people. When people, evil people, hurt us, when they kill our loved ones, when they subvert the law with impunity for decades, when they threaten to extinguish all hope, we hanker for revenge. Thus, when justice finally takes its course, no matter how barbaric it may appear, you cannot deny that it is cleansing, liberating and healing.

After four and a half decades of living on this planet, I still don't understand this place I call home. I don't understand how it has brought moments of such pure joy in my life, and such mind-boggling pain. I cannot comprehend how injustice can permeate throughout a society so flagrantly, and how, at the same time, unbelievable heroism can be an everyday occurrence here. By any objective, logic-based metric, this place should either not exist, or be the centre of a conflagration so immense that it would make *Dante's Inferno* sound like a Sunday walk in the park. Yet, people survive. Some even thrive. People fall in love, raise families, play cricket with eccentric friends on the weekends, and just live life like in any other part of the world. I certainly have.

The last few months have afforded me time for much reflection and introspection on the curious phenomenon that is Pakistan. They have implanted several mental snapshots that I will never forget. I meet my literature teacher from school, a magnificent old Parsi lady, and someone who evoked a terror in me that I have not even felt when confronted by Jihadi assassins. She was a member of a community that was integral to the fabric of this city once upon a time, but has sadly almost disappeared in recent years. Recently bereaved and in the late autumn of her life, she is encouraged by all her loved ones to leave this place. What's left for her here? She'll be more comfortable overseas, among family and community. And all this in the midst of an unprecedented economic meltdown and a resurgence of militancy so brazen that, the week before my meeting, a team of Taliban fedayeen engaged in a siege of the Karachi police chief's office. And yet she refuses to leave. Why? Because she says she knows no other home. This is where she was born and this is where she will die. This place, this insane asylum where nothing makes sense anymore, is part of her DNA.

On a cold February morning, I make the journey from Quetta to the Afghan border crossing at Chaman. At the border gate, two Afghan Taliban who could not be older than twenty, scratch their balls under their shalwar kameez and stare down at a group of dedicated but overworked Pakistan Army soldiers. To observe the border gate at Chaman for five minutes is to relive in miniature, *Dr. Zhivago* or *War and Peace*, or the works of Aeschylus, or indeed any of the great tragedies of human literature. A sea of humanity, desperate to somehow get over the border. A former colonel in the Afghan army, reduced to penury, begs the authorities to allow his pregnant wife to deliver their child in a Quetta hospital. I have seen Quetta hospitals and would never want to step into one for even the most minor ailment. This man's desperation is acute. Pakistani authorities relate stories about mothers trying to push babies into the arms of the border guards. Anything to get out of Spin Boldak. Stories like these give one perspective. No matter how insane things seem to be over here on our side of the border, there are always places where the insanity is at another level.

I'm a huge sports fan. People who know me, know this about me. I play cricket religiously, I have written books about match-fixing in sport, I was a Rafa devotee from the time when that was considered unfashionable, and *The Last Dance* is my favourite documentary of all time. I have an oddball theory: that a country's athletes are reflective of the national characteristics of that place. This is why, in my mind, China has exponentially increased its share of medals in recent Olympics, through plain industriousness and laser-like focus, even in sports like fencing and snowboarding, which were perhaps never played in China before the last twenty years. It is the unbridled pursuit of capitalist riches that allows the United States to continue producing world-class sportsmen and women. The driving force is perhaps less a nationalistic impulse for flag and country, and more the desire to have your face plastered on a box of Wheaties and an eight-figure deal with Nike. Similarly, this is why the Pakistan cricket team, that most sacred of cows, is considered a neurotic, almost schizophrenic performer. They break your heart again and again and again, over decades. Some of us have become generational sufferers. They keep doing that, until that one moment when everything comes together, and suddenly, instead of breaking it, they make your heart soar. That's Pakistan in a nutshell.

I started these ramblings as an attempt at an explanation for my son. To allow him to understand, in the years to come, a little bit about me, and a little bit about this place he calls home. Reading these words back, I fear my attempt has probably gone horribly wrong. Who knows? Perhaps, like the PhD candidate who once tried to prove to me that my books had veiled Marxist undertones, my son may find some hidden understanding that eludes me. I don't know if, when he grows up, he will choose to remain here, or makes a new life for himself elsewhere. I don't know if he will ever choose to come back, after leaving this place three times, as I did. I don't know how I will react to his choices, other than to accept that they will be his choices, and not mine.

The only advice I can offer is that Pakistan is not an easy place. Recently, after an interval of 22 years, I met the father of the young man who was murdered on my first day as a police officer. The father was an honourable and courageous man, and he fought long and hard to get justice for his son's murder. He said to me that at the end of his struggle, he had learned one undeniable truth about this country. To get justice, you must have feet of iron and hands of gold. It was one of the saddest things that I had ever heard. That's not to say that Pakistan is not worth fighting for, or having your heart broken time and again. All things of real value in life are worth fighting for, but that's a bit of a cliché. The real question is always about what value you place on them, and how long you are willing to fight. And those two variables often change with time.

I haven't done a very good job of explaining my relationship with Pakistan. It's because I don't really understand it myself completely. Let me try again, in a more succinct manner, in terms that are more recognisable to the social media generation. If this were a Facebook page (apologies in advance to my son, who believes Facebook belongs in the same generation as the transistor radio), my relationship status with Pakistan would read: *it's complicated.*

Omar Shahid Hamid is an acclaimed Pakistani novelist who lives in Karachi. In addition to his writing career, he has served as a senior counter terrorism police officer who, in between writing books, has survived several attempts on his life, investigated the international murder of a journalist in Kenya, and had his offices blown up by the Taliban. His first novel, *The Prisoner*, was published in 2013 by Pan Macmillan India, and proved to be a huge critical and commercial success. It has also been translated into French, German and Urdu, and is being adapted for a screenplay. His second novel, *The Spinner's Tale* (2015, Pan Macmillan), won the Italy Reads Pakistan prize and the Karachi Literature Festival fiction prize and has also been translated into Italian and German. His third book *The Party Worker* (2017, Pan Macmillan) won the Karachi Literature Festival fiction prize, making Omar the only writer to have won in consecutive years. His fourth book, *The Fix* (2019, Pan Macmillan) explores the world of match-fixing in women's cricket. His fifth book, *Betrayal* (2021, Lighthouse Publishing) won the Karachi Adab Festival award in 2023. His latest novel, *The Election* (2024, Liberty Publishing), looks at the rise of populist politics around the world.

Instagram: @theprisoner2310

In Stanzas And Cells:
A Journey Through Cancer Research And Poetry

Dr. Azra Raza

In the summer of 1996, my mother came to visit me in Chicago. We each had our fixed morning routines. I would do some work first, then go for a long run by Lakeshore Drive, while my mother read for a while after her morning prayers. Then she would make phone calls to Karachi and to her other children scattered all over the U.S., and finally, come what may, we would meet for our 10:00 a.m. Chai and Chat ritual. This summer, I was recording an oral history of her days growing up as a quintessential Sharifzadi who represented the prevalent culture of Aligarh in the 1920s and 30s, and her departure from this age-old way of living and eventual arrival in Pakistan on August 14th, 1947. We taped 5-6 hours of conversations on a daily basis, and some of these took odd turns. One morning, while talking about Ghalib, we got into a debate about how to interpret this sher:

نہ تھا کچھ تو خدا تھا کچھ نہ ہوتا تو خدا ہوتا

ڈبویا مجھ کو ہونے نے نہ ہوتا میں تو کیا ہوتا

When there was nothing, then God existed;
if nothing existed, then God would exist
"Being" drowned me; if I did not exist, then what would I be.

Over the next few minutes, each of us recited the sher several times. My daughter Sheherzad, who was barely two and a half, was playing on the carpet by us. My mother asked me for a glass of water as we ended our Ghalib debate, and to our delight, when I returned, little Sheherzad jumped up and recited the entire sher perfectly (except for the American accent!). My mother said, "Well, her memory is better than yours. You should start teaching her poetry now so that she can also develop the correct pronunciations. Otherwise, she will call a horse Gora and not Ghordha."

I took this advice to heart and began making Sheherzad memorize grand Urdu poetry for half an hour every morning. This ritual became so important to both of us that when she joined Columbia University as an undergraduate student, I took two apartments in the same building so she could have her independence, while at the same time, we could also continue our poetry sessions. Once, when she was older, I asked Sheherzad why she was so accepting of this particular ritual and never missed a morning lesson even through her rebellious teenage years of high school and college. Her response was spontaneous and insightful. "I don't know the exact reason, as I was too young when it started. All I remember is a great feeling I always had whenever I saw you and Nano talking about poetry and having such a good time. I instinctively felt that if I recited poetry with you, we would also have a great time. And we do!" So, here is a child born and raised in America, whose culture is deeply unpoetic, and yet, this year, her Mother's Day present to me was a vase she had thrown in her pottery studio, inscribed with the following sher along with its English translation:

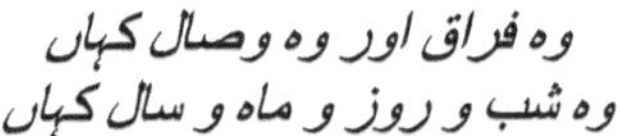

Where are those separations and those unions
Where are those nights and days, those months and years

I would say that these poetry sessions bonded mother-daughter in experiential moments that are hard to capture. You can imagine the exultation that comes with sudden comprehension. This is especially the case when the poetry you are reciting is using language that is grand, when the themes are noble, and when the message is universal, meant for all of humanity, and remains startlingly fresh for all times. Many a morning, we would contemporize Ghalib as we applied his thought process to extant situations of our own lives. I feel that growing up in Pakistan, steeped in our profoundly poetic culture, has informed not just many aspects of my own personal and professional life, but seems to now be affecting that of the next generation in my family as well. Instead of becoming a doctor like her parents, Sheherzad, showing an uncanny faithfulness to her name, has chosen to become a filmmaker and storyteller. Her scripts revolve around the existential themes that were so thoughtfully imagined in the poetry we read over the years.

My love for poetry also goes back to my childhood and my earliest memories. In a recent interview with the American Society of Hematology, I described the oral tradition in which I was nurtured. My childhood in Karachi was an extremely happy one, filled with excitement, energy, games, food and fun, in a family of seven siblings, adoring parents, countless visiting cousins and friends of my parents. No conversation in my family was complete without one or the other parent quoting an appropriate verse or two. I was made to memorize hundreds of verses of classical Urdu poetry from the time I could speak. It was their culture, their tradition. Even some games we played revolved around literary activities like staging famous plays, organizing stand-up comedies and, most enjoyably, splitting into two teams with one parent on each side and competing in poetry recitations called 'Bait-Bazi'. This meant having to memorize a whole lot of poetry, and it was great fun because my parents participated enthusiastically and made us feel appreciated when we rose to their expectations.

Perhaps one reason for their extraordinary emphasis on educating us in their cultural traditions was the immigrant's anxiety my parents suffered from. You see, they were raised in a storied poetic *Courtesy Culture* that had evolved in Aligarh and Lucknow over hundreds of years. Then the Indian subcontinent was suddenly partitioned. My father was in the British Civil Service and opted for Pakistan. As a result, overnight, my parents found themselves transported to the desert of Sindh, away from the grand old ethos and centuries-old codes of living that precipitated into a thousand nuanced mannerisms. Of course, Sindh had an equally rich and thriving local culture, but as freshly landed immigrants, they were unfamiliar with it. They became anxious to impart their traditional ways of living onto their children, as much as possible—especially the gallantry and poetry associated with even their most quotidian activities. In this curious way, we, the children born to immigrants in Pakistan, became the fortunate cultural beneficiaries of the Partition. And now the cycle has been repeated, with Sheherzad benefiting from being born to an equally anxious immigrant mother, plucked from the warm and cozy life of Gulistan-e-Raza in Karachi only to be dropped into a blizzard one cold January day, somewhere in the ice-drenched city of Buffalo.

Indeed, I am an immigrant, except I came to America not for political reasons but to cure cancer. Many people find it surprising that someone growing up in Pakistan would have such aspirations. This is why it may be worth recounting how I formed some of my early notions about what ended up becoming a lifelong quest. As a teenager growing up in Pakistan, I read a book that described two things about cancer which intellectually fascinated me: First, that within our bodies, we give birth to a cell that is 'Immortal'. This immediately suggested to me that if I can understand how a cancer cell learns to live forever, I will understand the secret of aging. Secondly, the book compared the human body to a State, with cells being its Citizens. And Citizens have to follow rules. A primary rule is that they must stay in their organs of origin; liver cells must stay in the liver, lung cells in the lungs, pancreatic cells in the pancreas. Only in one condition do they walk out of their "homes." Cancer. When I landed in America, this is the question I wanted to answer: how did cancer cells acquire both immortality and mobility? I had sighted my Quest. Allama Iqbal had already taught me that I needed to sight my quest i.e., my object of desire, very clearly, and once I had done that, even the blinking of an eye should be unbearable. Such had to be my commitment, such was to be my focus:

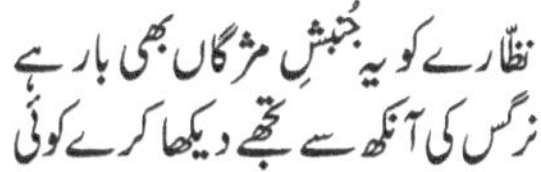

Even the eyebrow's movement is unwelcome to the Sight
With the eye of the narcissus should one see Thee

As if this intellectual challenge had not been enough to make a lifelong cancer researcher out of me, I was exposed to my first cancer patients as a third-year student in medical college in Karachi. This experience provided the final and necessary emotional impetus for my quest. I knew that from that moment on, everything I did professionally would have to be dedicated to reducing the anguish of patients. I came to America as a 24-year-old and volunteered to work at a renowned Cancer Center immediately. As I entered this grand old institution, I saw the following words inscribed on the wall in the lobby: "*If I had a choice between a walk on the Moon and saving one life from cancer, I would never look at the Moon again.*"

I knew I was in the right place. Not only because I was in a country that shared my ethos about the importance of reducing human suffering as the primary goal of our quest, but also because it was a country affluent enough to plan a moon walk. I started my serious cancer research work that very day at Roswell Park Cancer Institute, in Buffalo, New York.

For the last three decades, at every step of my career, both as a basic scientist researching cancer at the molecular and genetic level, and as an oncologist seeing 30-40 cancer patients a week, I am reminded of my real goal by reading the most sublime poetry in the world: an Urdu ghazal. And when I am really down and out because some grant got rejected, or a beloved patient died and I feel defeated, Ghalib comes to my rescue, reminding me that my job is not complete even if there is half a knot left undone in the Universe:

کاوش کا دل کرے ہے تقاضا کہ ہے ہنوز
ناخن پہ قرض اس گرہِ نیم باز کا

The heart makes a claim for scratching, for there is still
A debt of the fingernails to the half-open knot.

I am a hematologist. I see very, very ill pre-leukemia and acute leukemia patients. A critical aspect of a doctor's journey is to get the patient's story right, and to narrate it faithfully for medical records so that others can get an accurate picture. Narration is a central theme in medicine. When I was a young oncologist in training, I suffered from a perpetual anxiety about making sense of the fragmented information patients provide. Especially when the same events, described first by patients and then by family members, evolve as they travel from mouth to mouth, through different symptoms and signs, over the course of weeks and months. What did I miss? What did I not hear? What did they forget to report? How do I separate the noise from the real thing, the wheat from the chaff? How do I listen more keenly, how do I practice the kind of listening that the blind develop naturally? How do I listen for what is not said?

This is where poetry comes in. It teaches us to extract macrocosms of meaning from the microcosm of two lines in a ghazal. So much is said in so few words. One needs to be very attentive to the said and the unsaid. Then, there is the issue of dealing with soul-destroying moments, such as people running out of time who catalog their swelling regrets, seeing their options vanishing in the maelstrom of disease and disorder. How do I develop the self-control and equanimity to follow the advice of Emory Austin: "some days there won't be a song in your heart. Sing anyway"? In short, narration is crucial to medicine. Lives depend on what is said, and what is heard. And again, poetry helps.

For one thing, Ghalib has served (and continues to serve) as a guiding light during some of my darkest professional moments. Imagine that even while practicing medicine in Manhattan, I am able to invoke his poetry to explain, to my medical students, the many nuances of the issues related to dealing with terminally ill patients. In fact, my book on cancer, titled *The First Cell*, which is widely read by oncologists and the general public interested in cancer, is peppered with Urdu poetry. Why? Because no one, to my knowledge, has addressed the universal themes of humanity's pain, grief, suffering, loss and ultimately, hope, better than poets. It is also due to the ghazal tradition that speaks volumes to me, because it is part of my history and who I am, and because of which I know Urdu poetry best.

This is how I explain it in the book. I walk countless individuals to their deaths, escorting them through some of the most harrowing, painful terminal illnesses. There is a point, reached rather invariably in these cancers, when no further treatments can be offered. This stage is particularly distressing for young oncologists. They feel defeated, lost, bereft and paralyzed in the face of mortality. Spurned by the vigor of youth, some fight back, denying the inevitable.

Training young oncologists is part of my teaching responsibilities. I counsel them to accept the bitter truth, and instead of feeling crushed, I advise them to focus on making the final journey less painful for their patients, so as to bring a modicum of relief to their shattered spirits. I encourage these young oncologists to shift their attention from trying to cure, to trying to heal. Ghalib taught me how to make this possible. He points out, in a thousand nuanced ways, how compassion is just as important for the ill, the suffering and the afflicted, as the drugs administered to them. There is a couplet I recite often to my American medical students, residents and fellows that is so profound, so poignant, and so uplifting:

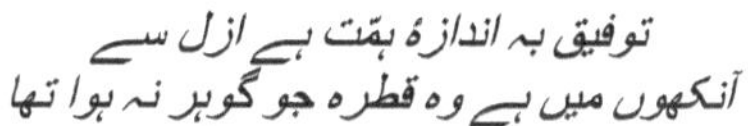

From infinity, accomplishment rests on endurance
Rain's triumph lies in becoming a tear and not a pearl

The myth in Urdu poetry is that only the first few raindrops from the very first rains of the season have a chance of becoming a pearl if they land inside a clam. In this couplet, Ghalib consoles the raindrops that missed being the first of the season, therefore having no chance of becoming a pearl. He reminds them that though they cannot become a pearl, they now have the possibility of becoming a tear that fall from a lover's eyes. Here, the cure is the pearl, and healing is the tear. We can and must do both.

I am who I am because I was born and raised in Pakistan. My psyche, especially at the emotional level, is largely determined by the centuries-year-old, refined, subtle and layered tehzeeb as well as the courtly, profoundly poetic culture in which I grew up. These influences have shaped not just my personal and professional lives, but also guided my relationship with my daughter in mysterious ways. What I did not anticipate was the influence this would have on Sheherzad's interests and even her career choice. In our case, this pronouncement would be true: you can take the girl out of Pakistan, but you cannot take Pakistan out of the girl. For generations. Pakistan Zindabad.

Dr. Azra Raza is the Chan Soon-Shiong Professor of Medicine and Clinical Director of The Edward P. Evans Foundation MDS Center at Columbia University in New York. A practicing oncologist who sees 30-40 cancer patients weekly, she also directs a basic cancer research lab with hundreds of original publications in high-profile journals. Her life is dedicated to the prevention of all chronic diseases including cancer by early detection. She worked with President Clinton designing Breakthrough Developments in Science and Technology and with President Joe Biden for the Cancer Moonshot initiative. Her latest book, ***THE FIRST CELL: And the human costs of pursuing cancer to the last*** is a national best seller and has been translated into nine languages.

Website: www.azraraza.com
Instagram: @dr.azraraza

Switchback

Sameer Khan

To leave Karachi on a one-way ticket; to come to New York—not the glittering city itself but its janky suburbs; to settle there (as if settling were an intention and not a survival instinct); to start trying to actually live there, in the fine state of New York, only to find that instead of being immersed in "America"[1], you are pulled towards certain neighbourhoods and localities (Hillside Avenue, Jackson Heights, Curry Hill, or Hicksville, or, in New Jersey, Edison and the contiguous Iselin), places where you feel a sense of comfort, an internal loosening, and to immediately know that this feeling, this relaxation, is borne out of familiarity and nostalgia—to do all this is to traverse the perimeter of a circle, or rather, a spiral, that by sweeping close to the point of origin, generates a fractured sense of belonging. "Fractured" because what couldn't happen at "home" is now happening at a place very far from home—there is a literal geographical break between where you were and where you are now. And "belonging" because the sense of familiarity comes from the evocation of that first point of origin. It is like receiving the gleam of a lighthouse from across the bay. It is so far away, but seeing its searching beam swing towards you feels like making contact, like you're there even as you still stand where you are.

And so, you go about your business where you are, you work,

---

1 Or as we would say in Pakistan, "AMARICA".

you hustle, you change, but you know you're not *just* where you are. There is some border after which the United States slips away, and one is left with Karachi, or Lahore or Tirah or wherever. The border is usually at the living room threshold, where somehow furniture from Ikea or West Elm manages to get configured in a way that evokes the chintzy, fusty Pakistani drawing room, and there is always, *always*, a kaleen. Sometimes it (the border) is laid down further away, spanning the whole neighbourhood, and in other cases, it is closed in tight, not a border at all but a knot (or a noose), somewhere in the body. It is like the drop in one's hip after carrying heavy groceries a long way, like the vindictive look after an insult— that is to say, in gestures or reactions that spring from one's ancestral land. But, in any case, it's there, it's definitely there, whether you try to escape it or embrace it or ignore it is as immaterial as your opinion of the faraway lighthouse's revolutions, or whatever path the Sun takes through the galaxy.

And you're left wondering: if one had to come back to that starting point anyway, what was all that distance travelled for, why couldn't I have just stayed in place? You end up feeling like a bowerbird – not building a new, original life, but taking familiar scraps, many less than ideal, and pasting them together to create some kind of illusion. An attractive simulacrum, but can you actually live in it?

In Jackson Heights, for example, fragments of the motherland come together in bricolage. Different fragments from different motherlands. A shoebox-sized storefront sells heavy ropes of paper flowers, stacked upon each other in thick profusion till they form a sort of hedgerow. You know which flowers are meant to be represented; the orange and yellow colours carry a specific meaning, but at the same time, this festive boulder is not something you would see in Pakistan, or at least not in the Pakistan that you experienced. Maybe it's an Indian thing? At a roadside stall, a man in a topi has successfully recreated the classic wheeled cart laden with produce—you expect him to break out the hawker's call at any moment. Except the cart is laden with unknown leaves, many different kinds of leaves—no tomatoes on board, not even onions—just leaves. They are large and wild looking—Bengalis call them shak. I tried looking up how to cook them once, and was alarmed to learn that they have to be soaked in alkali to be edible. It's a lore completely unknown to me, I cannot simply take these leaves and cook them like I would for aloo palak. A false sense of familiarity could poison me.

And yet these different fragments, scavenged from their home localities and reassembled here—sometimes with panache, sometimes with an unthinking sense of monotony, sometimes soaked through with homesickness—still form a legible whole that evokes the nostalgic feeling. Jackson Heights somehow feels like Saddar, despite the non-Karachi elements, maybe because the inconsistencies are smoothed over with the gestures and expressions that are endemic to the subcontinent. It's a physical vernacular, a way of carrying oneself (like that drop in the hip I was mentioning earlier, and almost everyone in Jackson Heights is laden with heavy groceries). It's a manner of bearing, one that feels so rooted in the subcontinent that it softens the unfamiliarities in the environment until they cease to matter. A hand on a furrowed brow, or safaidi being laid down over asphalt. Maybe if you put enough brown people in close vicinity, a kind of collective psychic process is instituted, with people falling into ancient and familial ways of being. A centripetal force is generated, and all involved start orbiting around the central axis of what feels like home. Certainly, the unitary 'me' would never have been interested in a place like Jackson Heights when I was back in Pakistan. I would have found the dirt and disorganization unappealing to my modern (Westernized? Colonized?) sensibility. Yet now, here I am. I drink tea twice a day and delight when qawwali comes on the radio. What I once disparaged now beckons to me.

It's hard not to feel duped.

Cross the street at the shoebox-sized store with all the flowers, go a few steps, and you will arrive at Maharaja Sweets. You're in for a treat, because at Maharaja, they have five different kinds of ladoos. The store assistant jokes with me that it's basically the same recipe with different add-ins. He lists off some examples – ground up almonds, crushed pistachios, or maghaz.

"Maghaz?" I exclaim. "But maghaz is brains!"

He laughs, yes, but it's also a grain. We riff on this for a little bit, using that particular strain of desi humour that works by successive embellishments of a small detail—in this case, the confusion over the word 'maghaz'. It is comfortable to lapse into the idiom of the subcontinent, to joke in Urdu, knowing that I will mostly be understood, and I feel I can playfully attack my interlocutor since my ignorance of the different meanings of a word are the basis of the misunderstanding. I am the one making the mistake, so I don't have to worry about coming off as disrespectful. On my way out, however, I check my impulse to say khuda hafiz. This is despite my knowing that, once abroad, there is a degree of tolerance to the expression of different national and religious identities, and the presumed-Gujarati shop assistant would probably take my farewell in the way it was meant. But I don't want to risk it.

Sometimes, I'm the one that gets offended. I was sitting in Bryant Park one day, by myself, when I heard two gentlemen behind me—well, really just one—the other was mostly listening. The speaker was bringing up the similarities among the peoples of the subcontinent, initially taking the fairly benign tones of "We have this, don't you have it too?" But then, he started bemoaning that Partition ever occurred, that India was ever separated. How wonderful it would have been if that hadn't happened, he said, it was all the doing of the British. Despite my pretensions to liberality and curiosity, I felt something in me tighten. Maybe it was the noose I described earlier. The man's words clashed against the ideology I had been raised with, that had become part of me, and any ability to listen or think ground to a halt. I didn't actually say anything to them. I tried to ignore them. But part of me wanted to get up and confront them, taunt them—were the differences that led to three countries coming out of one so insignificant? Were Muslims not being horribly persecuted in India as we spoke? And, in an even shriller tone, in my mind: if he wanted a return to the old arrangement, would he also consent to India being under Mughal rule? It was like some viciously patriotic tiger had leapt up in my throat, held back only by a sense of decorum.

I didn't like that I wanted to say those things. It felt unseemly, crude, unsophisticated[2]. It just wasn't cool to be so jingoistic, it wasn't the kind of person I wanted to be. It didn't feel like the kind of person I had been, even in Pakistan. Yet, it seemed unavoidable that, having grown up surrounded by so much nationalistic feeling, I had absorbed it into my cells, even while feeling consciously opposed. All it would take was the right kind of wound, and it would bleed out of me. It seemed that in the diaspora, I could get along and revel in my similarities with other brown people, until it felt like some crucial difference was being overlooked or dismissed—and then I would forsake my stated principles and join ranks with the ancestors.

Is the crucial difference Muslim identity? I think of all the relatives and friends I know, for whom Pakistan and Islam don't just overlap but overlay upon each other perfectly. The people who, even at mehndis, while enjoying the singing and dancing, the rituals with henna, paan leaves, and yes, ladoos, would still find a way to point out, "Ye Hinduana rasmey hain." ("These are Hindu customs"). They never went further, never tried to explain that if they were going to use this disparagement, how would they then explain their presence, their subsequent enjoyment? They seemed quite comfortable to let the conflict just sit (while they danced!). Or perhaps the disavowal of the mehndi back into Hinduism (if that's where it even came from) was a way of drawing a border between one's actions and one's identity. I suppose it's an identity that came out of Partition, except none of my elders ever wanted to

---

2   And, growing up in Karachi, I wanted so badly to be sophisticated. It meant showing that I was different than the squalor around me, that I could transcend it.

talk about Partition, let alone the time before. One's family history was connected back to the Mughals, or to the Prophet, but there was no sense of what came before conversion and no real story of what happened after either. It's sort of mind-boggling when you think about how essential culture and heritage seem to the subcontinent, that specific family stories seem to get lost, individual personalities eroded in favour of unquestioned customs. Or at least, that's what happened in my family. I suppose it's inaccurate to assume this was everyone's experience.

Maybe it would be better, then, to confine this discussion to myself, instead of trapping myself by making spurious generalisations about Pakistani culture. So, here's what I can say—in my family, we had little sense of our grandparents' lives, let alone the relatives that preceded them. I discovered the name of my father's village in India only in my late thirties, and not from him. He was only two when he left, but I had a whole host of aunts and uncles, all older than him, who never cast their minds back to that time. There was no mention of how the family of over a dozen children, in custody of only their mother (their father having gone on ahead) rode a donkey cart from their village to the town, where they boarded a train to the coast before taking a boat to Karachi. No mention of how this enormous family somehow lived in a two-room dwelling by Ranchorr Line. I still have no idea where Ranchorr Line actually is, but the way the name was uttered, with a contemptuous roll on the r's, made it sound like a desolate place, on the outskirts of the city. No mention of what had to be done to keep all these children clothed, fed, educated, or how my grandmother died of some kind of untreated oral cancer, her husband only deigning to visit a month after her death. Her children must have had to bury her, and who can say what else they buried.

As a child, none of this was accessible to me. There was no kind of family storytelling from any of my aunts or uncles. They did, however, have a lot to say about Islam: how to pray, the teachings of the Prophet (SAW), the ins and outs of various religious complexities. The connection to Islam was a living, breathing link to Allah, one's future, one's stated identity. The connection to one's history didn't matter much. Sure, there was a lot of talk about India versus Pakistan, about their governments and politics, but little in the way of personal narrative. There was a continuation of their way of life in Pakistan, and presumably their cultural traditions, but no searching look was cast out over the bay, at where they came from, at what their life in India had been like. Nostalgia was a threat to their going forward, and so it was rarely indulged. Maybe their family past was painful, leaving them with only the rope of custom and culture to hold on to. Consequently, now when I cast my mind back, and given that religion is far less important to me, the images I hold onto become moth-eaten, greatly attenuated. The kind of histories I want to bond with don't quite make it through.

Here's my theory. It was historically so important to protect Muslim lives and interests, and form Pakistan, that much of that prior "Indianness" had to be repudiated. Being Indian became synonymous with being non-Muslim, and there didn't seem to be a way to allow those differences to coexist, despite the symbology of the Pakistani flag, with its white margin for minorities. In a sense, the flag itself displayed separation, between those that were Muslim, and those that weren't. But what if this division was not just between different kinds of people, but internal, too? Did it become another fracture to carry around within us, mostly unawares?

These gaps widen when you leave home. Sometimes it's not clear if hidden faults are being exposed, or whether parts of oneself, one's history and ideology, are teetering over to fall into the gaps. In some ways, immigrating is a continuation of Pakistani culture— crossed a border once, why not go a bit further? There is a troubled past to escape, and always the prospect of a brighter future ahead. But the cracks accumulate. You adopt a recursive path, trying to go back and reclaim something, fish something out of the gaps. It was only in the US, when I started the decidedly non-desi pastime of hiking, that I learned about the switchback, a zigzagging path that allows you to traverse a height with economy. That feels like the process at play within me, a movement forwards and back, pieces jigsawed together, the dislocations shellacked over or sometimes spliced. Sometimes the old oozes out unbidden, like when you find yourself adopting a servile attitude to a white person, or when you mispronounce "America" and feel yourself darken with shame—not just because you made a mistake, but because you labelled yourself as Pakistani. What you want to hide is also what you love, what brings you comfort. You turn back to look for the lighthouse's rotating beam. You can see it, but you can't quite say what it really is, where it's really from.

Sameer Khan graduated from the Aga Khan University Medical College in 2007. He completed his residency in psychiatry at the Zucker Hillside Hospital, and his psychoanalytic training from the Psychoanalytic Association of New York (PANY), where he is now a faculty member. There, he teaches courses in Depression, and explores the differences (be they on the axes of race, culture, gender, sexuality, or class) between therapist and patient through the transference. He published *A Doer Doing,* a profile of Joseph Lichtenberg and his attempts to build a new psychological theory of motivational systems in *The Journal of American Psychoanalytic Association (JAPA),* in 2020. He has also contributed a chapter to Salman Akhtar's upcoming psychoanalytic anthology, *Marriage and its Discontents.* He is in full-time private practice in New York City, where he sees patients for psychoanalysis and psychotherapy.

Beyond Boundaries— The Cricketing Community
Ali Khan

What does being Pakistani mean? How is the relationship defined? For every individual, this will vary. In my case, I trace my engagement with Pakistan through a specific personal family history. In addition, there are factors that in my personal journey have taken me further away from aspects of Pakistan. But there are also other factors that have drawn me closer to the country. In particular, it was my following and support of the Pakistan cricket team that drew me ever closer to Pakistan. The global reach of cricket meant the connection to Pakistan could be played out even when I was not in the country myself. The emotional impact of sport binds me to the country. Here, I look at how my family history, an upbringing in a diplomatic household and cricket combined to define my relationship with Pakistan.

"What's your name?"

"Ali Khan ..."

"Oh My God, are you related to Imran Khan?"

***

"Where are you from?"

"Pakistan ..."

"You must be a squash player then."

***

I had never actively thought about the question of what being Pakistani meant to me. And when I did think about it, I realised that like many living relationships, 'Pakistan and I' was a bond marked by paradoxes. This 'complementarity' was exacerbated by the fact that while I was born in Pakistan, I was a dual national and that I spent half of my life in Pakistan and half outside. Yet, at the end of the day, I developed a strong bond with Pakistan, and I have never attempted to be seen as anything but Pakistani. I am not 'ethnically' Pakistani or of Pakistan origin. I am Pakistani.

Stereotypically, the paradoxical relationship would vacillate between 'love and hate'. It is important, however, to understand that both these extreme emotions require deep investment in the relationship itself. Moreover, relationships develop over time, influenced by personal circumstances and overarching events. In this reflection, I look at how my attachment with Pakistan emerged and developed.

Born into a family that migrated from India, the muhajir narrative of being the group that struggled to make the creation of Pakistan a reality, meant a strong association with the young nation of Pakistan. This was greatly exacerbated by the story of my paternal grandmother's dramatic migration to Pakistan. Princess Abida Sultaan was the heir apparent to the throne in Bhopal, India. Despite overtures by the Indian government, Huzoor, as she was known to her family and friends, declined a life of luxury and financial security and chose instead to opt for Pakistan. I reproduce below extracts from her autobiography, highlighting an exchange that Huzoor had with

Krishna Menon, the Indian High Commissioner in London in 1950 while she waited for the Pakistan government to grant her a visa:

"... why are you turning your back on your heritage, your life and your family in Bhopal for Pakistan? You are a brave and determined girl but there is nothing for you in Pakistan. Don't go. I can assure you that the Indian Government will look after you... don't be emotional. Stay in India. There is a great future for Muslim women like you."

"Mr. Menon ... I would never have decided to take such an important step purely on emotional grounds. My decision to go to Pakistan is based on deeper considerations that I have weighed heavily for months. They relate to my son's future as an honourable citizen, the destiny of Muslims like myself who are prepared to build a new nation on the ideals of Mr. Jinnah."

"But Jinnah is dead" retorted Menon. "There is no one to take on his mantle."

"Jinnah may be dead", I replied, "but Pakistan is alive—I have decided my future lies there." (Abida Sultaan, Rebel Princess, 191)

Huzoor would often relate the story of her arrival in Karachi to her grandchildren, alongside exciting accounts of shikaar in Bhopal. She spoke of the elation and feeling of freedom that came from becoming part of a vibrant new nation. We also knew that Huzoor had left Bhopal with not much more than some of her wedding jewellery and her Remington rifles. The house she built in Malir was funded through the sale of her jewellery. The rifles she would not part with. In 1951, Huzoor had moved from living in her palace in Bhopal to her modest half-finished house in Malir, where there was no electricity or water, no roof, and no windows. For years, she would eat by the light of a kerosene lamp and sleep in the veranda under a mosquito net. But she referred to her new dwelling as her beloved house and never complained or regretted her move. Bhopal House, in its minimalist splendour remains a serene dwelling.

Steeped in this history, my father, unsurprisingly, graduated from Cambridge, joined the Pakistan civil service and eventually the Foreign Office. He would go on to be Head of Permanent Mission to UN in Geneva, Ambassador to Jordan and France, and High Commissioner to the United Kingdom before finishing his career as Foreign Secretary. After retiring from the Pakistan Foreign Service, he served as UN Special Representative to the Secretary General to Rwanda (1994 – 1996) and was Chairman of the Pakistan Cricket Board twice. My maternal grandfather, Akhtar Hussain, was also a distinguished diplomat who served as Foreign Secretary and Ambassador to Italy, Iran, USSR, Algeria and Austria. *Bade Daddy* lived in Karachi but died early, and my interaction with him was therefore more limited.

The family history meant a close and emotional connection to Pakistan, which has continued to be passed down through the generations. Alongside the influence of my grandmother's personal journey to Pakistan, my father's appointments as Pakistan's representative abroad anchored my early relationship to Pakistan.

But being the son of a diplomat leads to the contradictions that I mentioned earlier. On the one hand, you are part of a family that 'represents' Pakistan abroad. In my formative years, I spent time in Pakistan's embassies and high commissions. There were celebrations for Pakistan Day, Independence Day and Eid. Foreign dignitaries and members of the local Pakistani community visited, qawwalis and cultural evenings were held regularly. I met distinguished Pakistanis from Pakistan as well as those who had settled abroad and were often hard working, generous and welcoming. In school, I was paraded out in my sherwani on International Day. At home, our staff was Pakistani. The cook's staple offering was 'aloo gosht', daal and a sabzi. Even our drivers at the Pakistan missions were Pakistani, including in Amman, where we had the striking 6-foot, 4-inches tall, Mohammad Khan, who had at one point been driver to General Zia. I formed an identity that revolved around the concept of a "Pakistan outside of Pakistan." With my immersion in a diplomatic family, came the feeling of being a representative of Pakistan, albeit in a more limited capacity than my father.

On the other hand, these foreign postings meant long stretches of time spent away from Pakistan itself. In my case, these absences from home were later exacerbated by my schooling and university being in England from the age of 16. Not being physically in Pakistan for extended periods did mean a distance from some aspects of Pakistani culture. On returning from Amman, I joined school in Islamabad, never having studied Urdu or Islamiat. The adjustment took time. My elder brothers had watched both Pakistani and Indian films in the 70s, but Pakistani film was in terminal decline when I started frequenting cinema halls. Indian films were also far more accessible in the VCR market, and as a result, Pakistani films were only seen rarely. Similarly, acclaimed Pakistani teledramas were less available away from Pakistan, their themes less attractive to young viewers. As a result, I never followed them.

But being back in Islamabad for a four-year stretch in my teens was a formative experience. At the time, the capital city was 'unexciting' for some, but for a teenager, I loved the greenery, the Margalla Hills hikes, the ability to walk to friends' houses without fear. Everyone lived within ten minutes drive. School brought close friends, many of whom were foreigners—Polish, Turkish, American, Iranian, Afghan, Peruvian amongst others. Summers were hot—sometimes the hills themselves would catch fire, the orange glow spectacularly illuminating the contours of the hills at night. But the fruit was better than any I had had before, and Polka's choc bars and jet sports brought relief, as did United Bakery's famous lemon tarts, which incidentally did not taste of lemon. Winter was glorious for its crisp days and pollution-free atmosphere and for the cricket season. Every weekend after dinner, we would make the trip to Rawalpindi to indulge in the best gulab jamans that the twin cities had to offer. On long weekends, there were trips to Peshawar's famous namak mandi for chapli kebabs and tikkas and onwards to Swat to see the snow-covered mountains and the majestic Swat River. We would consume Kashmiri tea and dry fruit from Aabpara during the 30-minute load shedding that would happen at 6 pm. And yes, chilghozas were affordable then. Jinnah market grew rapidly on the back of pirated films on VCRs—mainly

Indian, but also from Hollywood. The years spent in Islamabad ensured that I would return for holidays even when studies abroad began.

But there was one element of Pakistan that bound me inextricably to the country, especially after I moved to England for my A-levels and university. Sport was always important growing up. My grandmother was an outstanding sportswoman and played polo, squash, hockey, table tennis and even cricket. My father also played several sports, and as children, we grew up surrounded by sport. I followed Pakistan's success in hockey, watched Jahangir Khan win his 8th, 9th and 10th successive British Opens and followed Jansher Khan's subsequent domination. Importantly, my sporting heroes were primarily Pakistani and I followed sport where Pakistan was prominent rather than football, for example.

But it was cricket—a sport I both played and followed fanatically—that was the most important. Whether it was Amman or Islamabad, my father and I would look for two main features in a prospective house—space in the garden for 'net' practice and a room in the house suitable for indoor cricket. Inevitably, and much to my mother's dismay, this meant that our gardens were never well-kept, and one room was always off-limits to guests. But it was through cricket and my support of the Pakistan cricket team that my relationship with Pakistan continued to grow even while I was no longer physically in Pakistan.

It wasn't, however, an immediate attraction. My earliest cricketing loyalties were reserved—as for many cricket fans in the 70s and 80s— for the West Indian team of the time. How could you not idolise Viv Richards and Michael Holding? I supported West Indies above all other teams, including Pakistan, till well into the 1980s. But slowly my identification with Pakistan's team grew. From 1982, Pakistan was captained by the great Imran Khan and as Viv's career began to wind down, my loyalties began to shift.

Pakistan's cricket tour to England in 1982 was a turning point. At his peak, Imran Khan was an enormously charismatic cricketer—

second to none. Good looking, well-spoken and fiercely competitive, he was a Pakistani who stood out on the international stage. He was also one of the best cricketers of his time. From his debut as a 16-year-old in 1971, Khan transformed himself from a useful medium pacer to a devastating fast bowler and a genuine batsman. As captain, he brought a new combativeness to the team, making millions in Pakistan believe that Pakistan could win a series against England. It was no longer enough to win a match, or for individual players to perform, only for the team to inevitably lose to the former colonial masters. In the end, even though Pakistan lost the series 2-1, there was a famous victory at Lord's. Back in Pakistan, Pakistan Television would arrange an hour's live transmission after lunch. But otherwise, I listened intently on the radio as new heroes emerged alongside Imran. The dashing opener, Mohsin Khan, scored an elegant double hundred at Lord's to set up the win. The mercurial Abdul Qadir, with a magician's beard to match, was the wizard who reignited the art of leg spin bowling.

Later the same year, I watched Imran destroy India's famed batting line-up in Pakistan. There were memorable spells in Karachi, Faisalabad and Hyderabad, where Khan's late in-swing and pace castled India's finest, including the stunning dismissal of Gundappa Vishwanath, where he left the ball only to see it snake back into his stumps. "Little Vishy" was never the same player after. Stories were rife of a shirtless Khan purposely walking through the Indian dressing room in an attempt to intimidate the opposition—masculinity, fast bowling and charisma combining to produce a unique attraction to Pakistan and its cricket at the time. Which Pakistani teenage boy was not at this time imitating Imran's iconic leap at the crease? In fact, even the Indian cricketers were in awe of him, as is apparent in Sanjay Manjrekar's effusive praise of Khan in his autobiography *Imperfect* (Harper Collins, 2017).

But what started with Imran Khan became a lifelong addiction. Pakistan cricket is uniquely compelling. The team, so mercurial over the years, produces a rollercoaster of emotions—up one day and down the next. Nothing quite represents Pakistan as intensely and closely as Pakistan cricket. The exuberance, the vitality, the youth, the chaos and the unpredictability are hallmarks of Pakistan and its cricket. Pakistan cricket breaks your heart time and again but there are occasions where they do the miraculous—more so than any other team playing international cricket. They confound you in a way that Pakistan has done as a nation. And suddenly, the hearts of millions soar, and for a while, you forget all your cares. Win or lose, the heightened emotions that watching and supporting Pakistan generates, produce a very strong bond to the team and the country.

Pakistan's famous victories—and their disappointments—remainseared into memory. Most difficult to accept were losses in World Cups to India, particularly in the quarter-final in 1996 in Bangalore and the semi-final in Mohali in 2011. But also, Pakistan's semi-final loss to Australia in Lahore in 1987, in a tournament where Pakistan was hotly tipped to win the title. In 1999, arguably the best one-day Pakistan team ever again lost to Australia in the final, in an abject display having played consistently well throughout the tournament.

But there were also memorable victories. Two of these stand out in my memory. Pakistan's 1992 World Cup win remains a defining moment for cricket in Pakistan. Led, for the last time by Imran Khan, Pakistan's campaign had been largely shambolic. Having only qualified courtesy a shared point due to an abandoned match that they would almost certainly have lost, Pakistan eventually reached the final against England. I was in London at the time preparing for a panel interview for a potential Master's program in international development at the University of Bath. The match lasted through the night and a group of us watched it together eventually bursting into wild celebrations when Pakistan finally clinched the title. It was all the more sweet a victory as it came against England, while I was in England. I recall speaking to many Pakistanis in England in the aftermath of that famous win. All spoke of how they would return to work or school or university with their heads held high. Imran

Khan signed off on a high but left Pakistan's cricket-loving fans with players that would dominate world cricket last for years to come—Wasim Akram, Inzamam-ul-Haq, Mushtaq Ahmad, amongst many others.

The second unforgettable match was in January 1999 during Pakistan's memorable tour of India. The fifth day was evenly poised. I was in Cambridge at the time, working on my PhD and had subscribed to the one satellite channel that was showing the series. I had also emailed a few Indians and Pakistanis, inviting them to watch the match at my place if they wanted. On that fateful final day, on a bitterly cold and dark January morning, four Indians whom I had never previously met, cycled over at 5 AM. I was joined by Bazid Khan, son of the legendary Pakistani cricketer Majid Khan and nephew of Imran Khan, who had come down from Sussex for the match. By 7:30 AM—the lunch break—the Indians were conceding defeat and congratulating us. Being magnanimous hosts, we insisted that the game was still open while inwardly celebrating. By 10 am, Sachin Tendulkar's remarkable innings had turned the tables. Crestfallen, Bazid and I were conceding defeat while our guests were quietly confident. Eventually, Pakistan won a dramatic game by 12 runs and received a standing ovation from the Chennai crowd as they completed a victory lap. We watched the remarkable scene as Indians and Pakistanis and as fans of cricket. At the end of the match, we had made new friends and Pakistan had won both the match and hearts of the Indian public. It was a moment of enormous pride made more special as my father had been asked to be the manager of the Pakistan team by Prime Minister Nawaz Sharif, on what was also a critical foreign relations initiative between the two countries. When I spoke to my father the day of the victory, he related that in all his years as a diplomat, as someone who had been on so many Indo-Pak negotiations, never had he seen such a spontaneous outpouring of emotion and goodwill between the two nations.

Sport and religion both create emotional responses and demand passionate attachment. Gods and sportsmen are worshipped. The worshippers enter into communion with the players to produce moments of heightened emotion in a display of what the great French thinker Émile Durkheim termed 'collective effervescence'. Cricket was a colonial legacy that was enthusiastically embraced and indigenised both in India and in Pakistan. In fact, such was the level of cricket's adoption in the subcontinent that it prompted the Indian social theorist Ashis Nandy[1] to call cricket 'an Indian game that was accidentally discovered by the British'. The sport subsequently became a means of cultural expression and resistance against colonial powers, helping to forge a sense of national identity. As Pakistan's most popular sport, cricket has therefore played a significant role in defining the culture and history of the country, thus becoming an essential part of its post-colonial identity and national pride. In Pakistan, it has often been ascribed great power as a national symbol of unity, able to integrate a multi-ethnic, culturally diverse, and stratified society. Cricket, therefore, has come to define Pakistan. When abroad, like I was, Pakistan cricket was the most evident part of your national identity, as highlighted in the two quotes at the start of this chapter where my interactions with people in England were defined through the lens of sport.

It is also worth pointing out that support for national sporting teams (in comparison to franchise and club-based teams), does evoke strong feelings of patriotism and pride and becomes an avenue for people to express their national identity and unity. Cricketers are seen as representatives of their countries on the global stage and their performances can have a profound impact on national morale and the way the country is perceived internationally. Until recently, cricket has been a sport that has revolved around national teams and intense competition between them, with England vs. Australia and India vs. Pakistan being the most celebrated rivalries. This has meant that cricket is often seen as more than just a sport in many countries and is deeply ingrained in the cultural fabric of these nations with rituals, traditions, and values that reflect national identity. Matches between

---

1	Ashis Nandy, *A Very Popular Exile:* [An Omnibus Comprising] *The Tao of Cricket; An Ambiguous Journey to the City; Traditions, Tyranny, and Utopias* (Oxford University Press, 2000), p. 1.

arch-rivals are more than just sporting events; they are seen as battles for national pride and identity.

The team, then, represents the nation. Love and engagement with Pakistan comes to be transmitted and amplified through support of and engagement with Pakistan cricket, usually in the form of physical presence at venues where they were playing or through the knowledge that you were part of a community of Pakistan fans dispersed across the globe but unified by their backing of Pakistani cricket. It helped that this aspect of Pakistan was one where Pakistanis could speak with pride and a feeling of equality with Englishmen or Australians or Indians for example. Pakistan could compete with the best in the world.

It is not surprising, therefore, that when I returned to Pakistan after being abroad for many years, I ended up undertaking research on what cricket symbolises for Pakistan—how it reflects the country's politics, history and culture. To have an investment in Pakistan's cricket game is to foster an intimate connection to the nation itself.

I returned to Pakistan in 2004 to take up a position at the Lahore University of Management Sciences, and it has opened a new chapter of my relationship with the country. For close to two decades, I have taught and interacted with some of the brightest young minds in the country and have seen them go on to succeed in a variety of careers. Some have become internationally acclaimed academics, writers, film makers and musicians. Others have contributed to Pakistan through going into the civil service or have set up exciting new businesses or have worked in the development sector. Through teaching these students there is a feeling of contributing, in however small a way it may be, to Pakistan's progress. It is a step towards trying to create a more inclusive and progressive society along the lines of what Mohammad Ali Jinnah had envisaged. In between, there have been offers to teach abroad that, while attractive financially, lack the sense of purpose that teaching a generation of Pakistanis has. To date, like my grandmother and my father, I have not regretted my decision to remain in Pakistan.

And yet Pakistan continues to produce contradictory feelings. While there is a tendency to romanticise the past—and as a teenager, one is less aware of the political and economic health of a country— Pakistan in 2024 compares poorly with Pakistan before the turn of the millennium. Today, we stare into the abyss, as we stand on the precipice. I have never known, in my lifetime, the uncertainty and hopelessness that is enveloping the country today. The political, economic and moral decline that one sees unfolding in front of one's eyes is an ever deepening and increasingly painful wound. Pakistan has fallen so far behind regional South Asia countries in human and economic indicators. It appears that the world is progressing while we fall further and further behind. The economy is collapsing, poverty and hunger is rising, terrorism is once again on the march. Education and health indicators show the parlous state of Pakistan's next generation. Pakistan is one of only two nations that have failed to eradicate polio—the other is Afghanistan, which has been wracked with civil war for decades. Society is increasingly characterised by extremism and polarisation. Pakistan's record on gender and minorities is desultory. Corruption has hollowed Pakistan from the inside out. Where we looked forward to winter, it is now a season full of despair and discomfort. The pollution in the air chokes citizens, the depleted gas reserves mean no heating or cooking. Even the climate seems to be angry at Pakistan. The winter rains have dried up. The summer monsoons bring misery and destruction. People leave their 'home' at a rate faster than ever before driven by a sense of hopelessness. According to newspaper reports, 225,000 people left Pakistan in 2021. In 2022, this figure had risen to 765,000, and comprised highly educated doctors, engineers, IT experts, accountants and academics. It also included the more than 200 who tragically drowned off the coast of Greece in a desperate attempt to secure a better future in a new and unknown land. The exodus shows no sign of abating.

India and Bangladesh, poorer than Pakistan twenty years ago, have marched ahead. Not dissimilar to Pakistan in the 1960s, South Korea, Vietnam, Singapore, Thailand, Malaysia are light years ahead now. Dubai has risen from the desert. Arch-rivals, Saudi Arabia and Iran move towards reconciliation while Pakistan and India bicker endlessly, denying themselves the chance for stability and prosperity in the region. 132 children are killed by extremists in 2014 in Peshawar, but still Pakistan's influential and powerful leaders lead the country down a path of self-destruction driven by self-interest and support for hyper-religious obscurantists.

Pakistan has had two Nobel Prize laureates—Professor Abdus Salam and Malala Yousufzai. Both were forced to live outside their homeland. Where are our icons and heroes today? The decline in sports is reflective. In the 1990s, Pakistan held the cricket World Cup (1992) and the Hockey World Cup (1994). The great Khans— Jahangir and Jansher—dominated squash in the 1980s and 1990s, winning an astonishing 14 World Open and 16 British Open titles between them. Today, only Pakistani cricket remains an international force. Pakistan's hockey team has failed to qualify for the World Cup or the Olympics for years. Recently, Pakistan's Dutch coach resigned from his position, claiming that the Pakistan Hockey Federation had not paid him for a year's work. In squash, Pakistan's past dominance is now a faint memory. Between 1982 and 1991, Jahangir Khan won an unprecedented 10 British Opens in a row and remained unbeaten for 5 ½ years, dominating the world in a way that few sportsmen can come close to rivalling. His great rival, Jansher Khan, won 8 World Opens and remained world number 1 for almost a decade without break (1988 – 1998). Before them Hashim Khan, Azam Khan and Roshan Khan had laid the foundations of Pakistan's subsequent dominance. Today, Pakistan's highest ranked player is outside the top 50. A proud and unrivalled record is being painfully consigned to history. How we have fallen.

In times like these, when those you teach or work with—who are the hope for the future—begin desperately to find a way out of the country, you begin to question whether the commitment to Pakistan is something that you can afford. Is this the country that Jinnah envisaged and that my family sacrificed for? Has the dream turned sour? Why not leave rather than stay for some misplaced sense of loyalty for a country that seems to have forsaken the values on which it was meant to have been founded? Is there any place for those who still subscribe to those values? Many Pakistanis abroad have excelled but will not return because they feel there is no future in the country. It is heart-breaking. Oh, Pakistan, you make it difficult.

And yet ... in Pakistan, my family and I have received immense respect from people in all walks of life. This is a recognition that would not have been received anywhere else except at home. This *is* home. If we do not work to improve it, what hope is left? Maybe mistakenly, I feel, Pakistan is the only place that I can still make a small contribution. Pakistan must not fail. I believe that, like citizens of other countries, Pakistanis want a safe and secure country that invests in its people and their future, so that the vast potential of the country can be realised. We want a prosperous and progressive nation, that takes its position in the comity of nations as a respected and responsible member of the modern world.

Less than a year ago, my father passed away peacefully at his home in Pakistan. He leaves behind a rich legacy in terms of his contributions to the country. And today, as I watch Pakistan cricket struggle in a way not seen previously, my engagement with Pakistan— through my family history and cricket—remains undimmed.

Ali Khan is the Professor of Anthropology at the Mushtaq Ahmad Gurmani School of Humanities and Social Sciences at LUMS. He is also the Dean of the School. His research interests vary from labour issues to popular culture in Pakistan focusing particularly on cinema and sports. Ali Khan's book *Representing Children: Power, Policy and the Discourse on Child Labour in the Football Manufacturing Industry of Pakistan* was published in 2007 by Oxford University Press. He was also the General Editor for a series of seven books on Sociology and Anthropology in Pakistan. Two major pieces of research resulted in co-authored and edited books on cricket—Cricket *Cauldron (I.B.Tauris, 2013)—and* Pakistani cinema—*Cinema and Society* (Oxford University Press, 2016). A second edited collection on cinema—*Film and Cinephilia*—came out in 2020. His latest monograph, *Cricket in Pakistan: Nation, Identity and Politics* was published by Oxford University Press in 2022. Ali Khan has an MPhil and a PhD in Social Anthropology from the University of Cambridge, England.

Unlearning Elizabeth
Zain Saeed

My students are exceptional drinkers. They have rented out several penthouse properties in New York City, where they live alone at the age of 18, have an inordinate number of friends called Linda and Bob—who are also exceptional drinkers—and party into the long hours of the night. They only know Pakistan as a terrorist state. They have sex all the time, with everyone, including Linda and Bob, and also their friend Jennifer, who is a vegan and a human rights activist that frequents yoga retreats in Nepal.

This is the impression one would get if they read some of the first stories that undergraduate students, born and raised in Pakistan, write in my classes. A quick interview will reveal that they've never been to New York, that there is no Bob in their lives, and that they went to their first party that was not a wedding just the day before. They're supposed to be writing fiction, so I suppose everything goes, but then I ask them, "Why?"—as in, why are you writing this story, or why should I read this story about Bob's libidinous escapades in Hawaii written by you, Abdullah, a lifetime resident of Galaxy Apartments, Gulshan-e-Iqbal, Karachi—when I could read a similar story written by an actual Bob who's actually experienced things in the same vein in the places you're talking about, someone who knows how those places breathe, and how they shape the people who live there?

They shrug in response, then get back to their phones.

The shrug can be articulated as follows: those are the stories I have heard, read, and seen, so those are the stories I tell. A more nuanced interpretation would include the fact that those are the stories that seem "valid", "cool", "internationally accepted", "impressive", and so I'd be an idiot to not want to tell them. And this is where I begin to earn my big bucks, that sweet teaching-money-rupee-moolah (that, for some strange reason, keeps on losing value just sitting in the bank ... but that is a story for another time). This is where my job becomes one of helping them unlearn—to escape, once and for all, the mental dungeons of Buckingham Palace, and to begin seeing their own lives as infinitely interesting stories that are worth telling.

* * *

I became aware of this phenomenon as a student at LUMS, where I took my first creative writing workshop, not because I was really interested in writing or wanted to become a writer (I did not), but because I could not believe that I could get a grade in a class by writing and reading stories. I could not let such an opportunity go. I no longer have the first story I submitted, but I vividly remember that it contained a Mr. George, and that there was something seriously wrong with him, for which he kept visiting a Dr. Arzt (this is, indeed, the German word for "doctor", which I felt was a tremendously clever idea at the time) (still do). Mr. George was a straight-up Casanova, but also, of course, thought deeply about matters of love and deep personal connection (I was trying to impress someone in class).

I don't remember what people said about that story, but I remember that it required only a cerebral effort from me. There was no heart there, no need for it. I created a story like my archnemesis AI creates "original" media—I just took a piece from here, a piece from there ('here and there' being other things I'd read, TV shows I'd watched, Hollywood movies I'd seen) and put them together into a somewhat coherent whole. I thought that's what you did, what you were supposed to do. It demanded little from me, and I was unchanged by the experience of writing it.

<Begin tangent> I realize now that language definitely played a huge role in why I thought a story had to be so. English is the language in which I read and consume media. It is not the language in which I (and most of bilingual Pakistan) consume Life. It felt impossible, almost wrong, incredibly *useless,* to tell a story in English about people who did not speak it, about lives that did not involve this foreigners' language outside of the academic sphere. It was a strange block, and in fact, it still is. It is hilarious to me that this entire essay is written in English. It is an evergreen comedy I must deal with every time I begin to write. It is even more pronounced here because I'm trying to talk about learning—as a colonized subject—to leave the West where it belongs. I can't dwell for too long on the consequences of this liminal space or I'll never write again <end tangent>.

But everything began to change when I got the chance to read other students' stories, students who'd been writing for a while and had not just taken the class for its notoriously easy B+. There were stories of agoraphobic men in Gulistan-e-Jauhar. Someone wrote about an extended family living in an old haveli in Rahim Yar Khan (or was it Mirpurkhas?). The story that completed my rewiring involved a Pakistani couple that enjoyed putting out their local Marlboros on each other's bodies (I was scandalized and intrigued in equal measure). All I needed, then, was simply to see stories about my world talked about with love, being discussed as valid, as just as good as anything written by drunk white men on typewriters in the 60s, and I was on my way to leaving Elizabeth behind.

* * *

Like music, like visual art, like film, we need to consume writing unabashedly, almost obsessively, before we can produce anything of worth. I've lost count of the number of times I ask my class, in the very first session of every semester, what they've read in life, and they respond—chests puffed out—with *The Alchemist* (digestible fantasy) and *The Forty Rules of Love* (diluted, book-club-worthy spirituality). It is always these two books, no exceptions, and these two books only, for at least 95% of the class. They don't even seem to recall the *Wuthering* (clearly withering) *Heights* of their O-Level days. IBA, IVS, HU—it is all the same. It is these two books, and then everything on Netflix.

Out of the hundreds of students I've interacted with, perhaps only 10–15 have mentioned a Pakistani writer in response to my question. Maybe 30 have mentioned an Indian, and that too, most likely, Arundhati Roy. It is clear that local writers hold no appeal, that there is no draw in their stories (probably because most of us write boring, depressing political drivel, but also because there are not that many of us to begin with, and no forums to hype us up). So, if the first sentence of this section is taken as fact, then it is no wonder that they can't immediately produce Pakistani stories of worth. It would be like asking a musician trained exclusively in the tabla to suddenly produce percussions for a metal song, or asking a tech-reviewing YouTuber to not look smug—they are from different worlds, is what I mean.

A lot of art is mimicry. The task of an artist, then, is perhaps to seek the right things to mimic, and those are what I—and clearly, my students—miss so terribly when I sit down to write.

* * *

A student once submitted a story that was set in the future of Karachi. I was very intrigued by the premise—who wouldn't be? The fact that this city could continue to exist even a week into the future is a miraculous notion to me every time I think about it. But as soon as I began to read, it became clear to me that our proverbial Elizabeth reigned even in our local dystopia. Tall buildings (I can imagine these, flimsy and swaying), neon lights (we'll have electricity?), crazy gadgets (you'll get mugged!), brands (plagiarized), state-of-the-art surveillance (believable), an almost-flying-car (good riddance the potholed roads of my present), bars (here we go), robot sex clubs (here we go again), and a host of other things that confounded me so much that I called this student to my office the next day.

"Where are the floods?" I asked him. "Where are the broken

houses? The poor? The slums? The ill? The broken cars? The abandoned malls? The smog hanging over everything? Why is everyone speaking like they're from the streets of Los Angeles?"

He clearly thought I was losing my mind, poor thing, because his response was very softly spoken. "We will develop as a nation, sir."

Develop. What a word. "To develop" means pure, absolute progress. "To develop" means to move away from everything we are to something we can never be. "To develop" means to not just adapt to the lives of "the developed" but to *adopt* them, emulate them, in every way possible. The developed Elizabeths of this world are our gods and our saviors.

I couldn't really articulate any of this—my hands were flailing, strange noises of incomprehension coming out of my mouth like some confounded pterodactyl. I sent him on his way with a nod of my head and the customary B+, and he probably never wrote again.

* * *

I find it hard to fall in love with Pakistani writing. Just something I needed to say.

* * *

It may be too far along in this essay to finally make this admission, but I think I should clarify that I have nothing against people named Elizabeth—in fact, one Elizabeth is largely responsible for why I can (on a good day, of which there are very few) call myself a writer. My graduate supervisor during my MFA in Austin, Elizabeth McCracken, is an astounding writer, and one of the greatest teachers and mentors anyone can hope to have.

Fresh off getting a story published in an American magazine— and hence high on believing that there really was a place for "Pakistani" stories in the wider world of publishing—I enrolled in her workshop with a half-written novel, ready to amaze my almost entirely white American cohort with my authentic portrayal of the Karachi experience. Being the overachieving child that I was, I volunteered to be the first person to be workshopped that semester.

<Begin tangent> Another admission before we continue: I don't really care much for the "workshop" model when it comes to my own writing. Don't get me wrong, I absolutely believe that it helps certain types of writers really hone their craft (that is why I use this methodology in my teaching), but I have to say that it does next to nothing for me. Whenever someone offers feedback on my work, I am always amazed as to how someone could read something so carefully to come up with a point like that, and then confounded as to how I'm supposed to take what they've said and apply it to my work, when I don't know what I'm doing 99% of the time I'm writing. It's true: I have no idea what I'm doing. I just, well, do it, and then if I don't like it I do it again. My rational brain doesn't really come into the equation. I suppose some feedback may seep in through my subconscious and make me do things a certain way without my realizing it, but for the most part, I am more or less just improvising. <End tangent>

As usual, the workshop on my novel started off with glowing reviews about the *voice*, how *original* it was, how much power it had, how quickly it flowed, how well I swore in my mother tongue, etc., etc. At that point, I was already convinced that the workshop setup wouldn't help me in any way, but what I didn't expect is how quickly, on that day, I began to see it as something *dangerous, a* community that would—through no mission of its own—eventually rid my writing of everything I wanted it to be.

"I do not believe a person could be like this." This is probably the comment that did it for me. It was directed at a character in the piece that I submitted—someone who was, in a nutshell, so desensitized to violence that he went on with his life as if nothing had happened after witnessing the aftermath of a politically motivated killing.

I've always marveled at the confidence of Americans in claiming to know everything about the world (they call their national sports tournaments *World* Championships and *World* Series after all), but it has usually been something that elicited either a laugh from me, or an eyeroll. But this person's statement made my blood boil to a degree that I'd never experienced before. I wanted to say so many things, oh so many things. But I just smiled and nodded, and the workshop ended.

And then I wondered: a person less stubborn than me, a young Pakistani writer who had actually signed up to be "taught" by the workshop—what would've happened to them after that comment and the ensuing conversation, where most seemed to be in agreement? Would they have changed everything, mutilated the very experience and the person they were trying to describe, to fit into some unanimous worldview? A point of view they'd grown up believing was "superior"? And then would they've been published just like that, speaking a language that was comfortable to the Americans and hence sellable, but nothing to do with the stories they wanted to tell?

If I hadn't been who I was, the workshop would've destroyed me. For once in my life, I was happy about my crazy stubbornness.

Elizabeth (McCracken, not proverbial) did take me to the side after class to say that I didn't really have to take all of that advice, and I could see she was saying that because she didn't agree with most of it, wasn't happy with it, but couldn't say it because all opinions are valid etc. I really appreciated that moment. But I never listened to anyone in the workshop again, doodled incessantly in full view—doodling as resistance, hah—much to their chagrin. The only two people who "got" me were an ex-convict and a former marine. I will leave it up to the reader to imagine all possible implications of this, because to list them down would need a whole book or two, and I don't think my heart would survive writing it.

* * *

I suppose what I'm saying is that the unlearning doesn't really stop. If any of my students were to go to the same MFA program now, and end up with the same one-dimensional cohort, they will have to begin the process of unlearning again. And then again when they look for agents. And then again, if they're lucky, with editors and publishers.

They will need to be made of reinforced steel; they will need to resist again the very comfortable worldviews that they fought so hard to murder in their undergrad at every step, the familiar worldviews of the TV and the films they grew up with, if they want to stand a chance at telling a true story of the place and the people they are from.

* * *

I have cried in the process of reading stories submitted by my students several times. Most of the time it has been because of a deep, dark hurt that this generation in particular seems so proficient at conveying. And because I know them as people, their work affects me in a tremendous way. But sometimes I have cried because I have seen true unlearning happen on the page, whether it's mutant beings hanging out in a deftly painted Keamari, students driving to Sea View and doing what students do (the sea is everywhere and I love it), or just two people sitting on a rooftop talking about a future that is not the one you see on TV, that is dark and desperate in a way that is truly local, full of trepidation and unearned hope, the kind we are all so used to. I'm not even sure how much of that has to do with me, if anything at all, but it makes teaching worth it.

The consequences of letting Elizabeth run rampant in our stories are terrifying. Our imagination is all we have to understand who we are, where we come from, and how we find our place in the world, and if that too is imported, unoriginal, inauthentic, then we are merely uninspiring replicas of things we are absolutely not, which, to me, is worse than being nothing at all. Elizabeth is not going anywhere any time soon, that much is clear, but I pray we are on our way to producing a worthy opponent to stand up to her when the time is right: an imagination that values its own histories, its own people, its own landscapes, and its own futures.

Zain Saeed is the author of the novels *"Little America"*, winner of the 2022 KLF Fiction award, and *"The Year of Sound and Heat."* He earned his MFA from the University of Texas at Austin. His work has appeared in several places, including *Glimmer Train, The Hindu BL ink,* the *Kenyon Review,* and the *Freiburg* Review. He lives in Morocco, where he teaches creative writing at Al-Akhawayn University in Ifrane.

Instagram: @zainssaeed

The First Story

Bee Gul

My maternal grandmother was a migrant and she remained one till her last breath. She received a huge house in Model Town, Lahore, Pakistan, in return for the property claim they had left behind in India. The house belonged to a Hindu who, I heard, used to visit the house every year. He was never made to sit in the drawing room—how could he sit there? This was his home once. Instead, he would sit in the kitchen, talking emotionally and endlessly about the days he had spent in the house, while my grandmother cooked vegetarian meals for him.

I was told that he kept coming for many years. He took all the idols from the pooja ghar, a worship room in the attic. His frequent visits aroused my grandmother's suspicions; she was sure he had hidden some treasure in the house and now came to search for it. My grandmother would keep an eye on him as he roamed around the house, which was his home once. He said he could still hear the voices of his family, and he could still smell the memories of mehndi on his wife's hands. He would sit near the "mehndi" (henna) plant for long periods, without saying a word.

After every visit, my grandmother would have the floor dug up in many places, searching for the treasure she believed he had hidden, which she thought brought him back. He stopped coming after a few years, but my grandmother never gave up searching for the treasure—

the treasure of loss, abandonment, death, displacement, migration and nostalgia.

I grew up in the same house, which stood bravely and firmly until it was brought down after my grandmother passed away. The house had distinct features of pre-Partition construction, and intense nostalgia crept into every chink and corner. It had borne the pain of partition in 1947. It was an undivided structure divided in soul and presence. One part of it waited for its inhabitants who left in a hurry, leaving their gods in the pooja ghar in the attic.

My paternal great-grandfather, on the other hand, was a migrant from Afghanistan—a member of a nomadic tribe who owned and loved the new land as their own. Perhaps it was because they weren't forced to leave their previous homes; they were not pushed out in a rush. They chose to migrate, to seek new lands, and they brought their gods and roots along with them. I felt more at home whenever I visited his place at the border of Punjab and Khyber Pakhtunkhwa (KPK) in Pakistan. I sensed the trees around his house had deep roots to hold onto, and the little fishpond was inhabited by native fish, not migrants.

I want to confess that I grew bitter towards the pain of the migrants. I was worn out and annoyed by the constant sense of loss and nostalgia that overshadowed their lives and hearts. I grew impatient with their extremely calculative nature; they appeared to be borderline misers to me. I wanted to pack and send them back to their previous homes and lands. I didn't want to accept these victims of partition and displacement; I felt they didn't belong here. They belonged to a past that was killed during the riots of partition.

The perpetual conflict between the past and the present— navigating between departure, acceptance, reconstruction, and renewal—shaped a selfish attachment to my country within me.

I believed this land belonged to me, born and raised among the trees lining the streets. An intense sense of belonging enveloped me, solidifying my resolve to never leave my country.

And I never did. I adamantly decided and stuck to my decision to never live the life of a migrant. I had seen them bleed until their last breath, and I refused to subject myself to the agony of constant nostalgia for a home lost forever, existing only in the fragments of memory.

I was only a month old when my mother, under circumstantial pressure, had to leave me with my grandmother in Lahore. I had a sibling who was twelve months older, a father who was critically ill in a hospital bed, and a mother who had no choice but to give me away. That was when I first experienced abandonment, lying in my cradle at just one month old. Of course, a 30-day-old baby cannot differentiate between abandonment and security, between displacement and stability. Of course, a baby barely a month old cannot comprehend what it feels like to be moved from one home to another. I don't know if I was sent with the cradle I was familiar with , given a new one, or if there was no cradle at all. Are cradles important for a baby? If so, how important are they?

I wonder how important it is for a newborn to stay close to their biological mother. Does separation make the child vulnerable to a sense of abandonment? Does it affect the child's well-being scientifically? Did I also have to migrate against my will when I couldn't even talk or walk? Would I have been a different person if my mother hadn't given me away? If she had to drag me, too, through the dark and cold corridors of the hospital where her husband, my father, was living on the brink of death?

If it wasn't me, it was my year-old brother who took his first steps in the hospital corridors, who said his first complete sentences outside an intensive care unit. We were siblings in separation. While his was the tiniest and most supportive hand my mother could hold during those traumatic times; I was the only baby in that huge house. There, I lived with my dysfunctional, unhappy maternal grandparents and my four unmarried, struggling uncles, all trying to cope with their lives. The house was also home to a cow, a calf, a goat, a dozen wild geese, a room filled with rabbits (most of them had been dissected and repeatedly sewn back by my maternal grandfather, who was a biology professor), a whole generation of dogs descended from 'Lassie,' and a monkey.

The monkey was a female, and my grandmother named her "Shado" – which, in hindsight, meant nothing at all. However, Shado the monkey was quite a character. She and I never got along well; she would sneak away my frocks and vanish into the trees. She was mischievous, and my grandmother often had to field complaints from the neighbours about Shado stealing their belongings. But before my grandmother could address the thievery, the country went to war.

The country had already experienced a war, but I hadn't. It was a conflict between the two halves who were the same country, a few years ago, it was an "unavoidable" division that had escalated into a series of wars.

So, the garden was all dug up, not for treasure hunting this time, but for trenches to dive into during the frequent air raids. The sirens wailed as often as the blackouts engulfed us. Amidst it all, calming a mere few-month-old baby from crying was a struggle. I was told that I cried a lot. I wonder why. Why would a baby cry endlessly during an air raid, amidst wailing sirens and darkness?

I have been told that I used to sleep a lot—as in, I would sleep for 48 hours (about 2 days) straight. Was sleep my escape? During this time, my grandmother and uncles would keep refilling my bottle with milk and Rooh Afza, the sweet red sherbet. Sometimes, I wonder how I didn't end up being an obese, diabetic person.

I must have been sleeping when the country was divided once again—too soon and too brutally. The country was wounded, but my father recovered. They believed he was too resilient to succumb to his injuries or give up on life.

My mother conceived me when she was not ready for another child so soon. She was still obsessed with her firstborn, who was just a baby when she became pregnant again. I'm told she did her best to abort this unwanted child, even going to an underground, illegal abortion center to get rid of me. But I survived. The inherent resilience refused to give up on life. I survived, but that part of the country did not. The Bengali abortion center and I were separated by a war.

My father survived, recovered, and wanted to bring his daughter back. I was told to return to my parents, whom I didn't recognize. I was seven years old, I learned of my exact age when my name, age, and the clothes I was wearing were repeatedly announced through the mosque's loudspeaker.

Shado, the monkey, was also sent to the Lahore Zoo in a cage. She screamed, tried to bite, and to escape, but they took her away. Years later, my uncle took me to see her. In the large cage labeled "Shado monkey and her family," there were many monkeys that looked like her. But despite our shared past, we didn't recognize each other.

I sought refuge in the cow's room, nestled behind the haystack. How could I trust strangers at just seven years old? Distinguishing between a mother and a grandmother felt like an impossible task. "A seven-year-old girl, dressed in a floral shalwar kameez and a pink chappal, has gone missing," echoed the mosque's preacher through the loudspeaker. As I slumbered peacefully behind the haystack, my secret remained safe with the gentle cow. My grandmother had purchased that red cow from Sahiwal at the horse and cattle show. It was stolen one night but found by the police the next day, along with its calf. I wondered how the thieves managed to lift her; she was massive. Then I realized, they didn't need to. They simply picked up its baby, and the mother cow followed. But my grandmother didn't follow my father's car as they, my parents, drove me away from my home... My first home— the pre-Partitioned house that had witnessed its inhabitants leave hastily and against their wishes.

I conveniently kept falling ill and was repeatedly sent back to my grandmother for quite some time. Illness would come to me easily whenever I wished for it, and I wished for it often. Until I grew familiar with my brother, whom I hadn't grown up with, my mother, whom I could never identify as my own, and my father, who doted on me— he wasn't a stranger. I had seen the his photograph—this handsome Greek god—tucked between the pages of "Panj Surah," (a book of five surahs) which my grandmother used to read in the morning. She would ask me to pray for the Greek god who was battling for his life in the hospital.

The highlight of my childhood was visiting my paternal grandfather's farmhouse. He was an Aligarian, conflicted between the aristocracy of Aligarh University and the nomadic disposition of his tribe. He would walk through the fields to collect his post from the railway station—the final stop in that area, the last station. Very frequently, I accompanied him on those evenings, relishing the opportunity to carry his posts—latest editions of the *Reader's Digest, Times,* and *Newsweek.* It was a tiny railway station, where the train would hoot multiple times before approaching its final stop. As the train started to move, I searched for my grandmother. Though my uncle was sitting close by, I couldn't spot her. A woman—a stranger— was asked to engage me in conversation as my grandmother quietly slipped out of the crawling train. The loud hoots echoed through the Lahore railway station as the train departed. I was being sent back to my parents after recovering from yet another illness among many. In those times, trains played a significant role in displacing people. At my paternal grandfather's village, the train wasn't displacing anyone; instead, it brought us interesting posts, goodies, and unexpected guests. My feelings toward trains remained conflicted, as I couldn't determine if they were inherently pleasing or painful.

In those days, spending the scorching hot summer breaks at the village was all I longed for. That home, those people, those trees, and that final railway station provided me with a profound sense of security. The nomadic tribe embraced me as one of their own, never recounting tales of migration or harboring memories of displacement. They cultivated their own food, tended to their cattle, and gathered under the star-studded sky, living a life untouched by the looming shadows of nostalgia or abandonment. In their midst, I felt safe—safe from the poignant ache of a lost past. I grew up experiencing both city life and country living, embracing the migrant culture and the timeless values of nomadic life.

I grew up loving my country deeply, a love tinged with the fear of migration, displacement, and separation. Torn between nomadic values and urban sophistication, I clung to my motherland—a place where I could always remain without being sent away. I associated motherhood with her.

When I look back, I always see myself writing. Scribbling behind doors, inscribing on walls with coals and burnt sticks, my stories and poems spread across my world. From my paternal grandfather's village to my maternal grandmother's home in Lahore, my writing journeyed from folk to urban, from ancient to contemporary. I translated and reflected, weaving together my two worlds, both belonging to the same motherland. I grew up with storytellers who would recount tales of their past. I wanted to tell stories too, but stories of the present—of the people around me, of the people of my land, of those who didn't have a lost past.

And I did. I wrote the stories of my people, of my women, of oppression, my pains, and my experiences. Little did I know that every story carried a lingering shadow of pain, of unsettlement, of rebuilding, of reimagining, and of trying to forget the lost past. Little did I know that my very first screenplay, which won me the Best Writer's Award, would be a story of displacement and partition. I didn't plan it; I was unaware of its theme. It was simply the first story that flowed from my pen.

Bee Gul is an award-winning screenwriter known for acclaimed dramas like *Talkhiyaan, Pehchaan, Dar Si Jaati Hai Sila,* and *Raqeeb Se.* Her films include *Laloolal.com* and *Intezar,* with *Jamun ka Darakht* winning Best Film and Script at the 2024 Cannes World Film Festival. She earned a LUX Style Award for *Dar Si Jaati Hai Sila* and a Hum Award for *Kaun Qamar Ara.* A pioneer in original theatre, her works include *Bedroom Conversations, Marney Say Pehlay Janat,* and *Pandra Minute Aur.* Bee Gul teaches at the National College of Arts (NCA) Lahore, serves on its board of studies. Additionally, she leads initiatives as the project head for Khan Academy Urdu and serves as the country manager for ERA, a nonprofit advancing education, research, and the arts.

Being Pakistani Is
Never Enough

Arslan Athar

Many years ago, two men, unrelated to each other at the time, made identical decisions that were controversial for their times. Both had a lot in common; they served in the military and were part of a generation that saw the end of the British Raj and the beginning of independence. Their decision, even in today's light, is progressive: they did away with family names, *zaat*, and *baradari*.

This generation had the important job of bringing up the world's first-ever Pakistanis—a truly *azaad* generation. I appreciate the magnitude of that task, and how everything, down to surnames, would have felt like a heavy decision. It was a new country. In my family's case, their identity was formed anew.

How could my grandfathers have known that I, their grandson, would grow up in another country, finding comfort in my umbrella identity of being Pakistani, but upon returning to Pakistan, I'd be challenged on this overarching identity? That I would have to ask myself and my family questions such as "Who am I?" How were they to know *"Pakistaniyat"* on its own wouldn't be enough, that the cultural identities they were so quick to shed would come to hold great currency and relevance? A lot of my grandfather's children argue this was incredibly forward-thinking, to raise a family agnostic of *baradari* and *zaat*. It might have been easy for my grandfathers because of our family's army background. In reality, everyone else in Pakistan is still rooted in place in the country on their identity, their background and culture. The problem boils down to this: can *Pakistaniyat* be defined as a new identity in and of itself, or is it an identity made up of other identities, an amalgamation of sorts? The issue with the first definition is that it requires the sacrifice of one's own identity. The second definition juxtaposes the first in demanding a recognition of past identities—ones harkening to a time before the advent of nation-states. The first definition promotes *Pakistaniyat* as new and unique unto itself, while the second argues *Pakistaniyat* is built up of identities rooted not only in the nation but also in the region. State organisations prefer the first definition—*Pakistaniyat* as a unique and singular concept—whereas the people of Pakistan are still split. Some lean towards the first definition, while others lean towards the second, leaving a lot of Pakistanis in a strange grey area.

This story of understanding *Pakistaniyat*, as in my own journey, did not start in Pakistan. I grew up in Dubai, where people fit into very specific boxes. Your nationality defined your place in society, how freely you could move, and the social mobility you could achieve. My box was always "Pakistani." It was a simple box to remember and carry. It helped me connect with others in the same box. There, the intricacies of the box didn't matter; the many boxes within the singular "Pakistani" identity weren't relevant, or at least, acutely felt. This simplistic identity also led to something very interesting: the ideas of identity convergence and identity negotiation. This didn't happen exclusively to me or all "Pakistanis"; this happened to everyone in Dubai, and it can be argued that this phenomenon takes place in any "third culture"[1] context. The ideas of convergence and negotiation come from multiple research studies about third-culture kids and the general experience of being an expatriate. You "converge" your identity to the nearest available similar ones; so, for a Pakistani like myself, convergence would happen either with Indian culture (due to a shared history and culture), or with Arab or Muslim culture (a more

---

1 Kwon, Jungmin (2019), "Third Culture Kids: Growing up with mobility and cross cultural transitions": *Michigan State University*

faith-based identity). This effect creates a sense of losing touch with your own "box", trading it with a more pervasive or recognisable one. Where convergence seeks to merge and grow, identity negotiation highlights a sense of "loss", or a feeling of lacking something; some cultures might be more popular or pervasive, impeding on yours. You grow up feeling you have to fight for your identity or its continuation. Of course, when growing up in the UAE, I didn't have this vocabulary of negotiation and convergence. Looking back, however, it did apply to me. Not having a firm understanding of what being Pakistani meant, I felt untethered to my "box", and it needed to find a home. These dual feelings of negotiation and convergence lead to what is globally known as the third culture—shedding parts of your identity to join a more cohesive overall identity, becoming more universal rather than personal.

Our school in Dubai, on account of being predominantly 'desi', offered Urdu as a second language (the 'first' being English). A small circle of text indicated what grade level the textbook we were using was meant for. More often than not, that circle mocked us, always two to three grades below where we actually were in school. At the back of the book, there was a stylised version of the *Qaumi Tarana* written out. One day, I placed my textbook, *Tarana* side up. One of our classmates, an Iranian, glimpsed it and picked up the text. "This is Farsi!" she said, in shock. I clearly remember my first thought: "Oh my God, are we also Iranian?" I kept the thought to myself.

I also clearly remember once being asked where in Pakistan I was from. Our family was split so there was no simple answer. I said my grandparents lived in Karachi, to which my friend said, "Yeah, okay, so you're from Karachi then." This became my answer if someone asked me that question.

I don't want to associate the national anthem with understanding identity, but another memory about the anthem does illustrate my point. The UAE won a gold medal in the 2004 Olympics. That night, at a *daawat*, we discussed this win. One person laughed and said, "Can't believe we missed it! We could have sung the Emirati anthem. *Matlab*, it's the only one we know!" Another kid in the crowd took offence and huffed out of the room. The one who spoke earlier defended himself, asking, "Do you guys even know the Pakistani anthem?" The silence was telling.

My childhood was an identity storm; family history was rarely discussed, culture was rarely discussed, and the effects of a "third culture" acted upon us with full force. It sounds destabilising to read, but looking back, it was not destabilising to live through, mostly because "home", as a city and physical space, was constant. We lived in the UAE; therefore it felt stable. I had negotiated and converged my understanding of identity and there was nothing and nobody to dispute it; everyone there lived the same way. This isn't to say it was bad or good; only that it was and is a fact.

James Marcia[2], a prominent psychologist, built a framework to understand identity development. Broken down, his framework compared two questions:

Have you committed to an identity?

Have you explored identity options?

Your answer, a yes or no, would determine what stage you're at. A yes to both, which he theorised was ideal, is called "Identity Achievement", and a no to both is "Identity Confusion/Diffusion." He identified a lot of factors playing into both questions, ranging from the family you were born into, their identity, to the identity society ascribes you. I look at my time growing up through this lens. "Identity Diffusion" fits my feelings at the time rather well; I hadn't committed to one identity, and I hadn't explored much. I committed to "Pakistani", but I didn't really understand what that meant, and that "commitment" would unravel soon enough.

I would see the exploration side of things in play whenever we visited Pakistan. I mainly interacted with my cousins. My family was culturally and geographically mixed and the display of identity was always on a spectrum. My cousins had communities of friends, people they identified with—be it their friends from their building

---

2   Marcia, James (1996). "Development and validation of ego-identity" *Journal of Personality and Social Psychology*

block or other cousins they were close to. Early friendships are always formed that way. However, within this, tones of identity and sentiments surrounding them always played up. They came up when parents talked about who their kids played with, or who their neighbours were. "*Haan*, they're Bihari/Delhi-walas/Kashmiri/Syed/Hyderabadi." The list went on and on. As identifiers and differentiating factors, mentioning background could make sense, but the consistency with which this conversation came up made it seem there was currency in these identities. Hearing about an identity that isn't your own, you could, through unsaid rules and traditions, place that person in a hierarchy. Many people found themselves disappointed in my parents who carried an idealised version of identity without hierarchy, like their fathers. I'm sure this isn't what Marcia meant when he theorised identity exploration, but in the Pakistani context, people had explored—of their own volition or through learned stereotypes—what other identities were, and how to understand oneself better with or without them.

On one of these visits, and again later, when I moved back to Pakistan, I was given a reality check vis-à-vis identity. I told someone, "I'm from Karachi." I was taught in Dubai it was okay to say that.

The person I said this to asked me, "Have you ever lived in Karachi?"

"No." I answered shyly.

"Then how can you say you're from Karachi?" At that point, I was sweating bullets.

Therein lay the biggest unravelling of my identity. In visits to Pakistan, the question of identity could be escaped, but moving back there, it became unavoidable. Until then, everyone around me inhabited a "box", and everyone around us took that box at face value. This was the first time everyone around me shared the "box", —everyone was Pakistani— and I was faced with a question: *"What am I beyond that?"* I had no answer, and no one had ever prepared me to find one.

Big city identities such as "I'm from Karachi/ Lahore/Islamabad" were heavily dependent on the time spent in those cities. My claiming roots in Karachi because my grandparents lived there until 10 years ago was not acceptable; I had never "lived" there, nor did I understand the city. Both halves of my family were raised with an overarching understanding of "*Pakistaniyat*", with the reality that no one was rooted in one place, or one city. Saying my dad's side of the family was "from" Karachi felt disingenuous—they moved about, and considering my own father's movements, Karachi was the city he spent the least time in. The same applied to my mom's family, although she confidently identified with Islamabad as she did the most "living" there. The obvious conclusion would be, "I am from Dubai" but no one is really "from" there. The country doesn't offer citizenship, so how can one claim identity in a place that doesn't offer it back?

If not cities, then, I wondered if I could claim the "box" of broader identity. I knew my *dudyaal* were from Hyderabad Dhakkan, and that my mother's family was from Punjab. I shared this 50–50 split but I didn't neatly fit into any one identity. People didn't understand how to "box" me. I can think of two friends who taught me what it meant to belong to an identity and take pride in it. Their identity didn't infringe upon their "*Pakistaniyat*" but improved it. They were both from Bihari families and raised to appreciate this fact. Conversations with them often came down to talking about their family histories or cultures: what they ate as children or the Bihari phrases they grew up around. Their grandparents were the protectors and the propagators of culture. They held their identity near and dear and felt the responsibility to share it with their children and grandchildren.

In an assignment for our Pakistan Studies class, we had to write a family history paper. The recently-returned-from-overseas Pakistani in a class of 150+ students, I was utterly confused and asked the instructor to let me see some work submitted last year to get a sense of what might be expected. Paper after paper was about how culture and unique identities were inherited. Students who wrote the papers felt a strong pull towards their history, ancestors, and culture. When I returned the papers to the instructor, she asked if they helped.

I chuckled and said I didn't know how to answer the question, but that I'd figure it out. I wanted to say those papers made me incredibly sad. I didn't feel the things those students talked about. I didn't feel a connection with my past. Not to sound terribly cliché, but I didn't feel a connection with "the land" so to speak. Before that point, I didn't realise this was missing from my life, but once I did, it was all I could think about. Whenever I went home for the holidays, this feeling boiled under the surface. I asked why our family's relationship with identity was so weak, and my mother was a little heartbroken to hear it. For both my parents, still in Dubai at the time, the idea of *Pakistaniyat* taking precedence and importance was still salient. To hear me speak like that was disheartening. But one's identity was paramount and no *Pakistaniyat* was complete without understanding the cultures and identities within it.

My parents' response was simple: the intricacy of identity didn't matter. I retorted, asking how they never wondered what their identity was. There was always a baseline understanding of background, of knowing where the "original" family was from, but as my parents said, "It's in the past and we were taught not to dwell on it. Of course, life did not let us dwell on it either." Something else came through in their responses, the implicit understanding that identity was political. The political did not have had a home when they were growing up. Staying away from identity politics let them be safe—or at least, live in the illusion of safety. As mentioned previously, the definition of *Pakistaniyat* as a new and unique identity unto itself forces us to look away from our *zaat/baradari*. It forces us to look away from the privilege (or lack thereof) our identities carry, forces us to accept a narrative where identity is devoid of nuance and that somehow harbours peace and unity. Acknowledging the politics of identity unravels this narrative. For many years, that illusion of safety had, in some ways, stripped us of our identity. It became evident the change I was looking for couldn't have happened retrospectively but rather had to happen in the now, brought forth by my hands.

The process of understanding oneself began with a simple

question, "Who am I, and what importance does this hold for me?" At that time, I had neither answer and had to start from scratch. I was in Punjab then, and chose to start with that half of my identity. A few elders were still around, so I went and asked them: "What was life like back then? What memories do you still hold dear? Who were the elders when you were young?" I learned our family had a long line of hakims, and some members of the family practised *hikmat* (natural medicine) as a trade; they had mentors they learned from for over 5 years, and apprentices of their own. I even saw one of the few remaining handwritten notebooks on natural medicine. I learned our family's connection to land and farming moved them across the plains of Punjab to settle in the farmlands around Faisalabad. There was a special joy in learning the family had a long history of education and being educators too. Family elders wore their beliefs and politics on their sleeve, with pride, from the creation of Pakistan to the later turbulent eras of Pakistani politics.

On the other hand, conversations about Hyderabad and Hyderabadi-ness began and ended with food, or at least in my family they did. Understanding culture and our past came from food— the food my grandmother cooked and what her mother cooked, so on and so forth. A lot of contemporary understanding of Dakhni culture was also based on food since the region's cuisine is unique. Funnily, a friend's parents once remarked, "Oh Hyderabad. *Wahan ke log kaafi khattay hotay hai!*" (The people from there are quite sour). I laughed and said, "*Khanay jo humaray khattay hain.*" (It's because our food is so sour). We both laughed! It was a well-recognised point of discussion around Hyderabadis—*khattay log aur khattay khanay*! But beyond this, much of the understanding of the history and culture of Hyderabad was lost. On this side of the family, elders were far fewer and far between. The internet came to my rescue. Proud Hyderabadis on YouTube and Instagram showcased their city and its history. Walking tours were put online, with voiceovers talking about the unique Nizaami history and culture. Hyderabad, due to its geographical and cultural location, incorporated several traditions from the neighbouring empires and dominions of the time.

In fact, the internet helped me understand a lot about both sides of my identity. From ladies in Indian Punjab uploading videos of their everyday lives to in-depth analyses of Hyderabadi culture, the internet brought together elements of myself I didn't have access to earlier. My first exploration came through videos of women in villages in Indian Punjab coming together to sing and dance at weddings; it differed so much from the typical sit-down *dholkis* we grew up with. These women, of all ages, stood together in large circles, singing and pushing each other in the middle to dance. It made me wonder what a Hyderabadi wedding looked like and of course, YouTube delivered. The sound of the *dhol*, the tune of the songs—all changed. This led me to discover vlogs and even cooking channels with content shot in everyday kitchens. The voiceovers helped me understand variations in language, different turns of phrase, and the general ups and downs of how language and identity were expressed in how people spoke.

In a way, the World Wide Web also taught me I'm not alone in this feeling of being "unattached" to my identity; there are others too. They thanked the creators for their tireless preservation efforts in the comments sections. In a lot of ways, the creation of postcolonial states with singular "identities" relating only to the nation as a singular entity wreaks havoc on indigenous identities. With each generation, the question of allegiance is posed; do you stand with your inherited identity or do you stand with the monolith identity the state gives to you? The question forces a choice, but there is no choice. Both identities work together, not against one another. Learning about my identity in no way decreased or diminished my *Pakistaniyat*. If I had continued to ignore the other aspects of my identity, I would have continued being "Pakistani" but with an incredibly shallow understanding of what that meant.

Thinking back to the original decision my family made, a lot of the logic behind it relates to the question of allegiance. But it is also explained by the fact that for "new" Pakistanis at the time of Partition, it was a new start. They were truly '*azaad*'. The British Raj had left and they had the opportunity to govern themselves and shape their own destiny. It was time to put your head down and work. Conversations about identity and the past seemed to go backward rather than forward, especially considering their families and children were the new country's future. Then, as generations grew up, they were pressured to "make it" and build a life—the first generation of children born in the free land had to make something of themselves. A new nation, a new generation, it all had to work to keep the nation going. Here too, momentum was always forward, never looking back. Along the way, as more Pakistanis came into existence, they asked more questions about being Pakistani. The independence movement's fervour and the jingoism of the wars with India eventually died down; we had to define ourselves, for ourselves. This involves looking back and honouring our past. Many families did and continue to, but just as many don't. It isn't always malicious; the subject just doesn't come forth as important or worthy of discussion.

Pakistan today suffers from a considerable degree of identity crisis, from individual families to the nation. There is friction in where one begins to draw their history from. The answer in people's hearts does not match the overarching narrative. It is encouraging to see young people deal with this question, even for just themselves. Understanding yourself is incredibly important. For too long, we've tried to understand larger narratives around identity, rather than individual narratives around identity. In my case, understanding myself helped me place myself better, not only in Pakistan but also the world. History, as it pertains to me, helps form my worldview and where my personal politics or ethics lie. This isn't to say I fully know myself. It is a journey, and I'm committed to the journey—kind of addicted to it! I am a Pakistani. Within that, I am so much more. I couldn't be prouder.

Arslan Athar is a writer based out of Lahore, Pakistan. In 2021, he was a South Asia Speaks fellow, where he worked with mentor, Fatima Bhutto, as he wrote his novel. His articles and nonfiction work have been published in Newsweek, Narrative Initiative, GenderIT, and The News International. Additionally, his fiction work has also been published in international and local publications.

Instagram: @arslaniswriting

Home Is Not A Place

Seher Fatema Vora

My father's home in Karachi's Shabbirabad enclave always felt like an oasis at the end of the dusty chaos of Shahrah-e-Faisal Road, nearly a straight shot from Jinnah Airport. The once pale blue gate, now painted over in a charming but unfamiliar shade of purple. The towering langra mango tree in the courtyard, whose fruit—to this day, the sweetest I've ever tasted—I've not eaten in over twenty years. The creepers on the surrounding walls, tended so carefully by my cousin and the mali, the open porch where Dada used to hold court in his wheelchair. And the massive front door, heavy and hard to close, which stayed open and welcoming to visitors during the day and was painstakingly locked in three different places at night.

That was Abu's home. It felt like mine too, even though our visits became shorter and more spread out over the years, from three months every summer, to once every other summer, to once every few years in the winter, to once every few years for a maximum of a week. I only thought of that house when I thought of home. I sometimes do still.

Probably, my first memories of anything were in that house. Probably, I took my first steps there. Bits and pieces of the summers and winters of my life, forming more than mere fractions of who I've become. And yet, this place I still think of as home is a place that I don't seem to know at all. It is a place in which I do not feel comfortable to move freely, a place where I don't know anyone besides my family and their network of friends. And even that network wanes, as the search for a better quality of life continues to suction individuals, families, and even entire generations away from the homeland in the debilitating process known as brain drain. *I don't blame them*, is what I think. But what do I know? I am second-generation. Not an immigrant, but the daughter of immigrants. A visitor—a tourist. To some, an interloper, even. What do I know?

* * *

It's always felt like I was leaving my "real" life for a little bit whenever we made our preparations to spend summers in Karachi. Largely, this was due to the rigor of travel in those days: whereas now, you can hop a sixteen-hour flight to Dubai and catch a plane to Karachi from there, it used to be the case that at least two or three layovers were involved in the process. The first trip to Karachi that I remember clearly was one of these. It was a harrowing series of journeys from San Francisco to New York to London to Karachi, and the ordeal was made no better for the prospective boredom that I was sure awaited me in the next two months.

No matter if it was one layover or three, these cross-continental flights always seemed to touch down in Karachi in coordination with the sunrise. And so, the first sound that we heard upon arrival—apart from the pilot's greeting—was always the sound of the azaan, calling the people for Fajr prayers. Perhaps that's why we always met less than our fair share of Karachi's dreadful traffic on our way home; what made the route from Jinnah Airport feel like the descent into a different dimension, one deceptively tranquil until you watched it come to life from the confines of a car.

Those early trips are hazy in my mind, faded by the filter of time, certain threads of memories shining more brightly than others. But those threads remain some of the most durable parts of the fabric of who I am today, even as I continue to grow and change. Quran lessons with the local red-bearded maulvi, whose deep voice I feared, but whose impeccable tajwid and resonant qirat remain forever tied with my recitation of prayers now. Excursions to the local darzi, where the endless bolts of colorful fabrics and prints, rolls of lace and boxes, always ended up as a shalwar kameez of my own design, tailored just for me. Being ferried around in an ancient white Corolla with its wheel on the right side, ending up at some relative's house to be stuffed with samosas and biscuits and mithai. All surface-level recollections of a charmed life, if you could ignore the ditch-studded roads, the endless clamor, and the dusty surroundings.

This never bothered me, though. There was such vibrancy in everything: in the way people moved, in the sincerity of their speech, and even in the honking of their horns as they drove past. The resulting cacophony, mixed with the call to prayer emanating from a hundred different masjids at the same time, five times a day, became the backdrop of home. A place where I didn't stick out at all, because I was with my people.

But there were deep layers embedded into those surroundings, indications of discontents and the unsavory parts of life that are sometimes scrubbed from our memories over the passage of time. Karachi is filled with the contradictory sight of exorbitant wealth juxtaposed with the decay of extreme poverty, and it is not something that can be ignored, no matter how hard one tries. Displaced as the memory is in the timeline of my childhood, I will never forget the first time I registered it, and how I could never unsee it thereafter.

Abu and my uncle had taken me along to visit an old professor of theirs who was in hospice care at Anklesaria Hospital, a nonprofit facility located in the heart of Karachi's Saddar district. A major commercial area and home to the city's famous Empress Market, it was as wondrous as it was overwhelming. From electronics, to jewelry, to produce—anything could be found for sale here if you had the fortitude to navigate your way through the tangle of cars, foot traffic, alleyways, and storefronts.

Usually relegated to the car for trips through such thoroughfares, I was surprised when we parked off the side of the main road (what we called parking might well have been completely illegal anywhere else, of course), not in front of a hospital at all, but by a busy market street that showed none of the ordered sobriety one would expect to see near a healthcare facility. Abu took my hand, perhaps gripping it more tightly than usual, and began weaving through the throng, behind the shops and into a maze of alleys that were just as crowded as anything out on the open street. I clung to his hand like a vice. These sensations were new to me; I was filled with the visceral fear that if I let go, I might be swept away by the crowd, never to be found again.

We were about ten minutes into our walk when I first caught the smell. Raw and bloody, with a slightly iron tang of sweetness that comes with fruit gone bad, it was totally pervasive, wrapping around the senses like a cloud rather than creeping in whiff by whiff. I looked up and realized with horror that we were surrounded by hanging hunks of freshly butchered meat. Our route had led us directly into a butcher's alley.

Unused to such a blatant display of savagery, I was audible in my distress, almost crying with disgust. What other reaction was I supposed to have? The surface-level charmed view I had of Pakistan was shattered in that moment. As we tried to navigate around the pools of bloody mud that accumulated at the edge of the street, Abu reassured me that we would get to the hospital soon and not to fret, that we'd find a different way to go back.

When we arrived at the hospital at last, we were presented with the rather severe facade of a drab and slightly dilapidated building. I remember it being eerily quiet there, though we had not walked far from the market street. Yet the smell of raw meat lingered in my nostrils, overtaken though it was by the drying odor of antiseptic, and I could not forget it as we finally finished the visit and drove back home. I have not forgotten it since.

From that moment on, the quiet serenity of the house in Shabbirabad became an oasis of calm in the middle of the city. Beyond the cries of the sabziwala and the call of the azaan, the rest of Karachi, now characterized by its smells—the smells of freshly made pakoras and nihari, of hot salty Kashmiri chai, the smells of car exhaust and gas, too-sweet paan and garbage and raw meat—was a world away.

* * *

Like the majority of Pakistanis, I am Muslim. Unlike most Muslim Pakistanis, I am Shia, part of a small community of the Ismaili Shia sect known as the Dawoodi Bohras. And yet, none of those nuances mattered in the wake of September 11, 2001. To the faceless agents of the TSA and other airport security agencies, our Muslim-sounding names, our travel itineraries, and our brown skin were enough to send one message: threat.

I was nine years old.

We know this. We know the horror stories. How Muslim men were tormented and discriminated against, how women wearing the hijab were attacked and assaulted. How anyone adjacent to our communities, both in looks and by perception, was also in harm's way. All that, coupled with the very real horror of the image of the towers crumbling to the ground, like they were made of so many thousands of toothpicks, held up only by the most fragile thread. The hundreds dead, right here in the country I was born in—a country that was also my homeland. The icy fear of knowing that my uncle could have been one of the casualties, saved only by the grace of Allah and one late train.

We know what followed. The wars, the destruction, the collective trauma, whose aftereffects continue to reverberate arguably up to this very day. Almost every single one of my Muslim friends, no matter their ethnic background, has some tale of harassment at the airport, and now, over twenty years later, they still remain realities and not just anecdotes, not just funny stories, not just *remember that time when...?* For us, "that time" is still now.

Our routines of returning to Pakistan were not much interrupted; yet I think back to this time as when my perception of this travel was forever changed. We were not just travelers in the eyes of Homeland Security anymore. We were suspicious individuals, to be interrogated for the offense of having a homeland elsewhere in the world. I experienced this shift in December that year, as we made our way back to Karachi in the wake of Dada's death, and even though I was only nine years old, I remember that it invoked such anger in me. Anger at being treated as other in the country I was born in. Anger on behalf of my other homeland, judged unfairly for events that were out of our control. I was afraid of this new reality, and what it might mean for the future, for my family, for my friends. I remember the dreams I used to have in those days, of being carted off in the middle of night by faceless policemen, separated from my parents, all for the crime of having two homelands between which I could not choose.

But so too, I remember, for the very first time, feeling pride in being Muslim. In being Pakistani. In standing by my people, my religion, my culture, against all such odds. There was pride in being forthcoming about my faith at school and in speaking Urdu with my family in public instead of opting for English. Instead of complaining about having to wear brightly colored shalwar kameez to family parties and events, I wore them as a symbol of my heritage, and held my head high. And so, I looked forward to going back. I looked forward to going home.

* * *

Community is a different animal in Pakistan. It is hard to explain the overpowering feeling of belonging when everyone in a place looks like you, speaks the same language as you, follows the same religion and celebrates the same holidays. It is as all-encompassing as it is completely indiscernible. There is a feeling of wholeness that permeates the soul inside and out. You can forget all of a place's faults in light of these virtues; no matter how elsewise dissociated and distant you might feel, these commonalities sometimes can be enough, condensed into a moment that you can pocket and take with you to revisit when you are alone.

The holy month of Ramzan used to fall in the winter back then. The ritual of fasting was always a trial in California; in Karachi, it was torture. The days were comparatively hot and never-ending. Never before had I appreciated thirst for the killer that it could be. And yet, it was different from any Ramzan that I'd spent elsewhere. In California, we spent our evenings at home and weekends at the Korean Baptist church our tiny community rented in lieu of a proper masjid. In Karachi, the masjid was right next to our house, and family and friends would turn up on our doorstep at the drop of a hat, without so much as a phone call in advance, to have iftari together after sundown.

I was the appointed sentry back then—the doorbell was broken, and so whenever there was a banging at the gate, it was my responsibility to stick my head out the living room window and shout "Kaun!" at the top of my lungs. A ridiculous duty to give me, and how my cousins loved to laugh as I struggled! I didn't know anyone's names beyond 'Aunty' and 'Uncle'; I had no way to judge who was at the door. But I'd let them in regardless, pushing the button that unlocked the outer gate from the inside, and the guests would cross the threshold and greet me boisterously, surprised at who I was every time—" Younus ki beti, hai Allah kitni bari ho gayi ho, mashAllah, mashAllah!" No matter who came, this reaction was consistent: happy surprise at my being the daughter of the friend who had moved so far away, and shock at how much I had grown, by the grace of Allah. Food was exchanged freely, and talk would last late into the night before the cycle started all over again, a hearty breakfast brought in at sehri time before everyone went back to bed to sleep it off.

Each of the rooms in the house gained its own significance in these daily routines. There was the living room where we spent most of our time, watching dramas on *HumTV*, playing board games like Ludo and Caram and Dadu. The formal sitting room, with its stiff couches and greater dining table, where guests ushered in from the gate were seated, and the trolley featuring chai and biscuits and various other finger foods painstakingly rolled out. The three bedrooms, doors in a row used mainly for sleeping and storing our many hauls from bazaar shopping. The tiny kitchen, where we shared breakfast and dinner. Upstairs was the attic, used as a painting studio by my older cousin and decreed by him to be off-limits to the "babies"—he, in turn, had inherited it from Abu, for whom it had functioned as some sort of all-purpose lab for harebrained experiments in his youth. And, of course, the open rooftop, where a clear view of the neighborhood with its many houses and palm trees could be had amidst the backdrop of a dusky sunset. I loved the evenings spent there the most.

Between the call of the azaan five times and the two meals a day, community was a woven reality of everyday life. It remains a beautiful thing. It calls to the heart and sets itself into the soul. And the house in Shabbirabad, with the blue gate and the lone langra mango tree, with the broken doorbell and the always-occupied living room, was the fixed centre of it, around which my memories continue to revolve.

* * *

I always had a sense that Pakistan is what the world thinks of as a "third-world country," even though I didn't come across the term until I was in high school. Its difference from my Bay Area suburban bubble was stark—unkempt infrastructure and roads, beaten-looking cars, beggars on every corner of the street. But for a long time, Pakistan never fell into the category of what qualified to me as "dangerous." It was polluted and littered, sure. The electricity went out without warning, and every once in a while, the hot water shut off. No one was ever on time for anything and the shopping was cheap, clothes and shoes and jewelry always up for a bargain.

But dangerous? No. I, the child of immigrants who grew up away from Pakistan's political turmoil, had little idea about the many coups and rampant corruption that had become landmarks of the political landscape over the years since independence in 1947. I knew nothing of the regional wars that Pakistan had taken part in, or the atrocities its leadership were complicit in, because those things were not taught at school and were not spoken of at home.

So when, on December 27, 2007, we received the news that the popular prime ministerial candidate Benazir Bhutto had been shot and killed in Rawalpindi during a contentious bid for reelection, the immediate fear was not for what would become of the country. Instead, it was the sharp and primitive fear of the personal kind: all for Ami, who had gone to Karachi for a wedding and who, we feared, would not be able to get out.

I remember her account of that terrible week so vividly because everything about it was shocking to me. The news of the shooting, which was widely assumed to be an assassination. That even in Karachi, miles and miles away from where the killing had taken place, the entire city went from devastating chaos to the silent dystopia of limbo.

Here is what happened:

That day, Ami had planned to go shopping in the Zamzama Market in Karachi's well-to-do Defence neighborhood with her sister. Having been picked in the morning, the two, along with my aunt's son and another relative, made their way into Karachi's usual congested traffic, unconcerned with the world outside, keeping up a lively chatter as they made plans for the day's shopping for gifts, clothes, jewelry, and anything else they could find.

But when my uncle called, this rosy outlook withered within the span of thirty seconds.

"Come back, immediately," Ami recalled my uncle saying to my aunt over the phone. *"Don't you know what's just happened? They're destroying cars and setting everything on fire. Throwing stones and shooting. Turn around and come back."*

There was a commotion, and it was drawing closer, Ami and my aunt realized. Aerial gunfire that always accompanied a street riot. Cars on fire in the middle of the road. Looters smashing in windows, yelling various political sentiments. Panic, uncertainty, terror.

Coincidentally, my aunt lived in Naval Colony, a gated housing complex that happened to be on the way to Zamzama; and at the moment the call came, the car was just passing the entrance, located on the other side of the thoroughfare. There was a choice to be made, and without hesitating, my aunt made it. Instead of proceeding forward, she jerked the wheel in the sharpest of hairpin turns and drove the car straight into a cut in the road—and into the oncoming traffic from the opposite direction.

They made it to Naval Colony without further incident, but they had been extremely lucky. If they continued to the market, where they were later told rioting and violence had erupted, who knows if they would have been able to escape unscathed? "It was like hunkering down in a bunker that night," Ami said. No guarantee of safety. No idea of what was to come next.

What did come next, as she found out, was silence. I remember the haunted look in Ami's eyes as she told us what Karachi had woken up to the next day: streets devoid of a single human presence, not a car in sight, and total, complete quiet.

Perhaps you cannot understand the gravity of this unless you have experienced a city like Karachi. Silence is not a concept that exists. Not on the streets, where cars, pedestrians, and animals use the roads as they like. Not in the shops, where someone is always hawking or haggling. Not even in the masjid, where the azaan and the prayer bring calm, but not quiet, children laughing and shouting in the background always a part of the scenery. Certainly not at home, where someone is always speaking or being shouted at, the TV on, the stove running.

But when Ami ventured outside of her sister's house the next day, that is what she heard. Total silence. There was a creeping sense that no matter what happened next, our homeland was on the brink of an upheaval. There was no telling whether it would stand fast in the face of such a test.

And there was only one place to go—one place for safety. In Pakistani culture, when visiting, a wife usually stays with her husband's family, even if her own family is nearby. So back to the house in Shabbirabad she went, and there she stayed until the airports opened again a week later and she could come back to us.

* * *

The next time we returned to Karachi—three years later, suitcases stuffed to bursting with formal shalwar kameez, gifts for my cousin's wedding, and of course, a stack of books to pass the time for two weeks without internet—it was to a city completely changed.

Pakistan is considered by many to be a security state, where the army and intelligence services hold the power to determine the trajectory of politics. But it was the first time that I really understood that for what it entailed; the first time that I understood that the country that I loved—that contained the house I thought of as a home away from home—was in crisis.

Military presence was everywhere, from the moment that we exited the plane at Jinnah Airport. I had flown a week ahead of everyone else in order to take my Nani home, and it being just the two of us together, navigating the crush of people had been a daunting experience. The guns and leers of military personnel only compounded that dread. For the first time in my life, I was grateful instead of disdainful of the fact that so many in things in Pakistan were segregated by gender. The security guard at the customs line took one look at us—me, barely twenty and clearly an overseas Pakistani well out of her depth, and Nani, an elderly woman in a wheelchair—and directed us straight to the "Women-only" line, where we able to pass through easily enough.

The feeling of belonging that came with being among a populace that looked like me, the comforting blanket of hearing Urdu being spoken around me and reading signs that clicked and made sense as soon as someone read me the first three letters—for the first time ever, it did not come. I was in a hostile territory, but I did not know what I had done wrong.

The routine ride back to Shabbirabad was a new experience entirely. We had arrived early in the morning, as we always did, but traffic was terrible, people driving with reckless abandon. As if they wanted to get off the streets as fast as possible. As if they wanted to get out of the open, where a bullet could hit without warning, a car pulled over at gunpoint and the passengers beaten and robbed. I felt afraid for the first time. I wanted to go "home."

The next shock came upon arriving in Shabbirabad, where guards with machine guns now sat in front of newly built gates that blocked every entrance into the enclave. "Security," my cousin shrugged when he caught my incredulous look. I didn't know it then, but only recently our house in Shabbirabad had been robbed—a common story for many at that time. The number of locks on each and every door in the house had increased accordingly, as had my aunt's fanatical insistence on checking that each and every one was fastened tight before we all retired for the night. In the following days, I was not allowed to step outside the house without wrapping myself in a bulky pashmina shawl that hid all aspects of my body, and if we were going to an event, the jewelry was to be kept hidden in our purses until we arrived at our destination.

And yet, there were such beautiful moments of freedom and wonder too. The entire family—from across the USA, Canada, England, and other parts of Pakistan—had arrived in force, and wedding festivities were in full swing. We sang Pakistani folk songs, ate copious amounts of biryani with milk-based mithai for dessert, and stayed up into the early hours of the morning with our cousins, playing games and sneaking onto the roof to smoke shisha.

We went on outings to the seaside at Hawkesbay, where we ran freely on the beaches and yelled at the top of our lungs, or took boats out into the open ocean to catch tiny little fish and then throw them back in again. There was one memorable cousin's trip out of the port of Keamari, where we spent the entire day in a cheerfully painted wooden boat, drinking some of the best doodh patti chai I've ever had. How I miss the way the harbor lit up that day as the sun rose and went down. How magnificent the sight of light on the ocean, creating an inferno of color that was orange and red and yellow and blue-green and purple all at the same time. How easy I felt in claiming the space under that sky as my home.

These dual chaotic forces—one terrifying and one joyful—color the memories of that trip even now. And yet, when the wedding was over, and we all packed our things and made the journeys back to our real lives, back to our other homelands, I realized something. No matter how much I liked to think of it as home, the high highs and the low lows of Karachi did not make a place that could realistically ever be a home for me.

* * *

What happens to the bonds that tether you to a place in the years you are away from it? Do you begin to forget them, or do those bonds grow stronger as you pile on perceived remembrances to fortify them? Between 2012 and 2019, I traveled a great deal, but not once in the span of seven years did those travels take me toward the country that I still referred to as "the homeland." In those years, one by one my relatives in Pakistan began to uproot themselves and move away, in search of better educations, better jobs, better lives.

The house that I loved, with the blue gate and now-barren langra mango tree, lay empty; my aunt and uncle had immigrated to Canada to be closer to their children. The only consolation was that they had not sold it, and so the house remained an oasis in Karachi's increasingly volatile landscape, waiting for visitors to fill it. For that was what all of us—even those who had lived in the house, like Abu and my uncle—that was what we were. Visitors now, our stays finite, our time limited. Perhaps, innately, I knew at that time that an ending was coming. I didn't know when it would come: only that it would.

The precarious security situation that we had left behind us in 2012 only worsened in the following years. In 2014, a devastating attack was carried out in Karachi's airport, our one point of entry during visits. Extremist attacks on schools and other areas in the northern province of Khyber Pakhtunkhwa put Pakistan in the news frequently, reinforcing the image of it as a violent backwater that was doomed to tear itself apart. This reasoning became a justification for the deadly drone campaign in the same area, overseen by the United States, which took the lives of many innocent people. Even as I read these headlines, full of righteous fury at the one-sided callousness of western publications in whose eyes all people with brown skin looked the same, it became easy to separate ourselves and lament in our houses from oceans away. *What is the country coming to? How could people let this happen?* And of course, the favorite refrain of my parents: *This wasn't how it used to be. Hamare zamaney mein...*

But there were positive developments too, ones that made me turn my head and develop an academic interest in Pakistan for the first time. The economic initiative known as the China-Pakistan Economic Corridor, a momentous regional partnership between China and Pakistan, was born in 2015, and became one of the topics that I would dive into during the course of my first graduate degree program. And, for a diaspora Pakistani, the most promising development at all—the meteoric rise of star-cricketer-turned-firecracker-politician Imran Khan to national prominence, so much that he had become the top contender for the Prime Minister's seat in the 2018 election.

The amount of optimism and hope that we saw on the only Pakistani news channels that we received in the U.S., *ARY News* and *GeoTV*, could be felt in our living rooms as we watched the 2018 election results play out. I had not voted in this election, even though my NICOP—the National Identity Card for Overseas Pakistanis, my one legal connection to the homeland—would have allowed me to. I cheered Nani on as she cast her ballot for the very first time, and engaged in political commentary with my parents and relatives that made it seem as though my stake in this election was a vested one. And I rejoiced. Had democracy as I understood it then—a very western and frankly very narrow definition, given the hypocrisy in which it thrives—finally come to our embattled country? Imran Khan was famous for his outspokenness against corruption, for his lack of affiliation with the political dynasties that had bled Pakistan dry. Was this a new world? One in which we might return?

* * *

It is at the end of everything, in the present, that I finally got to visit the beginning: Pakistan's rich history and cultural heritage.

My return to Karachi at the end of 2019 brought a fresh

perspective, from newly gained academic knowledge about Pakistan to a newfound determination in seeing it properly for myself. There was a richness in my understanding of the homeland now, and I wanted to see things that would expand it—starting with a proper tour of the city, for one. Our usual itinerary in previous visits consisted of being ferried from one relative's house to another, with occasional excursions to the masjid or to the one landmark it had been deemed safe to visit: Mazar-e-Quaid, the glistening white marble mausoleum of Mohammad Ali Jinnah, the father of Pakistan. But this time was different. This time, I insisted on taking a tour of the city by bus, and I dragged my parents along with me.

Between the chai and paratha breakfast at Quetta Darbar Café that warmed my soul but upset my stomach, close-up views of Karachi's labyrinthine neighborhoods in Saddar and Aram Bagh, which were mirrored by the tangled maze of wires suspended above them, and most of all, the nostalgia this trip invoked in Abu as his own commentary about the places he remembered from his boyhood drowned out the tour guide—I felt like I was seeing Karachi for the first time. I was hungry for it. I wanted more.

And yet, as my fullness in this experience grew, the house in Shabbirabad was being slowly emptied.

Even though it had lain mostly unoccupied through most of the years we'd been away, annual visits and perhaps a visceral inability to sever the one connection to the homeland was what stayed my uncle's hand whenever the topic of selling came up. But it was on the table now as it had never been before. Though moving back had once been the agreed-upon final outcome, without our noticing, home and homeland had, somewhere along the line, become two fundamentally different concepts: the stable reality versus the romantic ideal. The house was becoming a financial burden; the family had put down new roots thousands of miles away. A decision had to be made.

How can I explain the utter heartbreak upon hearing these conversations? How can I explain the sheer helplessness that comes with not being able to claim that feeling? This was not my house. This was not my home. I had never lived in it, never experienced the ups and downs of life in it: not my first heartbreak or my first triumph. But in that house, my memories were there in the walls too—the echoes of those first steps that I didn't remember in the living room, of the wails when I burnt my hand on an iron in the bedroom, the lingering ghosts of so many words and laughs and meals exchanged over a tapestry of years. The house was being emptied, slowly. But do these things ever really disappear?

I had no right to a say. But as I imagine the prospect of Karachi without our home with the now purple gate, and the long-barren langra mango tree, and the line of open window shutters letting in the sunlight, I wonder...without it, will I be able to return? Has the concept of homeland become so deeply tied to this one place, this one house, that without it, a homeland does not exist? This is the tragedy of diaspora: existing in the limbo of being torn in two at all times, but having no real choice to make. The reckoning with this earth-shattering question: Is the image of home I have in my head not a memory, but a mirage?

As I continue to return, I see Pakistan more clearly, in a way that I never have before; and from this new vantage point, I understand deeply that I still have so much to learn. Perhaps that knowledge will be better obtained as a visitor than as an inhabitant, as someone filled with the dewy optimism of the tourist—as I found myself on my trip in 2022—rather than colored with the nostalgia of a homeland built on the rose-tinted panes of the past. Home is not a place after all, perhaps, but rather the feeling of knowing that the place existed. The certainty that no matter how far life takes me, if I look for home, I will find it in the spicy taste of nihari on my tongue, in the sweet lilt of Urdu in my ears, in the intricacies of the embroidery on the shalwar kameez I wear. In the beautiful recollections of my parents, and in the knowledge that no matter where I go, I still came from somewhere, even if it is a place to which I cannot return. Home.

Seher Fatema Vora is a Pakistani American writer and educator. She holds an MA in International Relations from Tufts University and an MFA in Creative Writing from San José State University. She currently works as the Coordinator for Online Writing Support at the SJSU Writing Center, helping students to find their way in a world where writing online is becoming the new norm. Seher's writing draws largely from her Pakistani background and upbringing. Her short fiction can be found in *The Baltimore Review, Carve Magazine,* and *Corvid Queen.*

Instagram: @sehervee

Dharti Ma

Farrukh Karim Khan

I lost my mother a few months ago, very suddenly and shockingly. A life-altering event many of us are likely to experience at some point. Barring the four years I spent at college, my mother and I always lived together (I was forty-one when she passed away). The grief, when it comes, is sudden and overwhelming and leaves me utterly forlorn. Although I am now back in the routine of life, a part of me continues to crave her presence, and I hope I always will. To miss her is to stay connected to our bond and our memories.

One of the most memorable condolences I received after my mother passed was from one of my wife's uncles. He wrote a message without the usual "sorry for your loss" and "stay strong for the family." Instead, with the utmost compassion, he explained how the loss of a mother causes a feeling of forlornness that knows no comparison and is a wound that opens up again and again to hurt us. He also mentioned that even though he lost his mother more than two decades ago, he calls for her whenever he feels despair, even now.

My mother's loss is personal to me and my family. But the other mother us 240 million Pakistanis collectively grieve is our *Dharti Ma,* our motherland—Pakistan. Pakistan has been dying by many accounts for the last five decades, beginning with the separation of East Pakistan in 1971. A steady decline has been visible through dictatorships and democracies alike. Our best and brightest have been moving to greener pastures since the 1980s.

However, in the recent past, there is nothing steady about the decline. It feels terminal and existential, with a sense of impending doom. Migration records are being smashed; the official data and the anecdotal evidence on the ground indicate that. My wife tells me she will not make an effort to get to know new people anymore. "What is the point," she argues, "when so many from our social circle end up moving abroad?"

That many Pakistanis with the ability and means have moved and continue to move out of the country should come as no surprise. Humans, like other animals, share an instinct for self-preservation, for themselves and, more importantly, for their progeny. With no road map and dwindling hope, who can blame them?

However, the oft-ignored aspect of this flight to safety is the emotional toll it takes on the nation and its family-oriented culture. So many families are divided across the globe. Parents living away from their children in their twilight years, siblings living their lives far away from each other, often at opposite ends of the world. Like so many others in Pakistan, my family is also scattered around the world. Of my two sisters, one lives in the UK, and the other in the UAE, while I remain in Pakistan. My wife is in a similar boat. The annual Eid gatherings of her childhood, she reminiscences wistfully, were vibrant and widespread affairs. Now, only a select few remain in the country. As Pakistan's trials and tribulations come to the fore and become obvious to all, Pakistanis both within the country and abroad feel a profound sense of loss. Some of us may not be conscious of it, but there is a weight and toll we all carry.

Is this concept of *Dharti Ma* relevant in today's globalised world? At some level, a country is an artificial physical construct, with borders defined arbitrarily. There was no Pakistan before 1947, after all. However, identity is such a complex phenomenon. Our identity is shaped by our land, our people, our food and our shared traditions. In the past, the affiliation was with the tribe. In the modern world, our tribe is our country. We can travel far and wide and live abroad for many years. Yet the soul's connection with the motherland and its people is not severed. Visit Pakistan in December and watch "Decemberistan" in action; people living abroad for many years visit family and friends, blending in seamlessly for a couple of weeks into their long-migrated-from residence.

While it is hard to be optimistic today about our country's prospects ahead, it is harder still to live devoid of hope. It reminds me of a quote my late father often brought up during testing times:

'Hope springs eternal in the human heart'
by Alexander Pope.

My quest for hope in my homeland is a real one, but not one I wish to conduct in a delusional manner, hoping against hope for miracles. However, I recently realized a most unlikely source of hope in our country. When Pakistan was dumped out of the 2024 ICC cricket T-20 World Cup ignominiously, our then-President Arif Alvi tweeted:

"Nothing in Pakistan works—why do I expect cricket to?"

I initially wholeheartedly agreed. Everything is hopeless; nothing works, and mediocrity is all around us!

But then I thought, wait. There *is* something that works in Pakistan. Coke Studio!

Coke Studio, which began in 2008 as the country's ultimate music jam session, has provided a plethora of memorable songs through the years. Spellbinding lyrics and videos touch a chord within us at such a deep level. Music for the soul, really. Appreciated by Pakistanis of all stripes, Coke Studio Pakistan has received much love and recognition from across the border as well. The Coke Studio franchise has been in many countries, including India, Philippines, Africa and the Middle East. But the magic of Coke Studio Pakistan has not been replicated.

Paradoxically, I think Coke Studio in Pakistan works not despite what is happening in the country, but because of it.

Percy Shelley, in his hauntingly beautiful poem *"To a Skylark,"* has a wonderful line my father often wistfully recited in my childhood,

"Our sweetest songs are those that tell of saddest thought."

Disastrous economic policies have resulted in stagnation, shoddy roads and runaway inflation. But it has given us some of the most awe-inspiring music. Truth be told, so much of the creative beauty of Coke Studio comes from a place of sadness and loss, of unfulfilled potential. Pakistanis have much to offer, but the space we find ourselves in is narrow and constricted.

I took a trip down memory lane and immersed myself once more in the Coke Studio songs of yesteryear. Tajdare Haram, sung by Atif Aslam in 2015, cuts across class boundaries and brings a tear to the eye of high society and their help. It also does not respect national boundaries either; at an Atif Aslam concert I attended in Abu Dhabi, it was the most requested song by Pakistanis and Indians alike. Bewajah from 2015, Faasle from 2017, Dost from 2017, and Tu Jhoom from 2022, to name a few, are music for the soul.

However, the most underrated gem from Coke Studio, for me, is a song called Mehraam. Mehraam depicts abandonment and emptiness, beautiful things neglected and left to decay and die. And yet, they retain a haunting charm. The song is written in the context of human love, but for me, it resonated in terms of my country. Pakistan is abandoned, decaying, and dying on so many levels. And yet, it retains an unspoken charm and beauty. Even when hope is diminished, the beauty remains.

Another gem of a song is 2AM Shah, from the Coke Studio season of 2024. A beautiful set depicting a neighbourhood in Pakistan, which provides a peek into the homes of many different families, united by the universal emotions experienced by all of us around the world. Two mesmerizing singers provide their perspectives on whether love (as the ultimate solution for this world) is to be trusted or not. The song is captured as a back-and-forth between the two singers and their divergent emotions, with an equally persuasive case made for and against. I am not sure which perspective to believe. There is optimism and despair at the same time. Optimism because the people of Pakistan are hugely talented. Despair because the system has not given them a fair chance to make it in life.

These songs arouse deep and conflicting emotions in me. They make me miss my mother and my motherland. At the same time, they make me value them, and our shared past and memories. In general, Pakistanis may be sad, disillusioned, even broken. But we find solace in our music.

There may be better professional prospects abroad, possibly a more secure future for our kids. But living in my own country has afforded me priceless pleasures. In their formative years, my children grew up around their grandmother, steeped in the culture and values of their ancestors. My wife and I could spend time with our parents in the winter years of their lives, and our parents experienced the joy of having their grandchildren around. There is no price in the world someone could pay me to give all that up.

I grieve our country and may hedge our bets by moving out as well. But what I cannot do is disown it. This is the land of my parents, of my childhood and of my children. It will always occupy the most special place in my heart.

Farrukh's professional passions include management consulting and portfolio management. Currently, he is the Chief Strategy Officer at one of the largest banks in Pakistan. He has a passion for non-fiction reading and loves to play Padel as well. Farrukh holds a B.Sc. (Honors) with a major in Economics and is a CFA charterholder. He lives with his wife and two children in Karachi, Pakistan.

Amainiris—The Second Day After Tomorrow

Sundus Saqib

It was the summer of 2013 when I decided that I would finally make the trip to Fairy Meadows. Everyone said I was crazy—Pakistanis don't trek, especially not with two kids under the age of eight. But I was determined. I had been dreaming of this moment for more than a decade, ever since I had stepped into college and every day since I left a year later. It had to be now or never. One might say I was being dramatic, but when life throws you a curveball, ducking won't always save you. Sometimes you need to know how to catch the ball, play the game, and hope to emerge victorious.

The first time I went trekking was in college, when my friends arranged a trip as a farewell. Sometimes, when I close my eyes, I can still feel that nineteen-year-old in me, exhilarated at discovering the feeling of liberation that accompanies physical accomplishment. Growing up next to a bustling road and the constant clattering of vehicles, the silence of the mountains was comforting. Fairy Meadows was supposed to be the next thing but it took me ten years to get there.

* * *

Standing on the barren ridge, the starting point of the trek, with my husband and my two kids, my mind drifts to my youngest, whom I have left behind. For a while, my husband and I debated whether or not to take him along. My husband was reluctant to leave him behind, and I was adamant to do so. At the tender age of two, he was too young to enjoy or to let me enjoy. So, I rallied against my mom-guilt and stood my ground. *I needed to do this for myself,* I kept repeating. And yet, standing among the vastness, I feel the inkling of guilt creeping inside.

Mom-guilt is a social construct, a realization that took a long time coming. Society expects parents—especially mothers—to feel guilty about leaving kids behind, even for a day, or indulging in any activity that brings joy if it doesn't involve one's child. I grew up seeing my mother sacrifice for me and my siblings; her daily life was dictated by what we wanted. It imbibed in me that this is what motherhood is. But I soon grew conscious that motherhood is also about carving out time for yourself. So that you don't transfer your trauma to your kids, so you don't blame them for everything that you wanted to do but didn't because you became a mother. It's about eating the last piece of chocolate, while also making sure no one catches you in the act! Thus, I left my youngest behind with my mother (who was still sacrificing so I didn't have to). Reminding myself again why I need to do this, I whisper a little prayer for him and blow it into the air, for the wind to carry it all the way to Karachi.

After a two-hour stomach-churning jeep ride of twists and turns through the most desolate landscape I had ever seen, we reached the starting point—a rocky ridge that promises to take us to greener pastures. On one side is the barren face of the mountain, and on the other the great descent, a murky river snaking through it. I imagined myself as Isabella Bird, an adventurer from England during the late 1800s, as she started on her horse ride through the Rocky Mountains in the Western United States—a feat no other woman accomplished before her. If she could break barriers and ride through difficult terrain on her own, that too a couple centuries ago, what was holding me back from trekking a small region, apart from my self-induced fears of what is right and wrong?

My backpack with all my belongings for the three-night stay weighs me down, but I am determined to go on. Carrying your own baggage is part of the appeal of trekking. This trip is about testing my limits, pushing past them and rediscovering myself. The trek to Fairy Meadows isn't going to be a smooth ride, especially with young children. But in my mind, I am prepared. We put the kids on horses (we are adventurous but not crazy to make our kids trek all the way up) along with their belongings and usher them ahead in the safe company of our guide.

Against the backdrop of the vibrant blue sky, I take the first step towards healing. We all have our own mountains to climb, and this trip is mine. Soon, my kids are out of sight, yet somehow, I don't feel panic gripping me. This mountain feels safe. I don't fear for their security like I would have back in Karachi. My husband and I walk on, our faces flush with excitement, as the sun shines upon us. It's hotter than I imagined, but I am too excited to care about the sweat sliding down my back. I like the slow pace of our stride, that rare absence of urgency. No chores to be done, no boxes to be ticked. The freedom from responsibility is comforting, but too deeply stigmatized for most mothers to pursue it from time to time.

My husband accelerates to catch up to our kids, but I am content with my slow climb. I marvel at everything I see: the huge boulders placed precariously on the slope, the occasional green jutting out amidst the desolation. The clear, pristine water bubbles over pebbles and then turns murky as it becomes part of the larger water body gurgling in the valley below. Shredding my inhibitions, I melt into the landscape and become part of something majestic. I have spent most of my former self being away from the confines of four walls, preferring to climb a roof or stroll in the garden, rather than being stuck inside a room. Even in university, I preferred being on campus, sleep being the only thing that forced me to go to my dorm. Things changed after I got married. I translated marriage into a state of being inside, away from the open sky, shunning the outdoors as if I were punishing myself. Free from the confines of walls, I allow my mind to question why I did so and yet fail to grasp anything concrete. Sometimes, we do things we feel are right without any logic behind them. The weight of expectations buries logic deep inside of us. Drawing from the experiences of women around me, I knew that marriage was going to be a cycle of sacrifices—mostly on my part. The first thing I had to compromise was a college degree.

* * *

For the last ten years, it seems all I have done is check items off a list. Go to college. Check. Leave college like a dutiful daughter after a year and get married. Check. Have your first child, a daughter. Check. Have another child—congratulations, it's a son. Check. For being a patient person—bonus, another son! Check.

At some point, in making sure all these people lived, my growth stood still. Time was passing. I could see its physical evidence on and around me—extra layers of fat on my belly, the tiny smudges of paint on the walls, the chipped wood on my side table, the rusting of the taps in my bathroom, the overflowing storeroom. Yet, my mind wasn't processing it. I was stuck in a time loop of existence, reliving my one year at college again and again. I knew I had to wake up from slumberland, where I would often sneak off for adventure. I needed to do something to break the monotony. From the fifteen-year-old who carried a screwdriver in her school bag and knew more about sports than makeup, I had fallen into a clichéd existence limited to kids and my home.

Being the youngest of three sisters, I grew up conflicted about my role in society. Early on I became aware of the fact that my birth was not a celebration. As a result, my existence became a quest to fight the system and the society that made me doubt myself for being a girl. I can pick up my own luggage, I can fix my own plug, and I can change my own bulb. I don't like cooking, I don't like sewing—anything remotely feminine, I rejected. I can play cricket, I can climb rocks and hills, I can explore caves, and I did. I understood there was more to being a girl than just dressing up and looking pretty. Girls could be strong and independent, and I set about to prove it. So, till the age of nineteen, I broke as many gender barriers as I possibly could, given the sheltered upbringing I endured.

I managed to get admission to a prestigious Pakistani university, where I did more than just study. I went rock climbing, explored caves and trekked. I walked alone on the road for the first time. I sat on the public bus for the first time. It was as if I was on borrowed time, and one day, this freedom would end. I was determined to do all that my heart sought after.

My parents encouraged me; they made sure I got to do all, be all. But society always lurked somewhere close by. People—their criticism, opinionated looks, and judgmental eyes—kept following me. They kept trying to censor my existence.

My parents were different, but only as long as society allowed them to be. So when I got an ideal marriage proposal at nineteen, I was expected to comply. I was expected to forget how freely I was brought up. I was expected to leave a prestigious university and the freedom I created for myself—and I did. Hard to believe, isn't it? It was a struggle. But I wasn't left devastated, and that is where the problem lies.

Why? Why didn't I object? People ask me now. Did I have a choice? No. Because no matter how much freedom my parents bestowed on me, society always kept me in chains. It was an illusion that I was free to be what I wanted. My parents played into the fantasy. But when the shackles were lugged, I obeyed. I didn't even know I had any degree of agency. I was conditioned, without me actively acknowledging it, that to be a 'good daughter' I needed to sacrifice, obey, then glorify that martyrdom. So I lied—to my parents, and more importantly to myself—that I was okay. Deep down I knew I wasn't. I was simply tired. Battling patriarchy, within the family and in wider society, left me haggard mentally and emotionally. I couldn't do it anymore. I succumbed to the societal pressure to conform. Maybe it was time for me to be the girl the universe was slowly nudging me to be.

* * *

The climb up is a meandering ascent of marvel as I witness the changing terrain. Soon, the bleak desolation is left behind, and I am among rows and rows of trees standing in an embrace, blocking the overbearing sun. Little streams of water running over pebbled soil add to the enchantment. Tired from the uphill climb, I pause near a shallow pool and rinse my face with the ice-cold water. Settling down on the floor covered with green foliage, I try to breathe in the moment, making sure it stays with me forever. Ten years of dreaming, and here I am. Alone in the looming landscape, I feel emancipated and embrace the freedom solitude brings. As a mother, the one thing I miss the most is not sleep but the lack of solitude—the freedom to be alone with my thoughts and actions. I can stop when I want to, run if I want to. No tiny legs are dictating my pace. It's liberating to feel like this after a long time. The only noise is from water flowing in the little streams around me. Occasionally, it's punctured by the squeals of local children as they effortlessly run past me in their rubber soles, making the weariness in my bones more noticeable. I feel a twinge in my belly I can't ignore anymore, and it grows with each passing minute.

I welcome the solitude with open arms, and yet, after a while, it feels frustrating; my lack of stamina for physical activities clouds my initial excitement. Conflicted at my wavering emotions, I quicken my pace and try to catch up to my family. The weight on my back becomes more pronounced, and I have a sudden urge to get rid of it. I deposit my luggage on a horse I accost on the way, and as my shoulders sigh with relief, I force my racing heart to do the same.

The twitch in my belly dulls a bit as I see my daughter running down towards me. I wrap my arms tightly around her. I smile as I see my husband and son a little further ahead, waiting for me. I feel strength returning to my bones. Soon, darkness starts eating away at the blue skies above me, and under it, we continue our trek. Though we went over all the details, the possibility that we would be trekking in darkness never occurred to us, and we didn't pack any torches. The only light illuminating our way is the pale glow of our guide's mobile and my own. I doubt if we can continue in this darkness, and yet the resolve of my kids pushes me on. My daughter refuses to get back on the horse, and after a while, we pull our son down as well. He is too weary to hold himself on the horse.

My lungs gasp for air, but my brain begs my feet to go on, and they reluctantly obey. My faltering tendons and sore feet make me realize how unfit I am for this journey, no matter how fit I feel in my mind. Maybe I was agile ten years ago when I went trekking for the first time, but I am no longer in my late teens. Walking uphill isn't easy, and the darkness is not helping. All the uncertainties of people flood my mind. Maybe I am crazy, after all. Maybe I overestimated my resolve.

* * *

Till recently, Pakistanis rarely traveled within Pakistan. This was especially true for people from Karachi's economically well-to-do families. If one can fly to Dubai for the same price and live in luxury, why would anyone spend the same amount to travel locally? It didn't have the same appeal.

Traveling is often associated with comfort, never with experience or adventure. To me, this is not a simple vacation. Having given up on my education midway, this is a means of learning from experiences, people and places. Now the whole world is my university and I am determined to learn as much as I can.

This part of north Pakistan is still a mystery for people in the south. The social media boom hasn't opened up the Gilgit-Baltistan area to commercial tourism yet. People don't know about the untouched glaciers, the hidden magical valleys, the fruit orchards, the pristine lakes, the waterfalls and the meandering rivers dotting the region. They are unaware of the hospitality of the people, the delectable flavors of their food or the different hues of its mountains. Not many have ever heard about Fairy Meadows and certainly don't understand the allure of trekking on their own feet to get there. A few even dissuaded my husband from taking his family along. 'It's not safe,' was the most prevalent argument. As Pakistanis, we like to play it safe, even to the point of suffocating our existence. Karachi has never been safe, but I have lived my whole life there, so why fear the rest of the country? A few even hinted at a boys' trip to him. I laughed at the suggestion. Was I now expected to live vicariously through my husband?

More questions followed. Won't you get bored? What will you do there? I knew that not everyone would understand the appeal. It was a milestone for me. To emerge from the shadow of the past that clutched me in its hold, to finally accept, move on, and forge a new path. But before that, I needed to do the one last thing connecting me to my old self. To prove that not all of my former self was lost. That I could still dream, hoping to make it a reality.

* * *

"How much longer?" I ask.

"Just around that bend," our guide replies for the umpteenth time, yet the elusive bend is nowhere in sight. My husband and I steal an exhausted glance. I feel crazy for doing this, and for dragging my kids along. Who willingly puts themselves through so much trouble? I wanted an adventure, and I surely got one.

We are hungry, haggard and cold. As the sun plunges, so does the temperature. The enticing, magical trees seem monstrous under the dark sky. The lack of human sounds creeps us out. The only thing making us march on is the encouragement from our tolerant and cordial guide and the promise of food.

"We are here," our guide finally announces. But 'here' is nothing but more darkness. Where is the majesty I had conjured in my mind, which propelled me, made me walk through tired legs? 'Here' is darkness and silence and a starlit sky. I feel robbed of my dream. My mind imagined a grand welcome, comforting bonfires, and the smell of chicken barbecuing on coal.

Our guide shouts something in his local language, and a dull light pierces through the darkness. I can make out a small clearing, and a few feet away, a wooden structure glowing with warm light inside. We make our way towards it—which our guide has told us is the dining area—and collapse on the floor, a bundle of weary bones and growling stomachs. I can almost smell the freshly baked naans and chicken tikkas. But instead, I get half-cooked, bland daal, not in harmony with my highly spiced-up palate.

"Where is the chicken?" My eyes question my husband.

"Oh, if you want chicken you need to order ahead, like two days before," the guide states, as if reading my mind.

I wanted the remote experience, and this is just the beginning.

The next challenge is the bathroom. I coped with walking in darkness and satiated my carnivorous appetite with daal. I survived. Onto the next battle. But how to teach a semi-conscious five-year-old to use the Pakistani toilet for the first time? Suffering from grand delusions like conquering a mountain, I pick him up in a squat position so he can go. But instead, he tumbles out of my grasp and falls into the toilet, as do all my hopes of rediscovering myself. At that moment, I feel betrayed by my physical limitations and my dreams. Was the whole trip an illusion, a mirage that shatters the closer you get?

I feel like the helpless ten-year-old girl who watched with terrified eyes as her younger brother plunged from above the circular staircase while she ran after him, and fell with a loud thud. *What if he dies?* She thought. Her parents would be left without a son. She blamed herself and prayed for his welfare, in her naivety beseeching Allah to take her instead—her parents have a daughter to spare but not a son.

My brother suffered from mild head trauma, nothing life-threatening, and yet, each time I recall the moment, I feel paralyzed with doubts, as I do now as I stare in disbelief at my son. Some memories have a way of resurfacing, creeping into the present and disturbing the peace you have worked so hard to build. I don't know why I am reminded of this memory at this particular moment. Maybe every decision I have ever made has crept from this place of low self-worth. Hot tears brim over, and with these doubts plaguing my mind, I fall into a disturbed sleep. For most of my life, my way of dealing with hurdles has been to close my eyes, hoping with new light things would improve, and that by morning I would be able to bury this memory again.

* * *

An intense light floods our cabin through the thin curtain, forcing me to peek outside. A flash of white greets my eyes. There, in all its grandiosity, stands the Nanga Parbat, the mountain captivating the imagination of mountaineers for centuries. Now, it has the same effect on me.

I step outside my small cabin and stand on the wooden balcony, the wood warm under my feet. I welcome the warmth of the sun. There is green as far as I can see, and in the backdrop, emerging from blue vastness, is the snow-draped mountain. Even under the bright sun, I feel its coolness slowly extinguishing the resentment I carried inside me for years. I am reminded why I embarked on this journey—not for the comfort but for the adventure, a second chance at happiness.

Over breakfast under the open sky, we strike up a conversation with the cook of the small camp we are staying in. "It's not an easy hike," he says. "Even adults find it hard to make the journey and turn back halfway. And you made it with your children." I look into his eyes and see a spark of amazement twinkling in them.

My heart smiles. I did it. I caught the ball and played the game. I emerged victorious. The little girl watching her brother falling wipes her tears and takes a step back.

* * *

I am standing in a corridor of the hotel we are staying at in Skardu. At one end, a glass door opens to a dining area. The floor of the room is covered with backpacks and climbing paraphernalia. Mountaineers, mostly of European descent, gather around tables, charting routes on their laptops. The light from their laptops illuminates their faces with an ethereal glow. The whole scene reminds me of the Hollywood movie *Vertical Limit,* whose setting was the K2 Mountain.

The walls of the corridor are adorned with pictures of famous mountaineers, and I am surprised to see Pakistani names up there, too. Why didn't I read about these heroes growing up? I feel nostalgic about a time I never got to experience. I grew up and missed the best part of Pakistan—its majestic mountains. Growing up in Karachi, I secretly dreamed of becoming a famous mountain climber. What if I had known about people like me scaling these mountains? What if I had not based my dream on a character from a Hollywood movie but on real people? Would I have actively worked to fulfill my dream?

* * *

I return home two weeks later. Am I healed? Was it the right time for the trip? What is next for me? I don't have all the answers.

The only thing I am sure about is my own ignorance regarding myself and the country I live in. Not everyone living up north in Pakistan is Pathan—a lesson I learned over a bonfire with the locals. Previously known as the Northern Areas of Pakistan, the region was renamed Gilgit-Baltistan in 2009.

I learned about the region's history and conflicted status. Despite government apathy, the people of Gilgit-Baltistan are extremely patriotic. They don't sit waiting for help but rather help themselves. They build small hydro plants on their small streams to generate electricity. They educate their children, even daughters, and send them as far as Karachi for education.

I learned I had stopped pushing myself and testing my physical, emotional and intellectual limits. For a long time now, I have been accepting things as they are. I stopped fighting the system. This trip changed that. I pushed myself, went past my physical limits. And I did that as a mother, with my children. I learned I have changed, and not all change is negative.

For a long time, I felt like I was just a prop. While my kids and my husband were the primary focus of the picture called Life, I just merged into the background—part of the picture but not really the main focus.

And there we were, getting snapped in front of the magnificent

Nanga Parbat, the most spellbinding backdrop I had ever seen. I learned the mountain is the hero of the picture. The background, in this case, was an integral part, setting it apart from the rest of the family pictures. Sometimes, what we think is inconsequential is the thing that makes it beautiful. Sometimes, things cannot always be quantified, measured and balanced. We need to feel them, breathe them, and make them a part of ourselves. I learned that I needed to enjoy the moment, and not always worry about what was to come next, or what I had left behind.

A decade later, my dreams have changed, and I have realized that maturity is about learning to shift your dreams rather than being stuck on something unachievable. For the longest time, I wanted to reach for the moon, and when I couldn't, I sulked in the corner. Now I know: the moon is a giant leap; before that, there are thousands of steps. I might still be thousands of steps from reaching the moon, but at least I have started my journey.

John Dutton, the family patriarch from the show *'Yellowstone'* once said to his daughter: "Solace is not found but discovered." To me, happiness is the same. You can't go looking for it, but stumble across it unknowingly. If not today or tomorrow, there is always Amainiris.

Sundus Saqib is an educator and writer from Karachi, Pakistan. She has taught reading, writing and literature to students ranging from junior to high school. Her work has appeared in *Lakeer Magazine, 'Pandemonium Journal'* and in the anthology *'Tales from Karachi'*. An avid reader, Sundus regularly holds book club meetups. She can be found on Instagram, where she documents social and historical issues.

Instagram: @narrativerevisited

Why I Stay On—Neither Unlovingly, Nor Unloved

Dr. Osama Siddique

I have a thing for colonial rest houses. It is not as if I am not well aware of their place in the larger architecture of exploitative extraction, and their location in the geography of colonial domination. I trace the resilient remains of haughty laws and haughtier attitudes of those these were built for in my scholarship and my fiction. Nevertheless, there is something deeply romantic about them. Dotted across the post-colonial landscape, alongside canals, hidden away in artificial plantations, nestled in wooded crevasses of the mountainside with their verandahs, high ceilings, and vast lawns adorned with beds of cosmos, cannas, hollyhocks, sweet peas, hibiscus and nasturtium, these crumbling edifices remind me of an era more gently paced, less cluttered, less noisy.

I set off with my mother one evening from such a place in the Pothohar hills to show her a wonderful ruin. We drove through that grand broken terrain, its tracts of acacia and wild olive, pangolins and monitor lizards roaming its gullies and ravines, Stone Age tools strewn along the banks of the Soan and other seasonal rivers, a mysterious landscape of caves, springs, undulating hills and jutting plateaus. The tenth-century Malot temples, combining Greek and Kashmiri architecture in the Hindu Shahi style are perched on the edge of the hills plunging to the Punjab plains.

Chest-high stone walls divided lush meadows; small cultivated fields sometimes interrupted the pastoral land skirted by wild vegetation. Bullrushes with white plumes swayed in the breeze. Thickets of invasive mesquite and tall elephant and pampas grasses blinded one on the narrow, winding road. There was hardly a soul to see except when passing through small villages with their green, banyan-shaded ponds that buffaloes and water chestnuts shared. Driving from memory, I finally approached a fork at the edge of the road, beyond which I could almost sense the dizzying drop. Unsure, I turned left. The road climbed. Suddenly, we were at the edge of a small village, more or less on the edge of the escarpment. The narrow space we drove into allowed little room to turn back. Embarrassed, I avoided my mother's eyes. The place looked deserted till we saw a middle-aged man walking towards us. He was shabbily dressed. With rocky terrain, small landholdings, and more or less exclusive reliance on temperamental rains, agriculture couldn't be all that bountiful. What a relief to see him in that remoteness!

I pulled down my window as he approached, greeted him and said, "I think we took the wrong turn. We were trying to get to the Malot temples."

He said we should have turned right at the fork. I thanked him and asked if he could help us reverse from that narrow, blind corner.

I have not forgotten our ensuing exchange, though it was hardly unusual in my experience. The man insisted we stay for lunch before proceeding to the temples. I declined, thanking him for his graciousness. Daylight was receding and, in any event, we didn't want to impose. He gently persisted, saying my mother would surely appreciate a little rest. How could he turn guests away? I made our excuses again but he said we wouldn't even be inconvenienced to step out. He offered to send someone to bring us a meal and tea right where we were parked.

Where I live, customary offers of hospitality are a way of life. Often, those who extend them anticipate future interface, if not a favor or good turn in return. At other times, there is some prior nexus, an association or linkage no matter how remote, or perhaps an interest in holding an enjoyable conversation. But here we were, accidentally in this remote corner of the desolate country, and this man—with precious little to share and no expectation of ever meeting us again—truly and honestly felt that he owed us this hospitality.

But we really couldn't stay and burden him. We thanked him profusely; he helped us reverse, and we left aglow with a warmth suffusing us even as we scanned the remarkable view of the sun sinking over a dreamlike landscape. The memory has stayed with us all these years.

As an old friend and I roamed the winding, narrow streets of Lahore, exploring its medieval quarters and hidden nooks, we were offered endless cups of tea and even delicious meals. Once, approaching the Ayubia end of the picturesque pipeline walk in the northern Galiyat, we saw a group of burly men squatting and having a mango party. I bet family members that we would be asked to join when we passed. I won that bet. I often make and win such bets, convinced of the outcomes. On another mountain walk, I came across two very young, apple-cheeked local boys collecting colorful local berries for their sister. When I asked if I could photograph the berries, they thrust a fistful in my palm, insisting I should enjoy them. People from all classes, but especially less affluent ones, routinely offer to share meals on buses and trains, or in waiting areas, should you be traveling with them. I could go on. The hospitality of Pakistanis knows no bounds—I haven't experienced anything like it anywhere else in the world. Even as economic woes force everyone to tighten their belts, it is in the very essence of these people to be generous and hospitable, especially if your demeanor is civil and pleasant, more so if you are a visitor or stranger. If you look even remotely distressed, many will fall over backwards to assist, even play host. For every conman and ruffian bringing down the national reputation and passport ranking, I have come across many others who lift one's spirits with their inherent warmth.

So, is that it? When asked why one stays—for reasons other than those of proximity to kith and kin—given past opportunities to move on, given the collective mounting frustration at the shrinking space for speech, scholarship, books, democracy, economic stability and decent governance, is this the answer? Why do I stay put by choice? It cannot only be the willingness of so many people to play the generous host and display largesse far beyond their means; it cannot only be that a smile, a pleasantry, an innocent joke, more often than not, is reciprocated by an essentially friendly populace.

Could it also be the tremendous sense of wonder evoked by living on a diverse and variegated terrain. Here, history lies layer upon seemingly interminable layer, vistas shift rapidly, and sceneries dramatically change as you travel. Ways of speech are many and equally sonorous to speak and melodious to the ear.

Could it be the irrepressible, sharp, self-deprecatory and vibrant humor of the Pakistanis? I recently saw a clip of an amateur reporter interviewing a handcuffed dacoit at the very site where he was caught red-handed, on the outskirts of Faisalabad.

The reporter asked, "What did you come here for?"

The dacoit's deadpan reply was one for the ages: "What do you think? Obviously to steal. Surely not to offer my Namaz (prayers)."

In times of crisis, facing adversity and oppression, Pakistanis have steadfastly retained and tellingly employed their sense of humor and biting sarcasm. The greater the odds, the more lethal their wit—they make the best memes and heaven help the person they decide to bring down. Humorous writers and poets, wits, mimics, traditional *bhands* and *mirasis*, satirists, parodists, jokesters, punsters, and even everyday people employ their different languages and dialects, displaying acute social and cultural observation, political nuance and brilliant sharpness. Pakistanis are arguably the wittiest people in the region. Is that it, then, the reason I like to live here?

Is it also how deeply Pakistan is steeped in poetry and romance? Its languages are easy on the ear—sensual, evocative and deeply profound. Why does a couplet from Rashid, Faiz, Majeed Amjad or Munir Niazi move one so? Such diversity, innovation, panache and pathos in their voices! Why do Bulleh Shah, Sultan Bahu, Waris Shah,

Baba Ghulam Farid, Shah Hussain and Mian Muhammad Bakhsh resonate so deeply? Why does a dastan, a qissa, a local folktale, a ghazal, or a qawwali cast such a spell? Certainly, early and regular exposure play a part—growing up with them has led to all the associations of familiarity, nostalgia and good times. But something deeper connects.

Is it because we have grown not only accustomed to our seasons and their various boons but embraced them wholeheartedly, despite recent assaults by pollution and climate change? Winter's foggy mysteries; summer's sensual lassitude; the brief but unusually joyous spring; fragrant, gentle autumn; and then those almost erotic monsoon rains?

Does identity tether us, that nebulous thing? In my case, it is a shifting composite of Harrapan, Gandharan, Punjabi, Indo-Islamic and Lahori roots, post-colonial sensibilities and nationalism when it comes to sports and some aspects of culture. Sometimes cosmopolitan, sometimes local; always striving to ensure it doesn't become parochial and remains in sync and harmony with the global and universal.

Is it the way we look and dress, which not just slots us with others who look and dress the same, but defines our special aesthetics? Is it my notion that Pakistan is full of "characters?" Our per capita idiosyncrasy is probably amongst the highest in the world. Our people love to stand out, even as they often disastrously give into one or another limiting and narrowing conformism. Dickens would find thousands of characters in our bazaars and courtrooms, our festivals and drawing rooms. Even a far lesser writer, like me, finds plenty. That, in itself, is a good reason for a writer to remain—no paucity of stories. Or characters.

These days, I make it a point to visit universities and colleges. Even better if they're public universities. Even better if they're in a small town or a remote area. It gets me away from the debilitating cynicism and naysaying of the chattering classes. I go in search of an older normative system: the mutual respect between teacher and student, and genuine thirsts to learn. I go looking for fresher, younger perspectives on life, the land we live in, the future. Never disappointed, I return recharged and galvanized.

Shifting to write in Urdu alongside English has put me in contact with a young and diverse readership sickened by the paucity of our discourses, the languishing of our idealism, and the crisis of imagination we currently face. But coming across and engaging with hundreds of bright-eyed and intelligent young Pakistanis has taught me many important lessons. One of the foremost of these is to hope—to think and talk positively, listen closely, keep the faith, and look ahead and above. I should be the one conveying these lessons to others, given the good fortune that I have enjoyed, the spectacular opportunities that have come my way, and the myriad insecurities, deprivations and anxieties I have thus warded off. To a considerable extent, I have. But these engagements, real and virtual, have reinforced my confidence in the merit and goodness of us as a people and our tremendous potential.

There has been a dismaying breakdown of our institutions and processes; many social norms and traditions worth valuing and preserving have eroded; the clamor of fools far outshouts and outlasts quiet words of the reasonable, dumbing down our discourse. Yet, beneath this decaying surface, I detect the possibilities of new beginnings. We are too vast, too complex, too gifted, and too ancient a people to be so badly governed and so poorly led for so long. Globalization, with all its banes, has made the exchange and dissemination of better ideas easier than before. Our democracies don't last very long, but neither do our dictatorships. We have had quite a few springs equivalent to the Arab Spring. We write poems of dissent and songs of lament that echo long after and resonate even beyond our borders. We are a truly resilient people.

Many choose not to examine all this. Many ought to—they are in positions to matter rather than merely conjecture. But theirs are days of despondence and dull depression. Their nights are spent scheming escapes, or, much worse, manipulating and machinating, and blatantly or inadvertently augmenting existing hegemonies.

We are at the disposal of many mafias. I have also seen and read too much to romanticize anarchy or idealize chaos. We seek order—fair, harmonious, equitable and benevolent order. I would rather spend the rest of my days doing my bit towards that end in a place where so much else allows me to relate, connect, and build on. And yes, the language I hear daily makes my heart stir. My senses answer to the lilt of the songs the wind carries. Every day, I come across three local jokes that make me laugh out loud. I can start a conversation with almost anyone, anywhere, and find something in common. If I lose my way, or if people think I have lost my way, I will be offered directions and a cup of tea. That leaves me with a warm glow.

Dr. Osama Siddique is a legal scholar and a policy advisor. He has also practiced law in New York and Pakistan for eight years, taught at the Lahore University of Management Sciences (LUMS) for a decade, and has many international research publications. He has authored novels in both Urdu and English, notably *"Ghuroob e Shehr Ka Waqt"* and *"Snuffing Out the Moon."* Dr. Osama Siddique has a doctorate in law from Harvard Law School, was a Rhodes Scholar at Oxford, and is also a graduate of LUMS Business School and Government College, Lahore. Legal sociology, ancient history, world literature, archaeology, creative arts, nature, astronomy and cosmology, are some of his many interests.

Instagram: @dr.osamasiddique

The National And The Personal
Nadeem Farooq Paracha

What does it mean to be a Pakistani? As things stand, to many in Pakistan, this question is likely to mean, "What does it mean to be a Muslim?" A decade or so ago, during a TV discussion held in front of a live audience, the intellectual Khaled Ahmad asked, "How many of you consider yourself to be Muslims first and Pakistani second?" A majority of the audience described themselves as being Muslims first. Most of Pakistan's Muslim citizens will find nothing odd in this declaration. Yet, the same folk often wonder why the country has struggled to construct a 'strong' national identity.

We are still not sure what Pakistani nationalism really is. So, how can this question—"What does it mean to be a Pakistani?"—be answered in a manner that is even slightly convincing? Actually, this is why the country's Sunni Muslim majority often ends up calling itself Muslim first and Pakistani second. The rest, well, aren't all that different either. My various personal interactions with Pakistani Shias suggest that they are likely to describe themselves as (Shia) Muslim first. And ever since the 1980s, the Shia have not been very happy with the country's Sunni majority.

Between 2010 and 2015, I was heading the media department of a large British organisation in Karachi. The organisation often funded studies, especially on Pakistan's 'youth bulge.'[1] Indeed, in these studies

---

1 The Pakistani Youth Bulge: E. Hafeez (DAWN, June 25, 2017)

as well, the majority of Pakistan's young Muslims preferred to call themselves Muslims first. But here's the interesting bit: it was mostly the non-Muslim citizens of the country who considered themselves to be Pakistanis first. And here's something equally interesting: another segment of the country which identifies itself as Muslim first are the Ahmadiyya—a community ousted from the fold of Islam by an act of parliament in September 1974. In 1984, an Ordinance further prohibited the Ahmadiyya from reciting the Quran (in public).[2] The Ordinance also disallows the Ahmadiyya from referring to their places of worship as mosques, or using sacred Islamic texts on their places of worship and on the tombstones of their graves.

Then, of course, there is always the matter of ethnicity. A Punjabi, Sindhi, Pashtun, Baloch, or Saraiki is likely to identify more with their ethnic group than with the Pakistani national identity. From the late 1980s onwards, many Urdu-speaking 'Mohajir' began exhibiting similar tendencies, despite them being at the forefront of the movement that initiated the idea of a separate Muslim-majority country in the region. They then migrated in the millions to this country, which was made up of regions where the Punjabi, Sindhi, Pashtun, Baloch and Bengalis had already been settled for hundreds of years.

Now imagine constructing nationalism in such a country! A direct contrast to this is the Republic of India, which is just as diverse with respect to religions and ethnicities, despite having a Hindu majority. India also has a significant Muslim population – at the time of Pakistan's creation as a Muslim-majority country, there were more Muslims in India than in Pakistan. Yet, the Indian government was able to mould an Indian nationalism which always seemed to be more robust than the nationalism assembled by the state and the nationalist intelligentsia in Pakistan.

Nevertheless, as of recent, the prevailing idea of Indian nationalism is being seriously challenged by a populist Hindu nationalist regime that has been in power since 2014. In 2018, when I was stationed as a Research Scholar in Washington DC, I was able

---

2   Ordinance XX promulgated in April 1984.

to engage with various Indian sociologists, political scientists and anthropologists based in various major US universities. Most of them noted that many Indians had begun to identify themselves as Hindus first. Some of the US-based Indian intellectuals that I spoke to had no issues with this. So, whereas the state in Pakistan has had a history of moulding and remoulding various ideas of Pakistani nationalism while failing to construct a single, cohesive spirit of nationalism, India is now re-evaluating its nationalism by experimenting with a more theocratic variant. The rationale given to me by the Indian intellectuals was that the largely 'secular' nationalism, which had served the country rather well for decades, was undermining the interests of India's Hindu majority. They saw nothing odd in Indians beginning to refer to themselves as Hindus first.

Unlike Indian nationalism, Pakistani nationalism has gone through numerous mutations. For example, the 'Pakistan Ideology'[3] that the state often evokes today is an afterthought. It is a term that is nowhere to be found in the speeches of the country's founders. What one does find in textbooks between 1947 (the year Pakistan came into being) and 1978, though, is the phrase, 'Two Nation Theory.' This 'theory' is said to have been formulated by the country's primary founder, Muhammad Ali Jinnah, who posited that the Muslims and Hindus of India were two separate 'nations.'

During the first 30 years of the country, textbooks and nationalist historians claimed that it was this 'theory' that propelled the 'Pakistan Movement.' A 1956 book, *Pakistani Way of Life*, by the late and eminent historian Ishtiaq Husain Qureshi, states that the country's polity is regulated by a nationalism inspired by the Two Nation Theory, and 'an enlightened Islam.' This was how the authors of the country's first constitution in 1956 had described Islam as well, after declaring Pakistan an 'Islamic Republic.' The constitution itself, however, was largely secular.

Yet, when President Iskandar Mirza and military chief Ayub

---

3   The official nationalist ideology which was shaped by the state to reinforce the raison d'tere of Pakistan's creation.

Khan, imposed the country's first martial law in 1958, they described the constitution as a ploy "to peddle Islam for political purposes."[4] When Khan got himself 'elected' as president, he changed the country's name to 'Republic of Pakistan.' In 1958, my father was a student at the SM Arts College in Karachi. He once told me that even almost a decade after the country's birth, most of its citizens had little to no clue as to what Pakistani nationalism really was. My father was an active member of the left-wing National Students Federation (NSF). He said he was aware of something called the Two Nation Theory, but like him, most other students at his college could not understand what this theory meant in a country that was now supposedly just one nation. According to him, the only people who used to call themselves Pakistani in the 1950s were the Mohajir. Others who had not migrated from India, identified with their respective ethnic communities. For centuries, these communities had been residing in what would become Pakistan. My father, who originally came from northern Punjab, was often referred to as a Punjabi. He was quite okay with that.

Ayub Khan lamented that the politicians had begun to move away from 'Jinnah's Pakistan.' Khan saw himself as Pakistan's Kemal Ataturk. To Khan, the country that the Two Nation Theory had birthed should have been organised as a national whole, navigated by a 'rational' set of ideas that were 'modern.' But this set of ideas did not include the concept of parliamentary democracy. To create a national whole, Khan began to ponder the possibility of formulating an overarching national ideology. He reached out to various intellectuals for this very purpose.

According to my father, when he and his comrades in NSF first heard this, they asked how the state could attempt to turn Pakistan into a *single nation* through a theory that spoke of *two* nations? This happened in 1960, when my father had joined the Karachi University (KU). He was nearly expelled from the university for asking such questions. Ghaffar, a friend of my father's at the university and a son

---

4   'Martial Law in the Indo-Pakistan Sub-continent': A Munim (University of London, 1960

of a small Pakhtun trader who had migrated to Karachi from Dir in the erstwhile NWFP (now Khyber Pakhtunkhwa)[5], began to joke that Khan was trying to reshape the Two Nation Theory into the 'Two Islam Theory.' Ghaffar's sardonic quip wasn't that far from the truth.

Khan began to evoke the 'Islamic modernism' that had been pioneered in South Asia by the likes of Sir Syed Ahmad Khan and other 19th-century scholars. Ayub Khan envisioned Islam as a nation-building tool, controlled by an 'enlightened' military leadership rather than by the clerics.[6] In a 1960 speech, Khan said, "Pakistan was not achieved to create a priest-ridden culture but instead, it was created to evolve an enlightened society. It is a great injustice upon both life and religion to impose on the 20th-century man the condition that he must go back several centuries in order to prove his credentials as a true Muslim." Even though the speech impressed young men like my father, to others, such as Ghaffar, the speech was taken as an attack on the 'traditional' ways in which most South Asian Muslims practiced Islam. What's more, Ghaffar quit the NSF and joined the student-wing of the right-wing Jamaat-e-Islami (JI). He also exhibited anger towards my father for praising Khan's speech.

In 1962, Khan lifted the ban on political parties and approved a new constitution. Ironically, the 1962 Constitution was quite similar to the 1956 Constitution. The National Assembly that came into being was packed with members of the party that Khan had formed, the Convention Muslim League. But some members of other parties, also managed to find their way into the assembly. It was in this assembly that the term 'Pakistan Ideology' (*Nazriya-e-Pakistan*) was first heard. The assembly had just one member from JI. During a debate, the JI member mentioned the words 'Pakistan Ideology.' When asked to define this ideology, the JI member responded by saying, "Islam is Pakistan's ideology."[7]

But the term vanished soon after this exchange. It returned six

5   North-West Frontier Province (NWFP) was a province created by the British in India in 1901. The region had a Pakhtun majority and still does. In 2010, the name of the province was changed to Khyber Pakhtunkhwa by the government. The name-change had been a demand of Pakhtun nationalists.
6   M Munir: *From Jinnah to Zia* (Vanguard Books, 1980). p.29
7   Ibid.

years later, in 1968, during the height of an anti-Khan movement. The Islamist ideologue Abul Ala Maududi—who was also the chief of the JI—began to speak of a Pakistan Ideology, knowing that the Khan regime was on its last legs. The Khan regime had banned the JI in 1964, but the Supreme Court overturned the ban. A vehement critic of Jinnah, Maududi, believed that he should be the one shaping this ideology. Another reason why Maududi urgently pursued this was because of the rapid rise of ZA Bhutto's left-leaning Pakistan People's Party (PPP), the growing influence of the Bengali nationalist outfit, the Awami League, in the erstwhile East Pakistan, and the 'leftist' nature of the anti-Khan movement.

Maududi emphasised the need for having a national ideology that could navigate the rulers to 'Islamise' the society and then enact a 'Shariah state', which Maududi called '*hakumat-e-ilahi*.' Ayub Khan resigned in March 1969 and handed over power to General Yahya Khan. A JI delegation led by Maududi met with the new military dictator and came out of the meeting looking satisfied. The delegation stated that unlike Ayub Khan, the new ruler had agreed to serve Islam and form a national ideology based on Shariah.[8] Ironically, though, the General who had agreed to do this was notorious for being an alcoholic and a womaniser.[9]

By 1969, my father was already a married man. My mother was studying economics at KU when she first met my father in 1964. She was a Mohajir who, as a child, had migrated with her father, sister and brother from Calcutta in 1947. The family was Urdu-speaking and originally from Delhi. My father joined journalism after he graduated from KU with a master's degree. He was also on friendly terms with the leftist firebrand activist, Meraj Muhammad Khan. In 1967, Meraj became one of the founding members of Zulfikar Ali Bhutto's PPP. He wanted my father to join the party as well, but for reasons that my father never fully explained, he decided not to. He did become a staunch supporter of the party, though. Ghaffar, who had joined JI's student-wing, never joined the JI itself. He opted to follow my

---

8   *Pakistan Affairs*, May 15, 1969
9   'Night of the General': A.Nasir (*Newsline*, May 2001)

father into journalism. The Urdu daily that Ghaffar joined was pro-JI. My father, on the other hand, had joined the progressive Urdu daily *Anjam.*

Just before the 1970 elections, 113 ulema, including Maududi, signed a fatwa declaring socialism as a great threat to the 'Ideology of Pakistan.' Bhutto's PPP was the target. The fatwa did not explain what the 'ideology of Pakistan' was. Of course, the authors of the fatwa would have replied by saying 'Islam.' But then, Islam to the founders of Pakistan and Ayub Khan had meant something very different than the way it was explained by Maududi, especially in the context of the faith's ideological and political roles. My father penned a long essay for the weekly Urdu magazine *Nusrat,* criticising the fatwa and laying bare the history of Maududi's criticism against Jinnah.

In response, Ghaffar wrote a letter to my father. In it, he boasted that my father's 'socialism' was destined to die just like Ayub Khan's 'modernism' had. In the same letter, he advised my father "to repent" and join "JI's mission" to shape a national ideology that was "truly Islamic."

In the 1970 elections, the Islamist parties were defeated. The Bengali nationalist party, Awami League, swept the election in East Pakistan, and the PPP won an outright majority in West Pakistan. My father told me that when he was watching the results being announced on the TV in the Karachi Press Club's canteen, he saw Ghaffar quietly walking towards him. He shook my father's hand and then promptly ordered two gin and tonics. "For old time's sake," he said (in Urdu). He then quickly added, "But only today, as you know I stopped (drinking) years ago."

My father replied: "You will drink to drown your sorrows, and I will drink to rejoice. That's not right." Then, giving the writing pad on which my father was noting down the election results, he told Ghaffar, "I'll have the drink, while you can jot down the results for me. I will take that as an apology (for the letter)." Ghaffar obliged.

Due to the inability of the military regime, the PPP, and the Awami League to agree on a 'power sharing formula,' violence erupted in East Pakistan. The violence soon mutated into becoming an all-out civil war in the eastern wing of the country. It was during this commotion that two books appeared, both titled *Ideology of Pakistan*. One was written by journalist and author Sharif Mujahid, and the other by Justice Javed Iqbal, son of the poet-philosopher Muhammad Iqbal. Justice Iqbal explained that the unity which binds the country's diverse ethnic communities together was 'spiritual' in nature. By this he meant an Islam that was not theocratic, but spiritual (*roohani*).

This is also how the ZA Bhutto regime (1972–77) would begin to explain Islam, mainly by romanticising the local folk cultures and Sufism. The result of the 1971 civil war saw East Pakistan break away to become Bangladesh, leaving behind a disoriented, disillusioned and angry polity in West Pakistan. Bhutto replaced Yahya as president. A new National Assembly came into being based on the results of the 1970 elections (in West Pakistan). The historian, Ishtiaq Husain Qureshi, saw the country sliding into an existential crisis. Qureshi posed the question: What was Pakistan now about? Did the acrimonious separation of East Pakistan signal the demise of the Two-Nation Theory? Would Pakistan even survive as a nation-state? In 1972, he answered them by writing, "Countries come and go, but religions stay." This was his way of recommending the dialing up of the role of Islam in the country's politics and curriculum. The same year, my father became the Kabul correspondent of *Musawat*, the PPP's Urdu daily. Of course, that was a very different Kabul compared to the many tragedies that it would suffer years later. I have vague but fond memories of the city, even though I was just five years old.

The defeat in East Pakistan opened a window for Islamist parties to sneak into the country's decision-making institutions. JI echoed Qureshi's laments. So, in the 1973 Constitution, the formation of a Council of Islamic Ideology (CII) was mandated to aid the government in 'Islamising' the country's laws in all areas. The same year, a department of 'Pakistan Studies' was established at the Quaid-e-Azam University in Islamabad, to officially formulate a 'Pakistan Ideology.' However, the government informed the Parliament that it would take at least seven years to 'Islamise' the country's laws. In textbooks, the notion that 'Pakistan was made in the name of Islam' was dialed up, but the term 'Pakistan Ideology' remained missing.

We returned to Pakistan in 1974, just days before the Afghan monarchy was toppled in a coup led by Sardar Daoud. Back in Karachi, I was enrolled at the prestigious Karachi Grammar School and my sister at a school headed by Catholic nuns. My younger brother too was born that year. My mother became a teacher, and my father launched a progressive Urdu weekly with a few of his fellow journalists. Meanwhile, Ghaffar had greatly expanded his father's business and then married the daughter of a JI worker in NWFP. He also began to donate funds to JI. He told my father, "I will donate all my money if it can rid the country of that alcoholic charlatan (Bhutto)."

Birth of an 'Ideology'

In July 1977, Bhutto was toppled in a military coup by his handpicked military chief, General Zia-ul-Haq. The very next year, Pakistan Studies was made a compulsory subject at secondary, intermediate and graduation levels. A 'Pakistan Ideology' was thus officially launched and embedded in Pakistan Studies textbooks. The first chapter was titled *'The Ideological Basis of Pakistan.'* This chapter has since evolved and frequently been added to, across the 1980s.

So, what was the 'Pakistan Ideology' delineated in these new textbooks?

Pakistan was made in the name of Islam.

The Two-Nation Theory is still relevant because India wants to reintegrate Pakistan into India.

Pakistani Muslims have deeper ancestral and spiritual roots in Arabia, Central Asia and Persia than in South Asia.

Muslims of varied ethnicities residing along River Indus were always 'different' from the people living in regions that are now part of India.

The 7th-century Arab commander, Muhammad Bin Qasim, first

sowed the seeds of Islam in South Asia. He was, therefore, a kind of a proto-Pakistani.

The main roots of Muslim nationalism in South Asia can be traced to the long Muslim rule in India, that lasted from the 13th to the 19th century

Muhammad Iqbal 'dreamed' of a separate Islamic republic and Jinnah toiled and turned this dream into reality.

Jinnah wanted to turn the republic into an Islamic state.

The ulema worked closely with Jinnah to help him create Pakistan.

Islam is at the centre of all state and government institutions of Pakistan and permeates through the everyday life of the Pakistani nation.

Pakistan Ka Matlab Kya, Laillaha Illahah (What is the meaning of Pakistan?: There is No God, But God).

Since Islam is at the core of this 'Ideology,' the authors conveniently forget to mention that the Islam which the founders of Pakistan spoke of was quite different from the Islam that the Islamists (and later Zia) looked to impose. In fact, both variants were hostile towards each other. The Islam of the founders was entirely anti-theocratic, whereas the Islam mentioned in the Ideology was one developed by 20th-century Islamists that looked to create a theocracy—or at least, a 'theodemocracy.'

Moreover, some well-known ulema and Islamist parties in pre-Partition India were opposed to Jinnah and of the idea of Pakistan. Only a handful of ulema agreed to support Jinnah. *Pakistan Ka Matlab Kya, Laillaha Illahah* was derived from a 1944 poem by an obscure poet. It was turned into a slogan by the Muslim League during the 1946 election, primarily to stir the emotions of voters in rural Punjab. Jinnah never once uttered this phrase. It was then completely discarded and forgotten about until it was revived 32 years later (in 1978) by the Zia dictatorship. Its grammar is awkward, and really, it means nothing. In 1983, the University Grants Commission issued a directive. It stated:

"Textbooks should demonstrate that the basis of Pakistan is not be found in racial, linguistic or geographical factors, but in the shared experience of a common religion. The *books should get* the students to know and appreciate the ideology of Pakistan, and to popularise it through slogans to guide students towards the ultimate goal of Pakistan: the creation of a completely Islamised state."[10]

The issue with the declaration—'Pakistan was created in the name of Islam'—is not only about the fact that the idea of Islam of the country's founders was different from the Islam that the state began to adopt from the mid-1970s onward. The problem with it is also about its inherent singularity. Arabs recognise their Arabian identity as a pre-Islamic construct; Iranians embrace their pre-Islamic ancient history, as do the Turks and Malays, but Pakistan, by being defined as a state for Muslims, denies Pakistani citizens any other identity that might complement their religious identity.[11] In fact, it seeks to erase it.

My father was 'blacklisted' along with numerous other journalists by the Zia regime. Unable to work as a journalist and remaining unemployed for almost three years, he decided to form an advertising agency with a friend of his. Ghaffar was delighted by Bhutto's ouster. Ironically though, now running a successful real estate business and wearing a much longer beard, he readily handed over his company's marketing matters to my father's ad agency. I entered my teens in the 1980s. After completing my O-Levels in 1983, I joined a state-owned college in Karachi and plunged into student politics right away. I fancied myself a 'Marxist' and joined a progressive students' organisation. In 1985, after getting arrested for the first time (allegedly for setting fire to a public bus), I was released after spending a torrid ten hours in a notorious police station. I was punched, kicked, spat upon and called a 'Russian agent' by the cops. A year later, I was back behind bars. A brawl with members of JI's student-wing turned violent and one of 'our' guys was stabbed. He barely survived. And guess who else was part of that brawl? Ghaffar's eldest son, Bilal. I had

---

10   P. Hoodbhoy: *Pakistan: Origins, Identity and Future* (Routledge, 2023)

11   'Internal instability in Pakistan': A Ali (Islamabad Institute of Strategic Studies, 2014)

no clue about this at the time, though. My father informed me of this only after I was released. He also said that Ghaffar (who was his client now) had called him to complain that his son had been attacked by a group of hooligans "led by your son."

Fact is, it was our group of 'hooligans' that was attacked by a much larger group because they wanted to stop us from holding a protest against Pakistan's involvement in Afghanistan. But my father never stopped me from being a student activist. However, he did request that I spare the 'mujahid son' of his client. We both ended up laughing. He also advised me to stop questioning the Pakistan Ideology which students were being compelled to study. He wanted me to just pass the Pakistan Studies exam, graduate, and pose my questions as an academic or a journalist.

Although the discourse on the 'Pakistan Ideology' had evolved between the late 1950s and the mid-1970s, its official unrolling was accelerated by the Zia dictatorship in 1978. The 'Ideology' did not have any grand or noble intention. It was shaped to legitimise a dictatorship that had overthrown an elected government. Its aim was reduced to provide the dictatorship a national—and even a divine—justification. After the Pakistani armed forces were defeated in East Pakistan in 1971, Islamist parties had lamented that since the soldiers weren't defending an ideology, they lost. This curious narrative then swept through the military, which became the first state institution to be indoctrinated with what was to become the 'Pakistan Ideology'.

Conclusion

From 1977 onwards, the armed forces were to "defend Pakistan's ideological borders" as well as its physical borders. Following in their footsteps, other institutions, such as the judiciary, the senate and the parliament, were expected to do the same. Yet, despite the fact that presidents, prime ministers, judges, Islamists, and military generals often speak of a 'Pakistan Ideology', they do not do so in a coherent manner. Just like Zia, whose regime moulded an ideology that could serve his political interests, judges and prime ministers use this term to suit their needs. 'Pakistan Ideology' is unlimited in that it could mean anything that can benefit a personal or institutional cause or desire. This 'Ideology' therefore, serves little or no purpose outside of being a convenient catchphrase.

The ambiguous, rhetorical, anti-historical and largely reactionary nature of this Ideology has also produced oddities in which various banned sectarian organisations have often raised their hands and willingly become its 'defenders.' But the most curious oddity in this respect is that both militant and mainstream Islamists believe it is not Islamic enough. Others, such as the liberals, moderates, and leftists bemoan it for being too Islamic—by this they mean Islamist. They stress that Pakistan may have been made in the name of Islam, but it was not made in the name of Islamism. And nor was it made by Islamists.

Pakistan is a Muslim-majority country that has been experimenting with parliamentary democracy and constitutionalism, which project themselves to be inclusive in that they respect the cultures of the country's various ethnic groups, Islamic sects and sub-sects and 'minority' communities. In his first speech as Governor General, Muhammad Ali Jinnah insisted that Pakistanis belonged to a specific physical territory, as citizens in a region which happens to have a Muslim majority, but where the state will remain impersonal towards the "personal" religious beliefs of its citizens. However, this narrative was never turned into a national ideology because the state increasingly began to co-opt Islamist ideas as a way to keep at bay the highly-exaggerated fears of a communist takeover, as well as the more realistic possibility of ethnic-nationalists undermining the federation. While democracy was supposed to resolve this, not only did it come too late, in 1970, but it also triggered a rupture in 1971 due to a total mishandling of rising ethnonationalism, especially in East Pakistan. The 1973 Constitution was thus authored, and it was passed in an environment pregnant with uncertainty and even paranoia. Two views emerged in 1972 on how to fortify the country's existence from further breakages.

The first view encouraged the complete acceptance of Pakistan's ethnic and sectarian diversity and the accordance of democratic rights to its ethnic groups in return for their allegiance to Pakistan as a federal unit. This view also treaded a middle-path between Islamism and secularism, adopting a modernism that respected local cultures while eschewing 'regressive' theocratic aspirations. This view understood Pakistani society as a combination of various historical influences that included South Asian, Persian, Arab, Central Asian, European, Muslim, Hindu, Buddhist and Zoroastrian currents. In 1967, the progressive Urdu poet Faiz Ahmad Faiz wrote that Pakistan's culture was a mixture of varied influences, and that while it was prominent, Islam was but just one such influence. He wrote that it was an important part of the body, but not the whole body.

After the shock of East Pakistan in 1971, such views struggled to compete with the second view. The second view derided the first view as the reason behind Pakistan's ideological weakness that had led to the defeat of its armed forces in East Pakistan. The second view bemoaned that Islam was not given any serious thought, nor was it used as a source to shape the country's state, governance and polity, which remained rudderless, vulnerable and disunited. It was this view that largely informed the contents of the 1973 Constitution, even though advocates of the first view managed to exercise some influence in this regard after pleading a middle path and not allowing democracy to become a theodemocracy.

Nevertheless, from 1974 onwards, this is exactly what Pakistan became. The 'Pakistan Ideology' became a tool to rationalise the further 'Islamisation' of the country's constitution and penal code laws, turning Pakistan into a theodemocracy with an ideology that fortifies it. Nation-states shape ideologies that seek to instill a sense of belonging and national purpose in its citizens. The 'Pakistan Ideology' is not about this. With its static, ahistorical Islamist disposition, it alienates various segments of its diverse polity. The 'Pakistan Ideology' is a caricature of what a national ideology is supposed to be. It is also xenophobic, as it seeks to create a chauvinistic Sunni monolith.

My father passed away in 2009. Ghaffar had remained a friend of his. Their friendship had been strained once more when Bhutto's daughter became prime minister in 1988, and my father became close to the PPP again—this time as a general manager of a semi-private TV channel called NTM. The friendship rekindled in 1990, when Ghaffar requested my father to help him retrieve a nephew of his from a jail in Kabul. The nephew had landed in Afghanistan in 1986 as a 'mujahid' to fight against the Soviets. Somehow, he had ended up in jail, despite the Soviets having left Afghanistan in 1987. With the aid of PM Benazir's mother, Nusrat Bhutto, my father was able to extract Ghaffar's nephew. Ghaffar came to our house to thank my father.

In hindsight, I am now convinced this is what Pakistani nationalism ought to be—people with different backgrounds aiding each other to construct a better country for future generations. My father was Punjabi, Ghaffar was Pakhtun. Both were Sunni Muslims, but while my father had remained a 'progressive Muslim' (as he liked to call himself), Ghaffar was an Islamist belonging to the Deobandi sub-sect. When Ghaffar passed away in 2019, I properly met his son Bilal. We embraced each other like siblings, knowing well that our ideas greatly differed. Two humans, each of us Pakistanis, who also happened to be Muslims. Parts of a body, but not the whole body.

Nadeem F. Paracha is a social and political commentator and columnist. He has authored eight books on the social history of Pakistan. He is also a widely read columnist for Pakistan's largest English-language daily *Dawn*, and Head of Ideas & Research at Adcom Leo Burnett. In 2018, he was accepted as a Research Scholar by the International Forum for Democratic Studies in Washington DC.

Website: https://www.dawn.com/authors/774/nadeem-f-paracha

Ordinary Lives
Amber Zaffar Khan

Between what is said and not meant, and what is meant and not said, most love is lost – Khalil Jibran

Fortunate are those whose kaleidoscope of the past is a beautiful sanctuary that brings them nothing but joy when they revisit it. For others, it is a mixed bag of painful memories intertwined with happy moments. Life's journey, whether tumultuous or orderly, when looked back upon from the present brings clarity to all that has transpired, whether it could be shelved as the result of fate or as a consequence of the choices we made at pivotal moments. Nostalgia is a complex emotion; it can evoke both pleasant and painful memories at the same time, such as the simple joys of those family breakfasts of salted butter on white toast, the whiff of freshly brewed tea, the rustle of the morning newspaper alongside a painful occurrence.

My story begins with my uncle, famously known as Nakhshab Jarchawi—a poet, film producer and director who started his filmmaking career in British India. Nakhshab was the pseudonym or *Takhallus* he used in his poetry, which stuck – a standard feature for most poets of the subcontinent. He got his first break in the Bombay film industry with the song lyrics he wrote for the film *Zeenat* (1945). He further established his position in films when *Mahal* (1949) did exceptionally well at the box office; its songs and lyrics, which he had written, were instrumental to its success. The famous track from *Mahal*, *"Ayega Aane wala Ayega,"* sung by Lata Mangeshkar, is considered one of her finest renditions. Many South Asian artists perform it in concerts as a cover song even today.

Once Nakhshab planted his foot firmly in the Bombay film industry, he took to production and direction and produced hits like *Zindagi Ya Toofan, Naghma* and *Raftar. Zindagi Ya Toofan* was his seminal project, loosely based on Mirza Ruswa's novel *Umrao Jaan Ada*. He got romantically involved with the famous actress Nadira and married her in a clandestine ceremony. The marriage was short-lived and ended in a divorce. It went against the family ethos to marry an actor, so no family member was informed or invited to the wedding, and it remained a secret for a long time even after the divorce. He migrated to Karachi, Pakistan, in 1962 with his widowed mother, aunt (also a widow and childless) and three married siblings. My father, the fourth and youngest sibling, decided to stay in India despite the entire family's exodus from India. The émigré siblings all had their own families and chose to live independently, whereas Nakhshab wanted to find a home he could share with his mother, aunt and my father – the brother with whom he shared a special bond.

He found an apartment on the top floor of a colonial building on MA Jinnah Road, also referred to at the time as Bandar Road. The apartment was huge, with three bedrooms, a sizeable living room, two vast halls, and two large balconies. A typical archetype of colonial design, it had high ceilings with wooden beams, wooden windows with textured coloured glass, and floors adorned with monochrome tiles. He turned the two balconies that overlooked the tramline passing through MA Jinnah Road into open-terrace sitting areas for evening tea, post-dinner *gup-shup* with guests, and business meetings with colleagues. Diagonally across the apartment was Radio Pakistan, Karachi.

After two years of interminable nagging by Nakhshab, my father decided to migrate to Pakistan. My father's first marriage in India ended in a divorce, so the grandmothers sought a perfect match this time. He was introduced to my mother through family friends. She was a beautiful twenty-year-old, timid, shy and twelve years younger than him. My mother, who had lost her father when she was two, lived with her paternal uncle and his wife. She had completed her B.Ed certification and was teaching in a school. Her mother, my maternal grandmother, lived with her other married daughter and wanted nothing more than to have her younger daughter settle down. Despite the age difference, she consented to the match. My father was an alternative medicine physician and had a clinic on Burns Road. He was well-versed in Farsi and enjoyed Urdu literature and poetry. He had a small library of scholarly and literary works by famous poets and writers like Dagh Dehalvi, Mirza Ghalib, Mir Anees, Mirza Salamat Ali Dabeer, Munshi Ahmed Hussain Qamar and Raees Amrohvi, which are only a few of the names I remember. He and Nakhshab were regulars at *mushairas* (an assembly of poets where they recite their poetry for an audience) – him in the audience and Nakhshab onstage as a participant.

Filmmaking was Nakhshab's passion and he intended to continue it in his new home country. Being a part of the film industry required a lot of entertaining; dining out was not an option in those times, so most of these soirees took place at home. There was a constant flow of guests and industry professionals in the apartment. The kitchen was customized with tiles, storage cabinets and a massive cooking range – very advanced for those times. Kaley Khan, a young lad of eighteen, originally from Abbottabad, was hired as the cook. My two grandmothers had to train him to cook large quantities of food. Kaley Khan possessed the perfect skillset for this role. He proved to be a virtuoso in the kitchen and managed to create delicious meals for a hundred people at a time. The apartment became a popular destination for actors, music and film directors, and singers like Nur Jahan, Naheed Niazi, and Saleem Raza. Overall, Nakhshab's home and kitchen played a significant role in the film industry's social scene. Kaley Khan cooked food in huge cauldrons every day to serve the guests. But all this glitz and glamour was restricted to the men;

the ladies of the household were not privy to entertaining any guests from the showbiz industry. They had to stay confined to their rooms for the duration of these fetes. The showbiz crowd was meant for the *men* to receive and entertain. There were no protests. It was a fully established patriarchal setup, and the ladies of the house were the citadels of conformity.

In Pakistan, Nakhshab directed two movies, *Fanoos* and *Maikhana*. The well-known actress Firdous debuted in *Maikhana* as one of its two female leads. Although the songs did well and Nakhshab was able to bag a Nigar award for *Fanoos,* both mega-budget films bombed at the box office. The financial loss put a big dent in his pocket and he didn't take it well. I heard he even flung the expensive Sapphire ring he wore for good luck onto the street in anger.

Nakhshab enjoyed epicurean fancies when it came to food, clothing and hobbies. He had a collection of high-end watches and wore only imported suits. He also developed a love for racehorses and gradually acquired several thoroughbred steeds. My father had simpler tastes but shared his brother's passion for horses. Together, they would christen the newly bought foals with tenderness and love, making sure the names represented meaningful characters which they believed affected their performance on the racecourse. They treated the horses like royalty, keeping them on a special diet of stewed apples, foxnuts and oat porridge. Kaley Khan's cauldrons were either simmering with apple stews and porridge for the four-legged babies, or with *nihari, qorma* and *biryani* for the guests.

Horse racing was an established industry in those times, and horse farms were an essential component of this operation. Renala Khurd, in Punjab's Okara district, has always been well known for its agricultural land. Renala farms in the district were also famously recognised for horse farming. Horse owners would bring pedigree horses and mares to this place for mating, and their offspring would get sold for exorbitant prices. The family tree of these foals played an essential role in determining their worth. The purest and best blood fetched the highest price. Our family's horses and mares also frequented this facility because of their pedigree ancestry. This decadent habit brought both joy and despair—joy when money was coming in, and despair when one was losing money or if, sometimes, after a race injury, a horse had to be euthanized.

Despite the domineering personalities of both brothers, they had a soft and philanthropic side; they were very generous and accommodating to the émigrés they knew who needed assistance settling down in the new country. They provided free accommodation to a distantly related family who, after migration, had no means of sustenance. The brothers had two rooms built for them on the rooftop, and the family, which eventually grew into a nine-member household – husband, wife and their seven daughters – lived rent-free in the same place for several decades. The sense of community was vigorous and strong post-Partition, and many families helped their immigrant relatives or friends settle down in the nascent republic of Pakistan.

My sister was born a year after my parent's wedding. There were celebrations, and she became the apple of everyone's eye. Nakhshab doted on her and declared he would officially adopt her. My father, whom we called Papa, couldn't refuse his brother, so he changed my sister's surname to Nakhshab, which she has stuck to till today. Throughout our school years, we had to explain why we had different surnames when we were biological sisters. There was disappointment when I was born a year and a half later. They had expected a boy and were let down. There were no celebrations.

I was a year old when Nakhshab died suddenly. He was only forty-two. In those times, such fatalities were termed as *death by heart failure*. It is hard to describe how the family reacted in just a few words—his death was so traumatic that no one ever wanted to talk about it, but it was evident it shook the entire clan. He had been the blue-eyed boy of the family. My grandmother's health began to deteriorate after his death. Papa's grief knew no bounds. He was heartbroken as Nakhshab meant the world to him and had been the sole reason for his migration to Pakistan.

A year after the 1971 war, we moved to Defence Society, Phase 1, now referred to as Defence Housing Authority. I was four-years-old at the time. Kaley Khan and my two grandmothers had not yet moved in with us. The caretakers of this large brand-new two-storey house were Rana and Rukhsana, both of whom were intersex. Rana cooked food while Rukhsana cleaned. As a child, I didn't understand why they looked and dressed differently from us. They appeared to be part women and part men, with long hair and feminine clothing, but with masculine features and voices. My parents told me they were special people of God. I now think about their response and love and respect them for it. They had no issues with their gender and treated them with kindness, allowing them to cook, serve and live with us. That generation appeared to have just another level of tolerance and acceptance. This arrangement lasted six months until the grandmothers and Kaley Khan moved in. The second floor, an independent unit, was rented out. In later years, this rent became our only means of survival.

My memories of the time spent at the race course are still vivid and date back to when we moved to our house in Phase 1, Defence. My father would take my sister and me to the race course and stables, where the horses trained and exercised daily. He had built a small animal farm at the stables which housed goats, ducks and rabbits. My sister and I would spend hours playing with the animals while Papa tended to his other babies: the horses. The vibe of these stables was something I can't describe. It was like living on a ranch, but the moment you stepped out, you were in the metropolis of Karachi.

Horse racing, an organised industry and a lucrative source of revenue was a popular sport in those days. The race course was built on a massive plot of land next to the Cantonment Railway Station. After it closed down, it became an apartment and villa complex of the Askari franchise. The stables next to the racecourse were rented out to horse owners. The administration hosted mega tournaments. Horse owners from other parts of the world also entered the competition. The grandest and most prestigious event was the annual Agha Khan

Cup. Jockeys were hired from the UK and other parts of the world and provided with lodging for months to train for these contests. My father, too, had some jockeys flown in as he prepared for the mega event. My sister and I were fascinated by these short, slim Westerners—their distinct anatomy was a mandatory professional requirement. We often went with our father to entertain them with movies or dinner, but Papa never included my mother in these outings. He also restricted our inclusion in these tournaments to the movies and dinners; the ladies and children of our household were not allowed to attend the main events.

Our connection to the show business industry was severed with the death of Nakhshab, but the trend of dinners continued. Papa had cultivated friendships with people of all social strata, and nearly fifty people would be over for dinner every fortnight. Kaley Khan's special *nihari paya* was the ultimate favourite. It was served with diluted lassi infused with roasted herbs, curated especially for digestion. My father had a natural talent for picking up the sweetest fruit, and it attracted people to come over just to indulge in the delicious treats. There were mango parties, and all varieties and specimens of the fruit were bought, washed and dumped in a bucket filled with water and ice. He claimed this was the correct way to eat mangoes. The irony was that he had diabetes and could not eat the fruit he loved so dearly. The big dinners were segregated gatherings, or only for men most of the time. The gatherings with close friends and family were more enjoyable because the grandmothers and my mother were also included and entertained as hosts.

Growing up in this corseted background wasn't easy. My father had puritanical and stringent rules for his wife and daughters. Some were motivated by false religiosity while others simply imposed cultural constructs. My mother was only permitted to visit her close relatives by herself. She either had no friends or was not allowed to meet with any she may have had from her school and college years. In all my school life, I only attended one birthday party of a school friend. Luckily, we made friends with our neighbours who lived diagonally across from our house. They had a similar setup—husband, wife, and three daughters. Their eldest was the same age as me. My sister and I could just walk over to their house in Papa's absence with our mother's permission. Their father ruled the house with a far sturdier iron fist than ours. They feared him like rabbits caught in a trap; as soon as his car honked outside the gate, announcing his arrival, they would turn off the music, stop everything they were doing, and stand at attention to welcome him. Their body language changed when he was around, and they would ask us to leave if we were visiting. I got very close to them—they are like family even now. In my heart, I found solace in the fact that our situation wasn't as bad as theirs. Many of my peers at school shared similar experiences, where male dominance was prevalent. The cherished values of freedom of thought and action were great as long as the men exercised it.

Commanding such control didn't mean my father didn't love his family. His definition of love was just different from ours. He was a family man and spent much of his free time with us. Every weekend, he would take us to visit friends and relatives. One of his admirable qualities was his ability to connect with people from all social backgrounds and treat them equally. He was very generous with his earnings towards the family, relatives and others in need. His friends and acquaintances both admired and respected him. Despite his strict rules, my mother loved him dearly. He bought presents for her, always jewellery in gold. Our house had a huge garden and a long driveway. He would play cricket, badminton and throwball with us, and my mother was always included in these family activities. Papa taught my sister how to ride a bike, but he wasn't interested when it was my turn to learn. He showed greater love towards my sister than he ever did towards me. I always felt unwanted in his presence. A couple of times, in anger directed at me, he made a comment insinuating that my birth's reward was his brother's death. I remember his first outburst when I was ten years old. I bumped my head into his jaw by accident and broke his front tooth. I had expected Papa's anger but not the comment he made about me bringing nothing but misfortune. On another occasion, when our car wouldn't start while going to a friend's house for dinner, I made a silly comment about it being better to break down now than on the road and cause an accident. He got furious and rebuked me with a similar hurtful comment. My sister was always the favoured one who got away with everything. Words spoken in anger by someone you love, especially a family member, can be forgotten, but the underlying subtext lacerates and weighs down heavily on the soul. I had always hoped that my father would treat me with the same love and affection as he did my sister, rather than just seeing me as a responsibility. My grandmothers felt this obvious bias and compensated me for the missing affection.

Papa made career choices for my sister and I. He wanted my sister to become a doctor and me an engineer. Once he had decided, there was no further discussion on the subject, only constant monitoring of our grades and reprimanding us for not doing our best. I would be lectured for not doing well even though I consistently came second in the class. My natural inclination was towards arts, and I won awards in drawing competitions. My teachers also discovered, I had a great singing voice, and I was always asked to perform recitals at school events such as *Milads* and *Youm-e-Hussain* in Muharram. But I never felt thrilled about performing on stage, perhaps as a result of my low self-esteem and dwindling confidence. My father, too, never felt proud or acknowledged this as an achievement; he didn't care for such trifles. He simply wanted the best grades in science and maths. The performing arts that brought honour and fame to his brother, and subsequently pride to the family, was undoubtedly unacceptable for his daughters. Neither my sister nor I fulfilled his dream!

Kaley Khan married and brought his wife Rusmat from his village to live with us. Rusmat was an invaluable addition to the family. She was tall and broad, with a pleasant disposition. She had never been to school and spoke only Punjabi. She loved to embroider flowers and birds on tablecloths and pillows. Everyone loved her and she became quintessential to our household, so much that we often wondered how we had managed without her all this time. She would prove her unquestionable loyalty and be my mother's companion in her older age. Rusmat was sharp and intelligent, and quickly adapted to the ways of city life. Within a few years, she learned fluent Urdu and became more independent than any woman in our family. My mother often said that if Rusmat had been born into a privileged background, she would have surely held a top position in a big organisation.

The 1970s are infamous in Pakistan's history for changing the political and socio-economic landscape of the country. Following the 1971 war, political turmoil was brewing. In 1973, Zulfiqar Ali Bhutto became the Prime Minister and started the Islamization movement to appease the mullahs. His government declared horse racing akin to gambling, and therefore "un-Islamic."They decided to ban the game, and the colossal race-course, bustling with activity, was reduced to a desolate edifice. The stakeholders collectively filed a case for renewal, gathering fatwas from clerics that stipulated its legality in Islam. The case went on for years. The lavish expenditure for the upkeep of the horses became burdensome for my father, and all his resources and savings started depleting. There were no buyers for these thoroughbred pedigrees, which were priced for lakhs in better times. My father downsized the staff at the stables as well as at home to cut costs. It was getting more and more challenging to maintain the horse's fancy diets, and as a result, some of them died. Each death was a massive blow to Papa. They were his prized possessions, and sometimes I saw him wiping tears from his eyes. During these troubled times, my grandmother suffered a stroke and was paralysed. She was bedridden and in diapers, and the responsibility of nursing her came upon her sister and my mother. After a few years of infirmity, she passed away. I was very close to her as she gave me the love that was absent from my father. It hit me hard, and I would lock myself in the bathroom and cry for hours.

Kaley Khan, who was a massive pillar of support to my father and our household, found a job in Iraq and decided to leave. This was when the Middle East was in an era of rapid development. Scores from the labour class were leaving the country for more lucrative work. Kaley

Khan loved us but had his family's future to think of. My parents understood this and let him go without any grievance. Rusmat would continue to live with us as a family member without drawing a salary. The housework and cooking were divided between my mother and Rusmat. Even the driver was laid off.

When Ziaul Haque imposed martial law in 1977, my father lost all hope of the regime restoring horse racing. The financial strain was too much to bear, and his health started to rapidly deteriorate. His diabetes could not be controlled and it started affecting his heart. The memory of his first heart attack still sends shivers down my spine. It was 3 AM in the night when my sister and I woke up to the noise. We saw my father struggling to breathe and our mother scurrying around the room in panic, handing cupboard keys to my grandmother. Then they both sat in the car and he drove himself in that breathless state for twelve minutes to his friend's house, where the friend administered an emergency injection to revive him. That gesture of handing the keys meant that my mother was unsure if they were coming back home alive. We sat in anticipation all night, petrified, my grandmother quietly wiping tears from her eyes and Rusmat trying to get us to sleep. It is difficult for me to imagine what my mother endured in those twelve minutes, with him behind the wheel fighting for his breath. The immense fortitude and emotional strength my mother displayed in such a difficult situation makes me ponder about what women like her could have achieved if they had been given a different life. She never allowed her vulnerability to show, even though she must have felt intensely anxious about the possibility of something happening to my father, who was the sole provider for our family.

A year passed by, and there was a similar incident. Papa was admitted to the hospital. The doctors said his heart had weakened. Three days after his stay in the hospital, he suffered another heart attack—this time, it was fatal. It was 1982, a life-altering year for us—my father left this material world for the eternal, leaving behind the women he had protected and sheltered all his life to fend for themselves. The day before he died, my sister and I were at the hospital and my mother had gone to organise his food. He asked my sister to lie down next to him, caressed her hair and hugged her. I could see his eyes welling up. Maybe he knew he didn't have much time left. I felt like an outsider during this special moment he shared with her. He didn't ask me to join them. I stood at the window in the same room, sneaking furtive glances at them while pretending to look outside. As I wiped my tears away, I wondered if I was invisible. Could he not see me? Did he not realise that I existed too? His death brought the brutal realisation—that I had been robbed of any future prospects of regaining his love.

Papa's passing shattered the protective shield he had provided us throughout his life, plunging us into a pit of sorrow and overwhelming uncertainty. My mother became a thirty-eight-year-old widow with two daughters, aged fifteen and seventeen, having no clue how to navigate the practical world on her own. The financial constraints were huge as we had lost our sole breadwinner. We needed to learn the basics of how things worked. How does one encash a cheque? How does one do groceries? How do you deal with lawyers for legal matters, and how do you pay the bills? The once patriarchal household was now a matriarchy, except the matriarch had no idea how things worked in the real world.

My only living paternal uncle at the time, a lawyer by profession whom we all respected and loved, stepped up and visited us regularly. He would bring basic groceries since my mother was practicing strict iddah and couldn't leave the house. This arrangement lasted only a few months as he couldn't keep up with it due to his wife's displeasure. Papa's *Nihari* and mango-eating friends vanished like spectres. A handful of them stayed in touch, and some took advantage of our inexperience. My father was fond of hunting and had invested in costly ammunition, all licensed. One of my cousins in the army came and took them all without making any payment, knowing fully well how desperately we needed cash. During my father's lifetime, the same cousin had pressured my father into investing in a commercial plot of land, which he could purchase at subsidised rates because of his army position. However, even after making the full payment, my father was not given the ownership documents. Not only did the cousin usurp that property, but at this critical time, he also took away my father's personal belongings. The MA Jinnah Road apartment was leased on *Pagdi* drawing a nominal amount of rent. *Pagdi* is a traditional tenancy model that was commonly practiced in the sub-continent in those times, where the tenant is a co-owner with the right to sublet. The tenant pays a substantial amount at the contract signing and the rent that follows is a pittance.

We kept a driver for a year, till my sister learned to drive, and tried to live frugally—our only source of income was the rent from our tenants on the first floor. My mother sold quite a bit of her gold to make ends meet and invested the money in Ponzi schemes on suggestions by friends. All that money was lost. After eighteen years of marriage with my father, her confidence was low and she felt insecure about stepping out into the world to take up a job, even as a school teacher. It took two years for the legal documents to come through for our father's clinic at Burns Road. The middleman who was helping with the documentation got it sold for peanuts. We invested the money and our finances improved a bit. Yet, throughout this time, I never saw my mother embittered or angry. She was a born conformist and accepted her destiny without vexation. Her strength and patience came from her strong faith in God. She endured immense social pressure and developed high blood pressure but tried to stay cheerful and emotionally robust for us. Everyone was around to give advice but not assistance. People were ready to cast aspersions at the slightest trigger, especially towards fatherless daughters. Such was the ethos of our society. All this was new territory for my mother, and she had to tread carefully. From the fetters of patriarchy, we graduated to worrying about the age-old question, *what will people say?* Even though she cared about maintaining a pristine reputation and was old-school about extending liberties to her daughters, she felt comfortable about my sister and I picking our spouses as long as they fulfilled the criteria of family values, education and our sect. That was one long battle I had to fight with her for my choice of husband in my twenties, whom she grew to love wholeheartedly.

When I started college, we had new tenants. The family comprised of a husband, wife and their three daughters, all of whom were around my age. They were music lovers; it appeared fate had brought them to our house. The eldest two used to learn singing from an *ustaad*. A year after they moved in, their father passed away from health problems similar to those of my father—diabetes that ultimately led to a heart attack. Now both floors of the house were solely inhabited by women. The families, theirs and ours, had transitioned into female-dominated households, and while we practiced different family values, our day-to-day challenges were the same. Both the ladies, homemakers each, yet so different from each other and leading contrasting lifestyles, were examples of strength and resilience in their own right. Their mother, an extrovert, had liberal views and granted her daughters a lot of freedom and space. She would allow them to sing at gatherings and hold musical events and parties at the house. The shared experience of grief creates an indescribable camaraderie between people, so it was a combination of that and our compatibility that led to us becoming very close friends. I took their encouragement and pestered my mother to hire an *ustaad*. I received an emphatic "no!" It took a few years before my mother relented.

After graduating from St. Joseph's College, my sister and I started working at a school. We had no money to pursue a professional degree and needed the cash. I used some of my earnings to hire an *ustaad* for music lessons. I received much praise for my singing and was offered twice to sing professionally, once for a movie and a second time for a famous TV show. My mother's response was always a "no", but this time with a warning to end my music lessons if I continued with such demands. Music lessons were integral to my being, therapy for me, so I acquiesced. She allowed us to hold musical events at the house, unprecedented in our family.

During this period, my sister got engaged and was married three years later. My brother-in-law was a liberal, fun-loving person and nothing like Papa. It was around this time that I formed strong friendships, both in college and with my neighbours. These were unequivocally among the best years of my life. We had transcended the limits set for us by our patriarch and forged our own paths forward. Life was different from when my father was alive—not lavish and fanciful, and we missed him, but we were enjoying our freedom and living our lives.

During these times, our friends who lived diagonally across our house decided to move out of their father's home. The decision was their mother's, who had never left her household on her own in the twenty years of her married life. She called it quits when the husband decided to marry off the eldest daughter, who was my age, to his nephew by force. She could tolerate the stifling and autocratic environment of the house but refused to compromise on her daughters' future. The move was a herculean act knowing the nature of her spouse, and had to be done in secret. They had no money and no resources. The mother sold off her gold and moved into a garage in Commercial Phase 2, Defence, with her three daughters. Her eldest daughter was nineteen, and the youngest, nine. Their struggle has been most inspiring. The eldest daughter, one of my closest friends, found a job at British Airways as a Flying Attendant, and this milestone marked the beginning of their journey of survival. The decline in social status and frugal living was a small price for their autonomy and freedom.

Although I never told my mother any of this, after my father's passing, I used to pray for my mother to be rescued by a knight-in-shining armour. Many years later, when visiting the same friends, over a cup of tea and chit-chat, my friend and I told our mothers about a mutual friend's mother getting remarried at fifty-plus. We were very happy for her and advised our mothers to do the same, to which they cringed and said, we have finally achieved our freedom, we do not want fetters binding us again! Despite their financial woes, these women, who had insecure childhoods and spent the prime of their lives cocooned in environments forced upon them by their male protectors had found peace and happiness. They did not want a man to rescue them. Sometimes it feels like the concept of happiness is overrated. It can be found even in imperfection, and they were prime examples.

Life moved on with its ups and downs, its twists and turns. I switched my job from school teaching to Human Resources in an engineering firm, where I met my husband. He was all I had vowed to look for in a spouse of my choice—a partner, not a master!

Kaley Khan had come back after a ten-year stint in the Middle East. I still remember, on his arrival, he opened his suitcase and asked my sister and me to have the first pick of the gifts he had brought back for everyone. How does one repay such generosity and kindness? He was around for my sister's wedding. Both he and Rusmat adopted his niece, so now there was a baby in the house. The decision was solely Rusmat's, who had been childless for a decade. Whenever the baby cried hysterically, Kaley Khan would reprimand her for separating a day-old infant from her mother. The baby's mother, her sister-in-law and a mother of five, had asked her to take the baby straight from the hospital. Rusmat had the parent's consent and her firm resolve. She would make it work and probably did better than the biological mother would have. Ten years later and twenty years into her marriage, Rusmat gave birth to another daughter.

After my wedding, my mother decided to learn how to drive. She always depended on my sister and me for commuting, but now we both had moved out. She was fifty-plus, and it was a challenging task considering the unruly traffic of Karachi. It took her a year to perfect her training; one of my happiest days was when she drove from Phase 1, Defence, to Phase 5 to visit me. It felt as if she had finally achieved true liberation!

Epilogue

I moved to the UAE in 2002 with my husband and two kids, and my sister migrated to Canada in 2009. Kaley Khan passed away in 2009; he was able to marry off his older daughter in his lifetime. My mother was alone with her companion, friend and sister Rusmat, and Rusmat's younger daughter.

Tragedy struck our family when my sister's husband was diagnosed with cancer in March 2014. He passed away within eight months of the diagnosis. I had to call my mother to give her this news, and her screams on the phone still haunt me. She had been the embodiment of strength and fortitude all her life but couldn't hold the fort anymore. She suffered in silence for her daughter's tragedy and her beloved son-in-law. Her biggest fear was becoming an invalid during her old age and dependent on someone.

On September 16, 2015, my mother passed away with dignity, in her home at the age of seventy-one. It was sudden, and neither my sister nor I were in Pakistan for this dreadful tragedy. She wasn't granted a privileged, entitled life, but God blessed her with her desired peaceful exit.

Amber Zaffar Khan is an art, culture and literature enthusiast and promoter. For the last fourteen years, she has been introducing and promoting musicians from Pakistan in the UAE and holding community events. She's one of the founding Directors of her event management company, Aashkaar.

Lost And Found:
A Life Between Two Worlds

Junaid Zuberi

I was born in a family that had been living in pre-Partition India for generations. The events of 1947 brought most of my extended family to the newly created Pakistan. My grandparents from both sides, along with their children and whatever memories they could get hold of, migrated to Karachi with nothing in mind about their future course of action. They followed Mohamad Ali Jinnah and believed his word. Pakistan it was. Once here, there was no looking back and in spite of all their struggles and challenges, they looked ahead and carried on. They eventually settled well. Their subsequent generations got to experience the best of comforts as they did not have to go through the travails of migration.

I was born in Karachi in the year when Jinnah sahab's famous quote *"There is no power on earth that can undo Pakistan"* was proven wrong. There was a power, or perhaps more than one, that broke the country's eastern wing and created Bangladesh. Without even moving from the house that they lived in for decades there were families that had become Pakistani from Indian in 1947 and Bangladeshi from Pakistani in 1971. The same house, the same neighborhood, the same city and the same air they breathed gave them a third identity. They felt like puppets whose strings were in unknown hands. My family was settled in Karachi, so they continued with their Pakistani identity and reinterpreted Jinnah's quote as having meant for West Pakistan, rechristened as Pakistan. In that fateful year my mother gave birth to me. My grandmother had already settled on my name, declaring if I was born a boy, they'd call me Junaid.

Karachi was Pakistan to me. The rest of the country was alien to us as we did not travel frequently for a variety of reasons. My first trip outside Karachi turned out to be in another fateful summer. The year was 1977 and we were staying at a guesthouse in Murree when all the guests were asked to evacuate on an immediate basis. None of us were given a reason. Later, we found out that the country's Prime Minister Zulfiqar Ali Bhutto was brought there to be kept under military custody. Martial Law was imposed. A diminutive army chief, who was promoted out of turn for the job by the same prime minister that made seven of his senior colleagues retire forcefully, backstabbed Mr. Bhutto and the rest is history. We came back to Karachi and life went on. My younger brother was born that same winter, making us siblings four. My grandmother lived with us, too, but the rented house we lived in never felt small. The old banyan tree outside the house and our intrusive landlords, an old couple, who lived in the upper portion, are deeply etched in my memory.

I can never forget those days. We lived in a protective environment. I was blissfully unaware of the sacrifices my parents made to raise their family and manage the household seamlessly. I was not even privy to the damage Martial Law was causing to the society at large. I lived in my own bubble and was oblivious to the world outside. From a rowdy, boisterous and loud child who often became a social embarrassment for his parents, I turned into a quiet boy who withdrew from the world and kept no communication with anyone. The boy I had become was alien to the child I was. Sometimes I could not recognize this boy. It's not that the boy did not want to communicate. He was shy and lacked confidence. He was a recluse and hated crowds. He did not like the limelight and wanted to wear what was known in the fables as *Sulemani topi* which made the wearer become invisible to the world. From an active and animated child to a deeply introverted adolescent, it was an unnerving transformation, not so much for me as it as for my parents.

My father was deeply concerned by my excessively introverted self and often lectured me on Sundays, for hours at length, on why I needed to come out of my shell. As always, I would listen without uttering a word. It had become a weekend norm and I dreaded those sessions. I knew in my heart that his concerns were legitimate, but I had no clue on how to act upon them. A person who is introverted cannot suddenly wear the extrovert cap and become chirpy, talkative and social. I attribute many reasons for this transformation. It calls for a separate chapter and I hope that some day I get the courage to write more openly about the reasons that led to this change.

From school, I went to college and then university, coming out with a business degree. I followed the easy path. In those days, cinema excited me immensely. I was awed by the big screen and often thought how marvellous it would be to make a film one day. That dream died within the confines of my heart. I was always fond of music even though there was no major inclination towards the arts in my family. My parents enjoyed music, but there was no culture of going to performances or having conversations about art in the house. We were the stereotype of a middle-class family, conservative but educated. There was a lot of focus on reading books and education as opposed to the arts and creative expression. I knew I had the germs in me, but I neither had the guidance nor the mentoring on how to navigate my path and bring out the artist. While the urge to pursue my dreams sank deeply in my heart, my love for the arts persisted and blossomed when I entered practical life and became a little independent.

One fine day, I received an anonymous message informing me about a certain classical vocalist and trainer. The message said that she ran a forum to promote classical music as our artistic heritage. The person who sent the message apparently knew of my passion for music and along with an introduction of the lady, informed me of an upcoming performance that she was curating, before urging me to attend the event. The venue was a private hotel. The lady in question was Saffia Beyg, the mother of fashion icon Rizwan Beyg. I recalled reading a brief profile of hers in a magazine called Newsline, years prior. I also remembered the profile mentioning that the senior Mrs. Beyg was a stylist and ran a salon at one point, but I didn't recall anything about her musical journey. Anyhow, I attended the evening and was completely smitten. It was my first proper introduction to live performances of pure classical music. I fell in love with it. Her rendition of *Raag Hansdhwani* stole my heart. Later, I found out that Saffia apa sang the Hansdhwani version of Begum Parveen Sultana. That is how I was introduced to the great diva of Indian classical music. Saffia Beyg sang classical in a way that resonated with the uninitiated like me as much as it swayed the purists. The evening was held in association with a charity organization called Raasta to support drought victims in Sindh. Raasta's founder, Simi Kamal addressed the audience before the music began. Outside the hall, Farzana Rashid and Nameera Ahmad sat at the ticket counter. Tickets were priced at Rs. 100 each. Later, I got to know all these ladies well. I was mesmerized by Saffia Beyg's singing and introduced myself to her during the interval. She promptly invited me to her house and I booked an appointment with her for the coming weekend.

I took my friend Razi Iqbal, who was also fond of music, to meet Saffia Beyg (by then known as Saffia apa to us). She asked me to sing something and I attempted Iqbal Bano's *Dasht-e-Tanhai.* She said I needed to learn classical and offered to teach gratis. I was too shy and non-committal and though I attempted a few lessons, I realized I could not do it. I lacked confidence big time and could not bring myself to sing without inhibition before Saffia apa. My voice would shake and I had no idea how to overcome this fear, shyness and self-doubt. By that time, Saffia apa had grown accustomed to my presence, and I was gradually becoming a regular visitor at her lovely home. There was a level of mutual comfort. She asked me to help her run Sampurna, a forum for classical music and thus began a long association.

Sampurna was only a few months old when I stepped in. I became Saffia apa's eyes and ears for Sampurna and helped her in every manner. I fostered relationships with music aficionados, and Sampurna turned out to the be launching pad of my formal association with music. There was no looking back. I became part of many other forums subsequently through the network I had developed during my association with Sampurna. Saffia apa did not know how much she helped me overcome my stage fright and timidity, both of which had started to bother me immensely. I will always be grateful to her for mentoring me in a way no one had ever done. Apa was the kind of person one could openly talk to about anything under the sun with no fears. I always thank my stars and that anonymous caller to have introduced me to Saffia apa. I did eventually find out the identity of that caller and confirmed it from the person directly.

It was much before I joined Sampurna and became socially busy that I had gone to see a clairvoyant in Karachi. The lady was recommended by a friend. I can never forget that experience. One thing that stuck with me from the conversation was, "the country of your death will not be the same as the country of your birth." I was well-settled in Pakistan, single and with no intentions or even thoughts of moving abroad. "So, does this mean I'll die in one of my international travels?" I asked. "You will move out of the country", she said. I found this absurd not knowing that a decade or so later I'd be migrating to Canada.

That decade saw me getting married and raising a small family. I can write a whole new chapter on my wife Sadaf and son Hamza, but all I would say in a nutshell is that I am tremendously grateful to Allah for the gift of a family that I did not think I deserved. To date, I marvel at how my wife carried herself and supported me even in situations where conventional partners would never do so. To give an example, post-COVID when my parents were stuck in Pakistan with none of their five children residing in the country, I felt that I needed to be with them and they also wanted us to be around. It was Sadaf who pushed me into making the decision saying I was more needed there. I took the tough decision of moving by myself only with her support. Hamza is the epicentre of our world. We live and breathe for him.

Rewind a few years, it was my wife who not only insisted but convinced me to move abroad for a better future for our family, especially our son. She took it up as a project and connected with an immigration consultant in Karachi who finally agreed to take up our case, when many others had refused saying that we didn't qualify. I had already crossed 40 and the mere thought of moving abroad scared me. Leaving a comfortable job at my age, leaving my parents in Karachi, leaving the active social life and the network I had developed—all these worries pulled me down, but I had no choice. Sadaf saw the future whereas I was fixated on the present. I relented and we moved to Toronto, where my uncle, my father's younger brother, also lived with his family in a suburban town called Mississauga. He had been settled there for over three decades. We started off at his place, and the way he and his wife, my aunt, took us in their wings merits a separate chapter. They helped us settle in the new land, mentored us, guided us, protected us and allowed us to explore life and reach for the stars. They gave us space as a family and allowed us to make our decisions. They supported us in so many ways that I won't be able to mention in these few lines. They helped us get our own place and I will always be grateful to them for making this transition easy for us.

My fears, however, continued to haunt me. The guilt of leaving my parents behind would always bother me. I missed the bustling culture of Karachi. So, while we focused on settling down in the new country, I took a step forward and started networking with likeminded folks or, if I were to put it differently, musically minded folks. By then I had created a virtual community called Sur Sangum that already boasted hundreds of members, all music buffs from different locations. I searched and found some members based in Toronto, and this became the trigger point. I started meeting people and soon Sur Sangum transitioned from the virtual to the real. The community had its first meetup at a newly acquainted friend's basement where amateur singers and guests sang to their heart's content and enjoyed a delicious potluck dinner. A cousin who attended the gathering promptly asked me to organize a second similar meetup at her place the following month. Another guest offered their place the month after. There was no looking back.

Sur Sangum soon became a vibrant, and fun musical community in Mississauga. Friends who joined talked about it in their networks and more people attended our meetups. In less than two years, I realized we had grown big and needed larger venues. It was then that I decided to register this forum as a non-profit in Canada and take it to the next level. We started organizing and curating bigger events at concert halls and each one was a success. The name was out there and people began noticing the community. In less than five years, Sur Sangum became a name to be reckoned with. With over 30 performances featuring artists from different backgrounds and ethnicities as well as a vibrant community, Sur Sangum was seen as an exclusive forum of music loving people coming together. Friendships were forged, new connections were made and many people associated with the forum found a group of life-long best friends they now cherish.

Friends and acquaintances always see me as the person who knows how to create communities and help people connect with each other. Just before my immigration to Canada came through, I had created a group of Qawwali loving friends and we jointly organized and co-hosted a mehfil that we all loved. The experience was great, everyone gelled with one another, new friendships were made. We had all vowed to continue hosting Qawwali mehfils with artists of our choice to hear the kalam of our liking. Soon after that first mehfil, I left for Canada, but the group continued and thrived in the years I was away. They became much closer and jointly hosted many Qawwali evenings. I was the connector and it made me feel genuinely happy.

And then, COVID happened. The world changed, and so did it change completely for us all. The first lockdown was scary. While the days reminded us of the classic film *The Groundhog Day*, we were scared of all that was happening in the world. Death and chaos all over. We prayed for our loved ones. I was extremely nervous about my ageing parents coping on their own in Karachi, with none of their children in the country. The many what-if questions kept bothering me day in and day out. In consultation with my family, I decided to move back to Pakistan to be with my parents during the uncertain COVID times. I did not know what it entailed. The thought of leaving family killed me many times. I was in a dilemma and found myself trapped in a situation that had me losing out no matter what decision I took. My wife and son encouraged me to take the plunge as my parents desperately needed someone around. In August 2020, I took the flight to Karachi on a one-way ticket.

I became a "Wapistani." Four years into this state, and I am torn between two worlds, two lives, two identities and two diverging paths. I don't even know who to blame. I have many acquaintances but hardly any friends who I can open up to without any fears. I don't have a solid group of friends I can regularly hang out with. I have too many acquaintances and often run into people I know at events, gatherings, malls or restaurants. But they are all acquaintances, not friends. I cannot pick up the phone to make spur-of-the-moment plans with them. I cannot visit them at any time on any day. No one who I talk to about my years growing up is ready to believe that I was once an extreme introvert. They only see a man talking to the public on the stage, making speeches and writing fearlessly. However, I know and I realize that my aloofness and inability to make "friends and not just acquaintances" is a manifestation of the same introverted self. I realize that I am still an introvert and as staunch as I had been, except that the way it manifests has changed.

Ever since I moved back, I have deeply felt that the Pakistan I left is history now. The country I live in is not what it once was. Its people are not the same. The environment is not the same. The country's attitudes, behaviors and class consciousness are unsettling to me. I struggle to bond with the country that was once my pride, my joy, my love and my identity. The Sur Sangum community that I built has moved on without me, and their bond without me is stronger. When I visit Toronto and meet them all, I do feel I am an outsider, and rightly so, as I am only a visiting friend. I am no longer a part of the inner group. Back in Pakistan, the Qawwali group I had initiated moved on in my absence from the country, and now I don't have a place there except as a very welcome visitor.

This was a natural progression and I do not regret or question it. However, I do wonder where I stand after all these years and doing all the work that I did. I am standing alone, whether I am in Pakistan or Canada. I am alone. I am still struggling to find my home.

While in Pakistan, I was hired as Chief Executive Officer of the National Academy of Performing Arts (NAPA), Pakistan's only conservatoire to educate and train those aspiring a career in the disciplines of theatre arts and music. While this position came as a godsend opportunity, it was the fact that I succeeded the iconic Zia Mohyeddin that remains my most humbling accomplishment. I continue serving in this position and, with my team, managed to take NAPA to new heights. This opportunity notwithstanding, I find myself torn between my two lives. Pakistan, with all its degeneration, sometimes appears as a dream gone sour.

My yearly sojourns to Toronto allow me to breathe in peace for a few days. I so look forward to returning to Canada. I often call it home. What is home? Once, Pakistan was my home when I physically lived in Canada. Now, Canada is home when I am physically based in Pakistan. What is home? Is it an illusion or a reality? Has God played a game with me by keeping me longing for home all my life? Am I born to uproot myself and start anew after every few years? What is my destination and where is this path leading to?

Is my reality to be found in the end of this mortal life and my transition to the permanent abode on the other side the life? But in the words of poet Zauq,

"Mar ke bhi chain na paaya to kidhar jaayenge?"

If even death denies us rest, Where then shall we seek respite?

Junaid Zuberi, a distinguished leader, currently holds the position of Chief Executive Officer at the National Academy of Performing Arts (NAPA). With a remarkable career spanning over 28 years, Junaid's professional journey has been marked by his extensive experience in the financial services in both Pakistan and Canada. His commitment to the preservation of cultural and artistic heritage has been a driving force in his life. Over the past two decades, Junaid has been actively involved in various cultural forums and organizations. In Canada, he served as the Vice Chairman of the Friends of the Museums of Mississauga, played a pivotal role as a Co-Founder of The Hunar Foundation Canada, and contributed his expertise as a Director for the IBA Alumni Canada Chapter. Moreover, his visionary spirit led to the establishment of the Sur Sangum Foundation in Canada, a testament to his dedication to the arts.

Currently, Junaid is a member of the Executive Council at the All Pakistan Music Conference. His past affiliations include Sampurna, Tehrik-e-Niswan, Mauseqar, T2F, Joy of Urdu, and Tehzeeb Foundation in Karachi, underlining his deep-seated commitment to cultural enrichment. In addition, Junaid Zuberi is a social media influencer and an avid blogger. His written and spoken words resonate with his profound passion for classical music, Urdu poetry, and the performing arts. His love for these art forms is not merely a casual interest but a fervent devotion that ignites his soul.

Website: https://www.sursangum.org/
Facebook: https://www.facebook.com/jwzubery

Do We Have A Choice?

By Zofishan Umair

"How will you ever birth babies?" they asked me. It wasn't really a question—I was six at the time and clueless about the concept of reproduction. It was more rhetoric, delivered by a well-meaning female relative genuinely concerned about my future.

Growing up, I heard that frustrated remark often from her and other women visiting our home. My skinny form, refusal to drown a glass of milk or any ailment that my immune system couldn't fight off in time, triggered it repeatedly.

I can't recall much from my childhood—and I'd like to keep it that way—but this is one of the few phrases that stick out in my memory. It defined the sole purpose of my existence: to marry young and reproduce liberally. All I needed was the 'right' upbringing to guarantee it.

And so, pressured by society, many of my life's decisions were for the benefit of my future spouse and unborn progeny. I could be smart, but not so smart as to intimidate and scare off a potential match. I could be educated, but just enough to help my future kids get into the college of their choice. I had to be pretty but not demand attention. I had to be weak and meek, and let my brother lift heavy furniture around the house, but strong enough to carry a 7-pound baby and survive childbirth without complaining.

Perhaps, it wasn't all that bad. Although my future as a mere vessel was never up for debate, society allowed me to eat as I pleased as long as it didn't make me fat. I could socialize with other women in limited spaces as long as I was chaperoned. After all, it was for my benefit. 'Survival of the fittest,' as Darwin called it. My desire to be anything other than a 'respectable begum' was not worth risking a stable future. Failing to marry early would result in the worst possible fate to befall a woman in this society.

A recent unverified figure published on a news site proved this true. It claimed that a UN report found 10 million Pakistani women over 35 are still awaiting marriage[1]. The existence of the said report was not important, it was what society needed to blow off some steam. The internet blew up, quick to blame women, their progressive thinking and feminism for this unbelievable figure.

I only wanted to know why these women were 'awaiting' marriage. What were they seeking from this legally recognized union?

True love?

A soul mate to grow old with?

Were they on a quest for idyllic domestic bliss or the elusive marital utopia?

Financial security, perhaps?

Maybe they wished to avoid society's pitiful glances and the label of bechari, a term reserved for single, divorced and childless women. Or, perhaps, they wanted the deserved respect this country refuses to give women unless they are accompanied by a man.

I don't drive alone in Karachi. It has less to do with my ability to navigate the chaotic traffic of the city and more with the men in this city. I don't argue when the 21-year-old male housekeeper slips into the back seat to chaperone a married woman in her thirties. On longer routes, I text my husband and mother 'Reached,' 'Left' and 'Home.' If I don't, they call to check in. I understand their concern so I apologize and assure them it won't happen again.

One day, a speeding car runs a red and rams into the passenger

---

1   https://thefridaytimes.com/14-May-2024/behind-the-numbers-reimagining-marriage-in-pakistan

side of my car. A middle-aged man steps out. He knows he's at fault but starts to shout. That should be enough to scare me. Before a crowd can gather, my chaperone steps out; the man's expression immediately changes. I glare at him and pretend to make a call. He hesitates, returns to his car and drives off.

That night, I bring up the accident, but skip details of the encounter. My husband will deal with the mechanic and the insurance company tomorrow. He will raise his voice and demand they deliver on time. I will continue to drive with a chaperone in the backseat.

It's a man's world and life is simply easier if you have one.

* * *

When pink boxes arrive at my house to celebrate the birth of a baby girl, the cards have her name. For nine months, the tiny XX-chromosome lived in her mother's womb, attached for comfort and nourishment.

Once outside, her umbilical cord is snipped. She becomes tethered to something else. This new cord is invisible. It attaches her to her closest male relatives: a father, brother, even an uncle or grandfather. For the sake of her protection, of course.

With age, these invisible cords morph into puppet strings, controlling her hemlines and speech, her well-being and life. They dictate how far she can venture from home, and how far she can go in life. Women need a *wali*. It makes no difference if this *wali* is old, blind, crippled, an addict, or a wife-beating husband. Deny them one, and a 6-year-old girl[2] disappears from her front porch to be found lifeless in a garbage dump days later, assaulted and strangled. A tiny mistake or a simple oversight, like an empty fuel tank on Lahore's motorway, can become a nightmare[3]. A woman without a chaperone is fair game.

And so, our men proudly serve as women's custodians. It's a given if she wishes to exist in this patriarchal Land of the Pure. Perhaps this is why we proudly rank 145th out of 146 countries[4] in the Global Gender Gap Index.

---

2   https://www.bbc.com/news/world-asia-45885686
3   https://www.humanrightspulse.com/mastercontentblog/sexual-violence-beyond-the-law-a-look-into-pakistans-motorway-incident
4   https://www.dawn.com/news/1760949

Sometimes, these cords become chains, denying women their freedom and choice. The most claustrophobic and typical minds in this society clench their fist and fashion these cords into a noose for women who dare stray too far. Every year, an estimated thousand Pakistani women[5] are murdered for dishonoring their families. A few, like Saba Qiaser,[6] shot point-blank by her father, refuse to die. Others like Farzana Iqbal[7] and Qandeel Baloch[8] aren't so lucky.

I live opposite a mosque. One of its speakers points directly at my window. Every mortuary tribute begins with the announcer clearing his throat and ends with him calling the community to join the *namaz-e-janazah* of the deceased. A man is remembered by his name and his nearest male kin. A woman is not. Instead, the speaker begins by addressing the nameless deceased woman as the wife of one man, the mother of another, a sister, daughter, or daughter-in-law to a third. She only exists in this country in relation to these men. I wonder, did Qandeel's mortuary tribute mention her by her name or as the sister of her murderer? What about Farzana, killed by her father for marrying of her own free will?

Google the words *'Shaadi koi gudda gurya ka khail nahi he'* and multiple YouTube snippets of Pakistani TV soaps will pop up. It's a common dialogue. Oh, *but it is! It is*! It is child's play. <u>19 million child brides</u> are married off, 1 in 6 young women[9]. Why? It is the only solution to prevent sexual transgression and keep family honor intact.

In metropolitan cities, arranged marriages pair offspring based on factors like education, financial stability, and family background. You are whom you are married to, so you marry well and do as you are told. Age and compatibility are mere trifles. Companionship and love

---

5   https://www.hrw.org/news/2019/08/22/pakistan-should-not-again-fail-honor-killing-victim

6   https://www.trtworld.com/magazine/pursuit-of-honour-in-pakistan-often-ends-in-murder-11201#:~:text=The%20young%20woman%2C%20whose%20story,%E2%80%9Cunacceptable%E2%80%9D%20to%20her%20family.

7   https://www.aljazeera.com/news/2014/5/29/pakistani-stoning-victims-husband-speaks-out

8   https://www.bbc.com/news/world-asia-49874994

9   https://www.unicef.org/pakistan/media/4151/file/Child%20Marriage%20Country%20Profile.pdf

are an afterthought or a bonus, but never a pre-requisite. The puppet masters proceed to change hands—passing the baton of power from father to husband.

How does the state feel about this? The country seems to support this play of marionettes, with every legal document replacing a girl's father's name with her husband's. Her safety, her future and her success are now tied to the latter. The state also doesn't wish to bother women with complicated decisions. For the longest time it has been believed by many in Pakistan, that an adult woman isn't capable of making her own decisions, such as choosing a spouse and marrying of her own free will[10].

In 1996, a father dragged his daughter to court, where the judge told her she was a disgrace[11]. The 22-year-old woman legally married a man without her father's approval. The father 'petitioned the courts to declare his daughter's marriage void' because he had not given his permission. After all, he was her *wali*, this was his right. And so, an adult married woman, Saima Waheed[12], of sound mind, stood in court and fought for her right to marry of her own free will. It was not easy, and her lawyer, Asma Jehangir[13], received death threats during the trial. An angry mob attacked the shelter where Saima sought refuge. But Saima fought and won. When a nation refuses to change, your only choice is to change the nation. Then, she and her husband left the country[14].

It was a good decision. Not much has changed over the years. The state continues to side with the marionettist: This year, police stood guard as one woman's relatives stoned her to death[15].

Female sterilization, one of the most common contraceptive

---

10   https://www.thenewhumanitarian.org/news/2003/12/30/supreme-court-legalises-free-will-marriages
11   https://www.aljazeera.com/features/2023/3/30/one-pakistani-womans-battle-to-marry-of-her-own-free-will
12   https://www.aljazeera.com/features/2023/3/30/one-pakistani-womans-battle-to-marry-of-her-own-free-will
13   https://brill.com/view/journals/yimo/3/1/article-p518_52.xml
14   https://www.aljazeera.com/features/2023/3/30/one-pakistani-womans-battle-to-marry-of-her-own-free-will
15   https://www.aljazeera.com/news/2014/5/29/pakistani-stoning-victims-husband-speaks-out

methods in Pakistan, still requires the husband's permission[16]. Since the country is obsessed with male heirs, a woman is only eligible for sterilization if she has 'at least two children, one of whom must be male[17]'. What if the husband decides to undergo sterilization? Does his wife get a say? While spousal consent from the husband is mandatory for female sterilization, the wife's consent is not required for male sterilization.

The state also discriminates when it comes to marriage with foreign nationals. The Citizenship Act of 1951[18] favors foreign wives of Pakistani men, granting them citizenship. The same rights are denied to Pakistani women married to foreign nationals. The reasoning: national security.[19] (Perhaps the real reason your blue-eyed, long-term boyfriend wants to marry you is because it's the only way to steal state secrets?)

These laws repeatedly reinforce the idea that a Pakistani adult woman, single or married, is incapable of making adult decisions. She is a vulnerable creature who can be easily manipulated into marrying potential spies. She may, in her naiveness, wake up one day and do something stupid like getting her tubes tied. And so, society and the state feel all eligible girls must continue to squeeze themselves into the molds of modesty and perfection. In turn, they will achieve marital and maternal bliss. Marriage is their best, no, their only shot at happiness.

Since I'm married, I often find myself awkwardly seated at 'social gatherings' with other married women. I don't want to be there but society demands appearances from married women. I sit and smile. The women share updates and occasionally, when the subject of a single girl is raised, they collectively sigh at her lack of *achay naseeb*. Some blame fate, others blame her. *"They're just not willing to compromise these days."* One of these specimen, a young lady nearing her 30s is often placed under the microscope to be closely

---

16   https://reproductiverights.org/wp-content/uploads/2018/08/pdf_wowsa_pakistan.pdf
17   https://reproductiverights.org/wp-content/uploads/2018/08/pdf_wowsa_pakistan.pdf
18   https://www.dawn.com/news/1819452
19   https://www.dawn.com/news/1819452

examined. Her faults and tastes debated. She's smart and financially independent. She has found freedom and happiness independent of a man. She travels and seems genuinely content with her life. I want to point this out but don't. I know their answer. *"True happiness only lies in marriage and motherhood."* To them, a single woman will always be a tragedy.

Despite society's relentless dedication, the biological clock's ominous ticking and well-intentioned relatives' snide comments, some women 'fail' to find a spouse. A demographic analysis found that the number of unmarried women saw a 30% increase in the years leading up to 2017[20]. Single by choice or circumstance, or because their 'standards were too high,' they find themselves at a crossroads. It is then, that some of them, for the first time, get to choose a path of their own.

The first option is staying single, leaning on the nearest male kin for financial support: an ageing father, a married brother. Economic dependence doesn't come easy and often costs her freedom. She becomes a liability or deadweight. The second choice is to marry the next bloke whom desperate parents or well-meaning relatives nudge her way. He could be twice divorced, or completely incompatible, but can she afford to be picky now?

The third choice is to become an independent, single woman. This is, of course, the least palatable path.

A single independent woman of marriageable age living alone in Pakistan is an anomaly, a creature who invites interest. Since no woman can live without a man, her existence demands concern and critique. All decent women are married or living with male kin, so this new organism must either be rebellious or of loose character.

A quest for a space of her own results in unreasonable rejections on "decent" properties because, again, "She probably has loose morals." If she is lucky enough to find a decent place and a landlord willing to rent to a single woman, she should not expect privacy. A married woman is a cliché. But the life of a single, independent woman doesn't

---

20   https://www.researchgate.net/publication/352350570_Dilemmas_ Of_Singlehood_In_Contemporary_Pakistani_Culture_A_Qualitative_Study_ Of_Unheard_Voices

warrant the privacy of a married couple. Her business is everyone's business: from the neighbor to the grocer, everyone transforms into her watchman. And since we've established adult women, married or not, cannot make big decisions, who will make decisions for her? Who will protect her from unwanted advances in the workplace?

The independent adult women living alone in a city are one misunderstanding or mistake away from a juicy scandal. Every move and misstep, online and in person, is fodder for gossip and judgment. The images she uploads of herself are an invitation to slide into her DMs. Why focus on the real issue when we can dissect the life of a single woman daring to exist on her terms? In this grand spectacle of societal expectations, her life is a thrilling drama for all to see. A woman without a husband? Scandalous! A woman making her own choices? Preposterous! In contrast, an unmarried woman dependent on her male kin: tragic, harmless, but perfectly acceptable.

An aunt recently walked out of a 40-year marriage. Forty years feels like a lifetime. She wanted to be single again. Her now ex-husband was and still is a great man. There was no abuse, no trauma, no affair and she continues to speak highly of him. She married young, birthed and raised four wonderful kids, followed the guidebook to the dot and was the definition of a loving wife and devoted mother. Then she demanded a divorce, choosing to live the single life. Family members called her decision stupid, even selfish, but she says she's never been happier. Did we take her word for it? Of course not. Our purpose is to marry, procreate and serve—not live for ourselves, unburdened by expectations. We must be obedient wives and devoted mothers first and foremost. The self is secondary.

Could it be that perhaps, deep down, we are afraid of the desi, single, independent woman? Her existence symbolizes freedom, autonomy and the power to live life on one's own terms. And that is something we've been conditioned to give up since childhood.

A single woman, no, a single and happy woman, whether by choice or circumstance, shakes the very foundation of what we've been taught to believe: maybe, we do have a choice.

NOTES:

1.	"To be eligible for female sterilization, a woman must have at least two children, one of whom must be male. The younger of the two children must be over the age of one. Spousal consent from the husband is mandatory for female sterilization, but consent from the wife is not required for male sterilization."

Memorandum from Interview with Dr. Khwaja Shoab, Joint Secretary, Ministry of Population Welfare, Government of Pakistan, regarding Ministry of Population Welfare policies, programs and implementation 2 (Apr. 18, 2001) (on file with Center for Reproductive Rights); see also CRLP Study, Health Policies (draft) from Seema Sharif, supra note 299, at 18.

2.	See National Commission on the Status of Women, Annual Report, Amendments to the Citizenship Act, http://www.ncsw.gov.pk/annual_report/annual_report_01_13.htm (last visited Nov.25, 2003).

Zofishan Umair is a columnist and satirist based in Karachi. She is emotionally attached to a cylinder engraved with the mythological siren and is dangerously dependent on the contents within. Her words have been published in Dawn, Khaleej Times, The New York Times and The Express Tribune. She is currently working on her first book.

Instagram: @zofishan.u

You May Say I'm A Dreamer...
Muhammad Ali Bandial

It's 8:46 AM. I'm one minute over my cut-off time, but I don't move. I sit inside my car in the parking lot of the Khaleej Times office in Dubai and scan my surroundings. I 'bag and tag' the other inhabitants of the parking lot as they make their way to the office premises in various stages of wakefulness. There are the early birds who walk with a spring in their step, ready to conquer the world, or whatever crap they tell themselves. There are those with heavy steps, who you can tell have resigned themselves to the next nine to ten hours of squaring their shoulders, taking it on the chin and moving on. And then there is the third kind, the ones who rush out of their cars with the engine still running, often with another colleague, punch in their office card and rush back out. Off to the latest trending breakfast buffet. My stomach grumbles in solidarity with them as my mind is momentarily distracted by the nihari and naan I had at Shehre Karachi last week.

I quickly re-focus, honing in on a colleague who works in my department. I try to camouflage myself against the background as I count their steps in my mind. Only after I make sure that I will not have to make eye-contact or talk to anybody do I exit my car and make a beeline for my cubicle.

The next hour and a half crawl by as I duck and weave through the double-entendres of my cross-border work colleagues. I keep my brows furrowed as though I am engrossed in some mind-bending task for the client; my nose remains pressed to the screen.

At precisely 11, I detect movement in my periphery. Like a scene straight out of a National Geographic documentary, missing only David Attenborough's narration—or if my inner child has any say, Uncle Sargam—I peer above the walls of my cubicle and sniff the landscape.

It's Ejaz bhai, the only co-worker in my department who shares my predicament. Through a telepathic connection that is restricted to our eyebrows, we agree on our rendezvous place.

We leave separately so as not to raise suspicion and meet in the store-room, which serves as Kutti's office and tea room. Kutti is our fifty-year old arthritis-fiddled office boy who can be found here most of the time, talking to his assembly line of children or with his better half. We have an unspoken arrangement where every day, in exchange for a small packet of Peek Freans Nan Khatai biscuits, he vacates the premises, allowing us to enjoy our tête-à-tête in peace. On our way to the store-room, we make our wannabe 'doodh patti' which Ejaz bhai perfected over 28 years on the job. It is a delicate job, requiring an eagle's eye and precise hand-eye coordination. The procedure consists of placing two teabags—any brand will do, but being the mohibb-e-watan he is, Ejaz bhai prefers only Tapal Danedar—dipped into scalding hot water in a Styrofoam cup. You then put the cup in a microwave and hit the stop button just as the tea is about to explode. It is an exact science and I have yet to crack its code, much to the consternation of Kutti.

That morning, there's no time for the extra kick, which involves re-heating the extra hot cups again. On most days, it is also accompanied by me humming the Mission Impossible theme as Agent Ejaz Hunt defies physics and Brownian motion theory. Today, we take our tea and head on to the store-room directly. Beneath old decaying newspapers that date back to Pakistan's Cricket World Cup triumph, the nuclear tests and the other highlights, I pull up a chair as Ejaz bhai fishes out a pack of Peak Freens Sooper. Only then do I exhale and unwind.

"What's going to happen now, Ejaz bhai?" I begin as we unravel the latest crisis, doing the rounds.

Welcome to another day in the hair-tearing life of a Pakistani expatriate.

***

A few years back I took the ultimate expatriate plunge: I agreed to go hiking with a friend who'd been doing it for years. I figured that four years was a long enough time to keep pulling out of any weekend plans. There are only so many times you can use the pulled muscle excuse before people mistake you for a masseuse. Or keep extolling the ethereal beauty of Trail 3 and the Margalla Hills without running the risk of totally alienating myself and our family. It was time. In agreeing, I also hoped that the heat and sand would do their magic and I might finally start feeling like an ordinary expatriate.

I soon realized this was a doomed enterprise. With each puff of the powdery dust that lifted under my feet and wafted into my homesick nostrils, I moaned and whined about the lush greenery of Islamabad – its singing brooks, the mischievous monkeys and the chai and pakora dhabas. The sandy dunes and rocky cliffs echoed with my loud sighs and I'm sure my co-hikers were not too impressed. Sometimes I'd just trail off, saying, "Never mind, everything's fine." But I'm sure I made my point because from then on, I never got invited to another weekend hike.

It is not that I'm ungrateful for all that the UAE has given me. I'm aware that there are worse things to be than a Pakistani expat in Dubai. You could be a Pakistani living in the Islamic Republic of Pakistan. It's a double-edged sword for sure, to be passing judgement from the outside. Having spent more than a decade in the public sector, I share the sense of cynicism and deep-seated distrust for those of us who've left but can't help making comments. So, I keep my mouth shut. All the same, as an expatriate, every time I uproot my family and move somewhere, I'm faced with the question that expatriates everywhere face: Shouldn't I be going home?

Like waves crashing against the shore, the Pakistani population in the UAE falls very broadly into three categories. There are the fatalists—people who took a gamble on the shifting sands and leapt off into the unknown decades ago. These are the ones whose second and third generations are enthralled with the idea of living here, their link with the motherland as tenuous as their Urdu accent. The moneyed version of this person lives as close as possible to the Burj Khalifa, their guiding star.

Then there are the denialists, often here for a job, the fates of whose extended families rely on the remittances they send home every month; they live frugally and on a very tight budget. They cope with living in the UAE by pretending not to be in the UAE, except once a month on weekends when they congregate to watch the Fountain show or sniff out some great deals on offer at big brand outlets. In their hearts, they're still in Pakistan, ears and eyes glued to the latest TV drama, with tempers flaring and mouths frothing at the latest political development. Even after 28 years in the UAE, Ejaz bhai falls into this group despite having no living family back home.

Finally, there's the third kind—people like me—who, like tumbleweeds on the wind, uproot our existence and let our whims navigate our destiny. We call ourselves searchers, untethered 'citizens of the world,' and yet deep below the surface we still remain anchored to a single place and ideology.

Though I have been in the UAE for six years, making me a guppy in comparison to some of the big fish in the sea who have been here for decades, I feel that I'm starting to get a read on the pulse of the country. Every day, I feel a little less like a stranger. While I still haven't completely cracked the codes, I no longer feel entirely out of sync: when the whole country goes into mourning after a beloved personality dies, for example, I know who they were and what the appropriate response is.

Still, no matter how familiar Dubai becomes, something always reminds me that I don't belong. The Sheikh Zayed can never replace the wonder and awe of the first time I drove my '74 Volkswagen

Beetle on the Grand Trunk Road (and was fined for speeding). The Burj Khalifa cannot come close to the Margallas as my pre-Google Maps North star for whenever I was lost. The road that runs parallel to the mountains also remains the best stretch of thoroughfare in my mind, the canvas for so many of my memories. The Dubai Mall might be the biggest in the world but it doesn't hold a candle to the manic festivities of Centaurus Mall on Chand Raat. In my mind, Krispy Kreme will always come a distant second to Jamil Kulfa or Grato Jalaibee on Murree Road, and all the books in Borders still pale in comparison to Saeed Book Bank.

But that's just me. A sentimental old man-child with his heart stuck in the past. When we first moved to the UAE, I wasn't sure how long we'd live here. The question of whether to stay is especially resonant for Pakistanis in the UAE. It could be because many feel that they live here by accident, that this is sort of a halfway house. A compromise, or an even an 'arranged marriage'. Not too far from home to be completely out of mind but far enough to be out of sight. A win-win situation. There's an initial period of denial, where we pretend that we're just here for a short period. But we're only kidding ourselves. Before we know it, we settle into a rhythm, a routine. Expatriates often say that they came for six months but end up staying for 15 years. No one is quite sure where this time goes. It's as if Dubai is a vortex that lulls you with its comforts, charms, safety and stability, until you wake up one morning, middle-aged, to a nine-year-old daughter with an atrocious Urdu accent and a vague idea of her roots. And you realize that every day, she runs the risk of ascribing to Pakistan all the one-dimensional stereotypes that are presented by people who have never experienced it like you have.

As a kid, I remember hearing an idiom: 'Kawa chala hans ki chaal, apni bhi bhool gaya.' I would roll around in fits of laughter, imagining a Heckle-and-Jeckle type of crow pretending to walk gracefully like a swan. Not only would it completely fail in its attempt, but would also, in the process, forget how it used to walk before. It was much later that I realized that joke had been on me. The irony of that image as I attempt to tell my daughter about her homeland dawns on me. As I watch the country I grew up in become a distant image to my reality with each passing day, the ache for what could have been is not lost on me.

Sometimes, I find myself yearning to be in a place where I don't just know more or less what people are saying but know exactly what they mean. But then there is another part of me, the part that has been keeping up with the news, hearing all the analysis that Ejaz bhai regurgitates over our doodh patti and Sooper sessions. That part asks me, "Are you sure you're fully in sync with Pakistan?" I don't have a really good answer to that.

***

When I get home, my daughter is on YouTube watching some US show. I'm sure she's told me about it but I have no memory of it. Lately, as the summer holidays approach, she's been coming home with lot of questions about Pakistan and all the activities we've got planned. When my wife and I shrug and look at each other, she pouts and says that all her classmates tell her about all the wonderful things they do when they go home and she has nothing. She makes a good point. I'll be damned if my kid comes second best. She's the daughter of a Pindi/Islamadi boy and a Lahori girl, damn it! Before I am done, her class is going to know that Jinne Laore nai takkiya, O jammia nai, so help me God. Sadly, there are no famous limericks about my hometown.

That night, after I've changed and washed up, we turn the TV and lights off and light a candle.

"What are we doing, Baba?" my daughter is excited that we're going to play some sort of Halloween-inspired game.

"We're going to play a game called load shedding," I reply matter-of-factly as my wife stifles her laughter by pretending to yawn. My daughter looks bewildered, so I press on, "It's a game that my parents, your Dada ji and Dadi used to play with us every evening where they'd tell us stories and jokes and riddles. The only condition was that it had to be in the dark with only a candle providing the light because these were stories that were meant to be told only in the magical glow of candles. Would you like to hear these stories?"

I don't know if she bought it or whether she felt sympathy for her dad who'd totally lost it, but she nods.

Game on.

"Hmm ok, so where do I begin?" I purse my lips and look at my daughter, who's all ears.

"Why don't you tell me about your first birthday party at Chucky Cheese?"

"It's Chuck E. Cheese and we didn't have those during my childhood."

"Claires?"

"No."

"Magic Planet?"

"Just listen to what Baba's telling you, baby."

As always, it's my better half who steps in and restores order.

Having grown up in an Army household, I've been all over the country, never staying long enough to make lasting friendships. But if I had to pick one city that had an enduring impression on me, it would have to be Rawalpindi. It's where I spent my most formative years. I was a Pindi boy long before the term became an insult or a catch-all for a type of behavior that had nothing to do with the city.

And so I begin.

The Pindi that I grew up in during the latter part of the '80s was one big walking track. There were hardly two or three cars on the tree-lined roads all day. If you were lucky, you cycled to meet and hang out with your friends. 'Follow the Leader' was a great way to cycle everywhere.

All the cool kids lived in Westridge or Harley Street or Chaklala Scheme III—the latter being hands down the coolest scheme in the world of schemes—or so I used to think. My opinions were based on first-hand accounts from my friend who would tell me about the latest activity in their park. But I had to admit, Lal Kurti, where we lived, was pretty cool too. There was a very different vibe to it. Religion never came up when I played street cricket with Christian and Hindu boys on my street. There were these tall Churches all around the city which seemed to have popped straight out of a Bram Stoker novel. Many a night, I'd sleep with garlic hidden under my pillow, much to the consternation of my mother. All my explanations of trying to ward off Count Dracula used to fall on deaf ears and I would receive a slap and a memorable tongue-lashing.

Party time meant heading over to Saddar Bazar for Softo ice cream. It didn't matter that there were only two flavours. The main thing was that you were there and you could boast about it the next day in class. If they didn't believe you, stationery bought from Idrees Book Bank next door would always do the trick.

Saddar Bazar really was party central as far as Pindi was concerned. On holidays like 14th August, there would be motorcyclists performing tricks and stunts, which usually consisted of only a couple of wheelies, all done with almost an air of sheepishness. No loud blaring or in-your-face noise.

My favorite time to go to Saddar bazar was on the weekend when the Sunday Book Stall was still a thing. The whole road from one end to the other would be lined with rows upon rows of second-hand books as far as the eye could see. It was a proper event where parents could simply leave their kids and go about their business. My parents would do just that as I squatted in front of piles of paperbacks, browsing through comics and haggling with kind-hearted uncles. They never seemed to care about the price, so long as you appreciated what a blessing it was to read.

There were plenty of snack options, but my favorite was Karim's or Kareemoo, as my father used to call it. Their samosas, dipped in tangy chutney, were the crispiest, and their lassi was to die for. Over the years, I saw boys who used to work there turn into men with their own kids in tow. They would always remember me and ask about my parents and my career.

On Sundays, there would also be a Landa Bazar, where used

branded clothes, shoes, belts, bags and everything else were sold at throwaway prices.

"Ooh, kind of like Brands for Less?" My daughter lights up.

"Errr yeah, let's call it that."

I once got some pretty cool tennis shoes and my first leather jacket from there using my pocket money there. You weren't considered cool and hip if you didn't buy a cassette or a poster from Bambino. I secretly coveted the Phoebe Cates poster my sister got from there. To this day, she thinks I stole it when I went to hostel. I did, but I'm going to deny it till my dying day. Might fess up on my deathbed, but no promises.

For movie buffs, Ciros Cinema was the place to be. I watched Hard Target and Jurassic Park there and both times I had the International anda shami burger from the cart outside. It didn't matter that I got violently sick both times, it was a rite of passage. You just had to do it.

For special occasions, there was always Pizza Kent. My dad used to tell us that it was a copy of the Pizza Hut brand, but we'd always roll our eyes. As if there could ever be a yummier pizza than the one at Pizza Kent. Plus, they had a Pepsi can at the cashier that would dance whenever you snapped your fingers. That alone was worth the price of admission. Beat that, Pizza Hut.

Haircuts were a family affair and Riaz was our barber. Not because he was the best. Heck, during those days, the 'pyala cut' was all the rage. So much so that even I could've done it myself! All I needed was an emptied out half-melon over my head and a trimmer to shave off the hair that fell below. But what made Riaz our designated barber was that he would give each of us a sweet after the haircut. As far as I was concerned, Willy Wonka had nothing on Riaz. He was my hero, and still is. I went to see him last year. He is almost blind and frail and his grandkids ran the shop, but he insisted on giving me my 'usual'. The two months I spent afterwards hiding my 'salt n pepper' 'pyala cut' under a baseball cap were worth the toothless smile on his face when he gave me the sweet at the end.

Waking up for school meant whoever got into the shower first got the warm water. Hot water was a myth, something only Richie Rich or Seth Abid could afford. If we were really, really lucky, we were able to catch the five-minute cartoons that Mustansar Chacha used to show in the morning. Running to catch the school bus was an art form, and you had to keep your knees up and elbows close as you made the dash. The three of us received ten rupees as our allowance, which got each of us a burger and coke from the school canteen and an orange ice lolly on the way back.

After-school chores included making a human chain as we shouted instructions at Dad on the roof, who would be trying to align the antennae so that we could catch cross-border channels. I used to get all my information from Neelam Ghar. Watching Tariq Aziz calling the newlyweds on the stage always used to make me blush. Whenever someone answered correctly or do something worth applauding, everyone would shout "Electra!" accompanied by banging on our desks.

If Dad was in a really good mood, we would all troop into our car and drive to Islamabad. The highlight of the trip would be to go to Jinnah Super Market. We would drive around the gol market once and stop for burgers and fries at Captain Cook. The evening would be topped off with a visit to Hot Spot if you could remember which street to turn into. There was something about sitting in that refurbished train cabin, eating ice cream and playing your favorite song on the jukebox, that just made you feel invincible. Some years later, the cool, hip venue would change to Shaheens at Super Market, and being out and about would mean hanging out at Mama's ice cream.

Weekends and holidays meant going to Ayub Park or Chattar Park. Getting Savor Pulao for the trip was always a hit. Sometimes, Dad would get a couple of days off and we would make camp at Lady Roberts in Murree. That walk on the Mall Road, checking out people from all over the country and screaming our lungs off on the chairlifts used to be a yearly summer tradition. It would also mark the end of summer holidays. The last night before school would see a mad dash to the local stationary store to get glue, notebooks and khaki wrapping papers. Dad would be laughing as we stayed up all night finishing the homework which we'd kept putting off.

"Gaya waqt phir haath aata naheen," he'd say in his mock baritone voice.

"Dad, stop it!" we'd scream as we scribbled essays and pasted hastily trapped insects and flowers in our biology journals.

"Saada aesh e dauraan dekhata naheen," Dad would finish in a more somber tone.

Today, as my nine-year-old hangs onto every word of my childhood, I finally understand what our father was trying to tell us.

I catch myself as the candle burns out. We carry our sleeping daughter and put her to bed. She half wakes up and makes me promise to tell her more tomorrow.

"You never told me about the Murree escapades," says my wife.

"What happens on Mall Road, stays on Mall Road," I reply in my best Ashton Kutcher accent.

* * *

While we expatriates don't like to admit it, the truth is that the thought of becoming an ordinary Pakistani again scares us. Being foreign makes us feel special. I guess it's that crow in me that refuses to grow up and still dreams of strutting about like a crane.

Having grown up on a healthy dose of Enid Blyton, Roald Dahl, The Hardy Boys and Louis La'mour, I always smirked at my class fellows who discussed the latest Naseem Hijazi or the Inspector Jamshed series. All I ever wanted was to be a cowboy in the Wild West or a member of the Famous Five and go on all those adventures. It seemed as if nothing interesting ever happened where I was.

I remember this one time when we were back in my village. I was being a little brat, whining to my father about how the American Wild West was so much cooler. He told me there were cowboys and outlaws all around me. Just because they wore dhotis instead of chaps and spoke in Punjabi instead of English, it didn't make them any less cool. I scoffed and laughed it off, as nine-year-olds often do.

After all these years later, I realize that the joke's on me. Now the identity-conscious crow has a young one who has all these questions and no idea about where she comes from. But it's not too late for my daughter to appreciate her history. I might be the identity-confused crow, but I also know that subaah ka bhoola sham ko ghar ajaye tau usse bhoola nai kehtay. I don't know when—or if—I'll be home, but as long as I know my way back, there's always tomorrow. And so, like a modern-day Hansel, I scatter these breadcrumbs of memories so that my daughter will know her way back one day.

It's my duty to at least tell her about all the things that my parents told me as I grew up. Whatever she chooses to do with that information is up to her. I'm not so disillusioned as not to notice that the Pakistan I tell my daughter about isn't the one we visit every time we go home. In fact, it seems more and more like a complete stranger. It feels like the child of a distant relative who's been away too long. And that's okay, too. I remember my dad telling me about how things used to be at all the places we used to revisit as a kid. There'd be more books and less cars at the Sunday bookstall. The movies were better at Ciros Cinema, the samosas at Kareem's were crispier.

I've realized that for an expatriate, coming back to Pakistan every time is like a daredevil climbing up a ladder and diving into a bucket of water. Each time I come back, it's like I've climbed one more rung. The bucket is a little smaller.

Talking about the Pakistan we remember, keeping up with the latest happenings, and passing down our memories of the place we grew up in, is our way of reassuring ourselves that the bucket is still there. There will be water at the end of our jump. It doesn't matter how small the bucket is or how far reality gets from the version of the homeland in our head. There is something magnetic in its pull that keeps us grounded. I can't say that it's always smooth-sailing, but the highs make up for all the disappointments. There are moments when the lows seem never-ending, when you seem to hit rock bottom only to find that there's more.

And then, just like that, something wonderful happens.

* * *

It's 8:45 AM and I'm scanning the parking lot for someone to accompany me on my walk to our department. Presently, I see a colleague from across the border. He's walking with his brow furrowed and head down as he purposefully strides across the lot.

Oh no, you don't. Faster than you can say 'Shaheen Afridi', I'm out of my car and in his path.

"Hey, Sanford! Good morning! Did you see the match?"

Sanford hems and haws but to his credit, does not run away. I drape my arm around him and extol the virtues of Babar Azam's batting and Rizwan's sheer belligerence. Inside, Ejaz bhai is personally distributing jalaibees at every table as he adjusts the green and white flag around his shoulders.

Welcome to another day in the ~~hair-tearing~~ chest-thumping life of a Pakistani expatriate.

Muhammad Ali Bandial is an award-winning author and former Civil Services Officer. He comes from a rural background and spent his formative years at Cadet College Hasan Abdal and the Lahore University of Management Sciences. Muhammad Ali earned his Master's in Public Administration from the Lee Kuan Yew School of Public Policy at the National University of Singapore. Before leaving the bureaucracy, he worked as a policymaker in several important posts, such as Deputy Director of Trade Policy at the Ministry of Commerce and Assistant Director of Extremism at the National Counter Terrorism Authority (NACTA).

Website: www.muhammadalibandial.com
Instagram: @muhammad.ali.bandial

Kaleidoscope Of Dreams
Khaled Anam

My early memories are nothing less than a beautiful dream. I, born in 1959, being just twelve years junior to Pakistan, have taken the roller coaster ride of growing up nearly together with my country. How beautiful our childhood was. Growing up near the pier—Passenger Pier Keamari to be precise, as my father after leaving the army had joined the Pakistan customs—the refreshing westerly wind bringing with it the sounds of sea gulls and haunting ship horns. Every new year's eve, at the strike of twelve, all the ships docked at the pier and would blow their hooters in unison, heralding the coming of the next year.

During the early sixties, Ayub Khan was ruling the roost. I remember the election symbols of the Lantern and the Rose. So the Rose beat the Lantern. How? I came to know about it much later. As far as I remember, everyone was happy. The reason for it might be that where we lived and the people we interacted with were all government employees with a few army officers in the neighborhood, so everyone was happy that the General had won. Even then, I guess the landed gentry, so to say, were scared of "real democracy", and that's what Fatima Jinnah represented—the real Democracy. People power and bureaucracy don't go hand-in-hand, thus the divide.

In 1947, two independent countries, namely Pakistan and Bharat, came into existence. In Bharat, politicians ruled supreme and still do, in collusion with the bureaucracy. Whereas in Pakistan, the bureaucracy abandoned the politicians and sided with the military, and what followed is obvious. Nonetheless it was a beautiful dream. Colorful, vivid, and full of hope for a magnificent future. Little did we know where all this would lead to. A freight train used to pass right in front of our house. All the kids would get excited at seeing these beautiful, almost new locomotives chugging on the tracks. These were given to Pakistan as a part of USAID. I vividly remember the emblem on it, a handshake of the Pakistani flag and the American flag and a slogan saying "USA-PAK friendship."

It all felt very real. Suddenly, an ample supply of foreign goods was readily available in the market. I would hear the elders discussing how the country is progressing in leaps and bounds under the marvelous rule of Ayub Khan. We, the school-going children, were all for the military rule. For one, we didn't know anything about democracy, and then there was a grandeur attached to the military establishment. My father was a royal Indian army officer who migrated to Pakistan and joined the Pakistan Army. Those early days were filled with the exuberance and optimism of youth, waking up early in the morning after having a good night's sleep, dreaming of a utopian land which seemed so close at hand. Now, I realize that most dreams are best left alone, as they are just that: dreams.

Today, I know for sure and can easily recall all the lies I was told to live and was living. "What fools these mortals be" rings truer with each passing day. It's not that we never had it, but somewhere very early down the road we seem to have totally lost it. How fondly I remember the feeling of being a citizen of a progressive, modern, moving in the right direction country. There was no bigotry, no obvious intolerance, no religious or ethnic divide as such. There were night clubs, discos, bars , proper liquor shops and even proper designated red light areas. Even the mosques, temples, churches and synagogues coexisted as in any developed country.

Reality has now been replaced by delusion, truth by lies, sugar-coated at that. With every despotic dynastic democrat I would associate hopes of a newer, better tomorrow, only to be disappointed yet again. The beautiful dream turned into a nightmare, a dreadful one at that. Now, it seems it was a bad idea for the countries to separate. The divide, and all that ensued after it, looks like an evil scheme to weaken a strong home.

I saw further rot in '71. The majority of the population decided to part ways with the minority. Speaking of minority, I, along with many others I know now feel like a minority in our own home, in our own country. I feel safer when I'm abroad on a trip. Why? When these foreign lands give me a false sense of safety and well-being, why can't my own country give me the same? As of late, it seems like the whole country, down to its systems, institutions, and people are naked. You can see through them clearly. The rot, the decay, the stench, it's all too real to ignore. Every day, the not so pleasant reality hits you smack across your face, telling you to wake up from this comatose slumber, this zombie-like existence, and face the fact that the dream might have been a pretty one, but that's what it was... just a pretty dream. There is not an iota of the kaleidoscopic effect in this real world that I call home. Hope, too, seems like just a pretty word. Just when you feel you have hit rock bottom and cannot sink further down, that soon the turmoil will settle down and enable us to rise like a Phoenix, a deeper, darker crevice appears out of nowhere to remind you that this is a bottomless pit—and we have hit a new low.

How long must we wait to wake up in a brighter, newer, better world? Seventy-seven years old, and we still are staggering to find the right footing. How long will it take for us to walk tall and straight? We have countries much younger but stabler than us, following the path that takes them to unprecedented success. We, here, on the other hand, seem to have not even decided which direction to move in. We suffer from a major identity crisis. What are we? Sometimes we are Arab, other times Persian. It reminds me of an old song: "torn between two lovers."But ironically, neither of the two is our lover. At best, they can be our strategic partners, and only when it suits them. That's about it.

We have failed to evolve as a nation. Much worse, maybe this is what we have evolved into. A bunch of crooks and looters. A hoard of Benedict Arnolds. So easy to buy. Yes, that's what we are as a nation. The "PAK" in Pakistan literally stands for "pure."Pure, we definitely are not. It boggles my mind as to how any one can be so adamantly corrupt. We are so persistent in being on the wrong side of history. Can you imagine that even seventy-seven years down the road, all we have to show in the name of culture is loot, bigotry, avarice, and so on and so forth? The dream has definitely turned into a nightmare, and no early respite from it is in sight. The weak and incapable only look skyward, waiting for a messiah or some God sent relief. But we don't even deserve that. Oh, what a foul has it been, my countrymen, what a foul. We've been had, and of our own accord.

The way out? Just relax and enjoy till your miserable existence comes to an end. But maybe there is a way out. Partition was a political requirement of 1947. Come 2024, the political scenario has changed. The unification of Germany has given me hope. How about we unite with India again. It is possible. We let go of the concocted animosity and we get rid of the imaginary border. We just throw away the bulging armies and bombs and nukes and soldiers and guns and warships and fighter jets and reinvest all that money into the people. Education, health, clean water, food, a roof above everyone's heads. Utopia. Yes, we can and we should combine our resources for the betterment of people. Let peace rule. Can someone please let me know what we have gained through these arms and ammunition in these seven decades? Misery, pain, death, hunger. One man's hero is the other man's terrorist. Enough dreaming. Wake up, people. Wake up to the fact that we're all one and the same. There is no point in dreaming more. Look where the previous dream landed us. Reality is totally the opposite. Wake up, I say. Enough of this dreaming. The map of the world has seen constant changes and shall continue to do so. Not because the change is good for the people, but only because it suits a few who rule the roost. My home, my house, my country, my continent, it's all been brutally ruled and divided by the powers that be, but I say: enough. I know people hate the ones who try and wake them up from a deep slumber, that too when they are having a kaleidoscopic dream, but I fear that if we don't wake up now, we will end up in oblivion.

I know I sound bitter, but what can I do? I have seen spring turn into eternal autumn, flowers withering away, waterways drying up, systems collapsing. I have seen cheating, looting, and daylight robbery becoming the norm. And the guilt, that I am the one responsible for passing on this moth-eaten, truncated country to my next generation. It's a killer. My elders surely gave me a much better country. I feel like going back to the drawing board, erasing all the previous diagrams and drawing again, or in this case tearing down all that was built in the past, getting rid of the debris, leveling the ground and rebuilding, and this time only a young master builder would do so. He should be around for a considerable time to make the necessary changes in the master plan as and when required.

I am not against dreaming, but it should end when we wake up. Only take cues from your dream and build for a real world.

So what now? Do I surrender to the present dread, or is there a light at the end of this darkened tunnel?

The map of the Indian subcontinent changed on the 15th of August, 1947, creating two sovereign nations, not for the love of anyone but on the notion of hatred and animosity between people having a separate set of beliefs or religions. It defies common sense as to how people having separate religions and different ethnicities could, for centuries having lived together in relative peace and harmony, have one day decided that their hatred for each other has no boundaries. Hatred based in religion. Friends for centuries turning into foes. The very existence of India and Pakistan is based on Hindu-Muslim hate and divide, and the moment anyone realizes how silly this made-up hate and animosity is, those in power will start some silly conflict and flare up the fire of hatred again. The powers want us to continually hate each other and be at war with our neighbors. Isn't it silly? We can't relocate ourselves. We can't change our neighborhood.

For how long can two neighbors, speaking the same language, being of the same ethnicity, sharing the same history, be at loggerheads? For how long can we keep on stoking the burnt-up common sense to try to flare up a fire that is waning away with time?

Everyone makes mistakes, but only the stupidest continue to insist on living it. Repeating the same folly over and over again. Passing on the hate to every coming generation, because if common sense prevails and people on both sides of the border decide to put an end to this hate-based divide, there remains no justification for having a divided home at all. We don't hate each other, we are not judging each other; we are accepting each other for whatever and whoever we are, so keeping the dividing line doesn't make sense, does it? Oh, how most of us long for an uninterrupted spell of peace and tranquility across the subcontinent. I, for one, long for one undivided Indian subcontinent.

How many billions have we spent on armaments, nukes, and all the wars we have never won. If only we had spent even half of it on health, education, and the people, it would've been a different world altogether. A once agricultural land is being turned into a concrete jungle just so a few powerful individuals can further fill up their already overflowing coffers.

Well, one thing is for sure. We have mostly been fed lies about how glorious the tyrants have been and what great leaders they were, that they were the ones who put us on the path of progress, winning wars and laying their lives down for us and the motherland (maybe a few in their simplicity did so). We have been lapping it all up from the state-controlled newspapers and television. We were taught these lies in our schools and history books. Don't we know that Pakistan was attained by a lawyer through a very well debated and fought legal battle, and that there was no armed struggle for it? So civil and scrupulously honest was Mr. Jinnah that even his detractors today call him an arm of the Raj.

You want to build anew. Not on the same crooked, bent and moth eaten foundations. Dig in deeper. Wrench out, obliterate, do away with the old one and build a new, sturdier, stronger foundation, based on real people-power, and not powerful people.

Every wrong in the society is our own fault. We are the ones who have always paved the way to get rid of democracy and real democrats in the first place. Aren't we like the rats who gnaw at the floor of the ship, and as it starts to sink we, the rats, are the first ones to abandon the ship? Do we want to be remembered as rats in the history books? The choice is ours and ours only.

With a Master's from Karachi University, **Khaled Anam** has done various theatrical training courses with Grips Theatre in Berlin, Germany. As part of a core team responsible for translating and adapting over 100 episodes of *Open Sesame* of Children's Television Workshop into Urdu—he was solely responsible for translating and re-recording the songs of all episodes. A founding member of Grips Theatre, Pakistan, he has performed in children's and regular theatres all over Pakistan, India, UAE, and Germany. In recognition of his services to children's theatre and education, Anam has been conferred the Goethe-Institut Award of Merit. Author of *Bachon kay Geet* (OUP, 2014), he is also an ambassador for the Children's Literature Festival. He has been awarded the President's Pride of Performance by the Government of Pakistan.

Instagram: @khaled_anam

Home Is Where The *Bahus* Are

Aisha Sarwari

I have not been able to escape Pakistan.

All escaping starts with love of some kind.

Like all love, there is magic at the start, a ripeness that follows, and in the end, a natural death.

My first love was a country, Pakistan. I differentiate it from infatuation, because you have to do the work in love, and often you find yourself laboring without a deliberate will. A free fall. On the other hand, when infatuated, you construct your wants and direct your attention to an object. It's conscious and calculating with the end objective of a reward.

Being in love with Pakistan and being in love with a man have very similar textures—first, you must believe their stories, then you must believe in them. You cannot want something in return.

Both need escaping from when you realize you skipped a step.

You escape Pakistan much like you escape a man—by running away, physically like migrants do. Like women with broken hearts do. We all need to escape men when their promised grandeur fades, and we learn that the things they wrote in books and spoke emphatically in speeches are not entirely true. The stories of countries and men are told to others as the truth, but how can they be true when they exclude women, exclude the people on the fringes of political power?

Women and minorities are not even important enough to be excluded deliberately. They are but a minor inconvenience, in a category of their own. Like background noise.

Pakistan as a collective culture is patriarchal, one that we need to survive regardless of gender. It smashes all dreams and opportunities equally.

The state dishes out women's rights like it's a bad dream and treats minorities like they are worse than women. In 2022 alone, 34,000 honor crimes against women took place in the country. Women sometimes survive with appeasement, at other times by freezing their dreams. Sometimes we bolt out of here.

This is not how it began.

It begins with parents like every origin story does.

I was pushed onto a stage and asked to recite hours of poetry, prose, and speeches from Pakistan's founding fathers. I was a little girl with a missing front tooth, a lisp, and two fashion-appropriate pigtails tied with red silk ribbons. I was asked to speak, from my guttural existence, about how lucky we are for being born Pakistani and for having ourselves a nation-state that does not persecute us for being born Muslim. Those are big ideas for a girl that tiny. I understood each of those ideas like I understood sunsets and the colorful marzipan that my mom made for Pakistan Day cakes—very green and white, very self-evident. Everything was sweet, including independence and freedom. Kids like the idea of belonging and doing as they please while still belonging.

Incidentally, the stage I was singing from was in East Africa. Even though I was born a Pakistani, I was not born in Pakistan. I was the last of the Ugandan expatriates from South Asia before they were asked to leave *en masse* by then-dictator Idi Amin. We lived a parallel life—one where we enjoyed professional lives in Uganda, the host country, and another where we had left behind something precious: family. We told ourselves a story, that home is where friends are.

Kampala's Makerere University auditoriums echoed Pakistani national anthems and Allama Iqbal's poetry. We were not alone. My parents had a few hundred families that wanted the same thing—a memory. My father was the President of the Pakistan Society in Uganda. So, he worked on my Urdu pronunciation, enunciation and delivery. He also taught me reverence when I bowed my tiny head as I said any important man's name—the Holy Prophet (PBUH), Quaid-e-Azam Mohammad Ali Jinnah and Allama Iqbal. I was free-falling. Love began. The work began.

The marzipan may have been sweet, but I learned from these speeches that we had enemies who didn't like us having all those lovely things like freedom—The Indians. They wanted a hegemonic, Hindu-dominated state where Muslims would be second-class citizens. India for Indians. It wasn't personal, but for the majoritarian Hindus, Muslims were a similar inconvenience. So, the Indian National Congress tried to tell us, by rejecting the truce-like Cabinet Mission Plan, to go to hell and stay there. My parents took that a bit too literally, making Uganda their primary home for 35 years.

My dad was from Ajmer, present-day India. My mom was from Konkan, present-day India. After the partition, Dad moved to Karachi and then Uganda. Before partition, Mom's parents moved to Kenya. I was born Pakistani. I had a hyphenated identity, which was not hard to pull off when my father was alive. If Uganda was open to non-Ugandan friends.

Sadly, Uganda was war-torn in the 80s. It was unstable and had a currency that could buy you neither dignity nor milk; often, Uganda was hostile towards its brown and white communities of expats—Uganda for Ugandans was the new song.

My dad had a sword mark on his back from trying to escape Ajmer during the bloody partition. I used to look at it as a kid when he took his naps and wonder if he was afraid of anything more than migrating and being destabilized by the things that come with it—loss of one's own room, loss of siblings, of bookshelves, and loss of continuity. This was why he cared so much about my Urdu. It was to be my anchoring if I ever had to escape.

As a woman in her middle years, I have now lost my silk ribbons and my pigtails. I no longer lisp. My beginner Urdu is helpful, but I could never learn how to read it. My lessons were interrupted by my abrupt move to neighboring Kenya after my dad died. I was only eleven. Time froze. So did I.

My dad is buried on a university campus where he once taught. My passport may as well have been invalid without a father to vouch for all the hyphens. I wonder how unstable Pakistan may have been for him that he came all the way to Uganda to make something of his life as a teacher, hoping that his new passport and his newly adopted home would not betray him. Even in his death, he refused to be moved to Pakistan to rest in peace. His peace, at all costs, belonged in Uganda.

Nations betray. United India betrayed him. Uganda betrayed him, too. When neighbors turned on neighbors, and Ugandans were convinced that anyone who wasn't Ugandan was an enemy to be "shot at sight", my dad refused to believe in the anger. He wouldn't budge.

The Pakistanis in Uganda, however, were more responsive to the guns. They immediately stopped singing and dancing about their freedom in 1947 and ran back home because they had one. They rushed to Entebbe Airport after they dropped off their belongings at our tiny faculty home and said they would write us from home. They never did. My dad, given the sword, made fear his home and stayed frozen.

One day, his fear almost got us killed. A couple of Ugandan militiamen, in their teens but armed with automatic rifles far larger than their emaciated bodies, stepped into our house and shot at my mom. My mom was being confrontational with them because they were blocking my path to her. I was tiny as a rabbit, screaming at the top of my voice, begging to go to my mother. This was before my pigtails era. I was holding onto my blanky, having just woken up into the nightmare I had every night—army men pointing a gun at my mom.

They shot near my mom's foot and missed it. They didn't miss reminding us that fear, indeed, was our home.

We still did not leave Uganda. There was either something so safe about Uganda or there was something so unsafe about Pakistan that made my parents stay in hell. Whenever someone sings praises about escape from tyranny, it means someone has won, and it is often not the one singing that wins.

My ancestors were settled in India for generations, then over the course of one generation, they ran for their lives and were forced to look down the barrel of a gun in Uganda. My ancestors lost, someone else won. My dad only got to keep the songs and the stories. He got to keep the enunciation of Urdu, and the reverence for flags. He got the land and the stability that comes from not being evicted. Escaping meant moving from a bad world to a worse world, and then having no world to return to.

Why was there no home to go back to for my dad like the rest of the 80's Pakistani expats in Uganda?

My father, as I recently learned, left Pakistan because of a family feud in Pakistan. Just as there are voiceless Muslims, there are oppressive Muslims.

Just as there are voiceless women, there are oppressive women.

When my dad was a child, he was raised chiefly by this one particular sister-in-law or *Bhabhi*. She was his *de facto* mom, because his real mom remained invisible with housework and children. He morphed into an angry young man but retained his love for books. It was his *Bhabhi* who protected him with her constant maternal nurture, patience, and love as he got into fistfights. When the women in his family had wronged his *Bhabhi*, my dad responded like any disenfranchised young man: with proportionate anger.

In a typical desi family, there is a hierarchy of women: the *nanands* (daughters) eat first, and the *bahus* (daughter-in-laws) eat last. The women closer in blood relation to the father have more power, more resources, and thereby, more wagging tongues. If my dad wanted to return the protection he got from his mother figure, *Bhabhi*, he had to take on the ultimate patriarch—his dad.

My dad was caught up in domestic politics, a drudgery no less toxic than world wars that men were sent off to, wearing helmets and dodging bombs in bunkers during endless winters.

My dad declared war on his dad.

This is the elevator pitch my dad made to his dad: *Bhabhi,* who practically raised me, is always picked on, humiliated, and disrespected. She is doing endless work in that over-heated kitchen, all night, all summer. Every day she kneads dough and bakes warm rotis. That too at the beck and call of other *nanands* in the house with undisputed higher status. Some of those *nanands* are far removed in relation, yet they still live in our home and mistreat her. The housework must be divided equally among the women. This slavery must end. Reign in those mean women by asking them to leave, or I leave.

Maybe it was the books or the loyalty towards his *Bhabhi's* maternal instincts that made him see oppression wherever it appeared, but my father showed sensitivity to something his privilege permitted him to ignore. My dad stood up for the *'bahu'* no one stands up for.

My grandfather, known to be a scholar and a respected headmaster back in Ajmere, was on his own trip. He was not going to be told what to do by one of his many sons, let alone the angriest. He told my dad that his home was a sanctuary for all. He said no woman would be kicked out on his watch. He also asked his son not to meddle in women's petty affairs.

My father left. He swore never to return because his line in the sand was drawn. My father did not return. His father passed. Then his mother passed without seeing him.

My dad finally began visiting Pakistan.

On one such visit, my father wept. I now know why. I understand the sword scar. I understand the grief. I understand the bravery. I understand the sensitivity to the internal politics of how the *bahu* often absorbs the hate and wrath of the family she marries into. She becomes the object of all the anger ever felt towards all the powers that be.

That is not at all okay.

If the adage "The personal is political" is true, then my grandfather had the power, yet he chose not to fairly distribute it, just like the

Indian National Congress did. If "The political is personal", Jinnah walked away from his ultimatum to Congress because that was his line in the sand. Full circle. If "The personal is political", Jinnah stood up for the underdog, the proverbial *bahu* which is Pakistan.

This is no puzzle. It is simply the human need to leave when expelled.

Not every expulsion is by the sword, sometimes all you need are words. Harming human dignity is a form of physical violence.

Jinnah and my father fought for the *Bahus* against the dominant structures. They ended something that was passed down like undisputed caste systems. This is despite them never having shared the underprivileged life of women or minorities. Jinnah was never a practicing Muslim. And yet, he foresaw the ironhandedness with which Congress would form a new order to make the majority of Hindus reign after the British leave, so he walked away. My father had asked for a just demand from his dad—you have the power to rectify this inhumanity towards the underdog women—and my grandfather had said no. Then my dad too walked away.

The home Jinnah made for my dad did not give him enough freedom to stay.

In both walking away, there is a refusal to sign up for the indignity to witness indignity. In both walking away, there is an acceptance of a war already declared. The line in the sand was already drawn by somebody else. When someone doesn't want you, you leave.

In my father's case, he just could not be asked to leave home the third time. His first time was by some politicians on a Hindutva wet dream. The second was by my grandfather who thought it wise to segregate women's issues from men's issues. The third time was by an African mad king who declared Uganda was best without any Pakistanis, Indians, or Bangladeshis, who lived there for generations.

My dad chose to sit it out for the last one. I understand that so much of the freedom and independence we sing about is not bravery but defeat. It is not valor. It is resignation. It is not balls. It's balls-up surrender.

The glorious stories are only reserved for the ones that fight and not the ones that escape.

I cannot escape Pakistan.

I am done being expelled.

Naturally, to me, Pakistan was first a vehicle to escape patriarchy. But an expat like me can only live in Pakistan by legal marriage to a Pakistani. With a dead dad, the hope was that I would find a husband who wouldn't die on me and would grant me some freedom. As a young Muslim girl, this was my only possible route to a home I was repatriating to.

As for freedom, that only comes to women through power. Women who are Muslim living in patriarchies have only one inalienable right to boundless power—that is when they become mothers to boys.

I seem to have three strikes against me by the patriarchy—Dead dad, sick husband, and no son. I had to turn to some other ideals. I had to manufacture infatuation and discover feminism. I'd run out of men to protect me.

In my memoir *Heart Tantrums and Brain Tumors*, published by Penguin India and Hurst UK in 2023, I speak about a strange idea of Muslim Feminism. A story of reclaiming my own indigenous anger and fight, one that is unimported and homegrown. One that allows women to survive when the men are missing, mean or ambivalent. The book I wrote is about being in a spinning web of endless, invisible labor of work, mothering and caregiving, mounting expectations, and relentless criticism of how I was failing in a patriarchal world. I have spoken up in my book. I have protested a joint family setup that doesn't share power equally and dishes out blame asymmetrically. I became an angry young woman making use of the one way my dad taught me—with books and words.

I protected the *bahu* in me.

In rushing to transfer power from dad to husband, I missed a step—my mother. It is always mothers that help us find our way back home to ourselves. To love ourselves.

My mom's nurturing and patience allowed me to want something better for myself.

But mothers have no power. Therefore, they cannot light the way for us, nor can they walk away, throw tantrums, or leave. The firepower has to come from the men who have power and then share it.

My dad was the founding father of my freedom. It was this posthumous story about his own self-inflicted exile that drove me to my own exile from my own home, my own country, my own people.

Founding fathers deserve respect because they saw something everyone would rather not see. They are considered mystical because they possessed a hidden life force that allowed them to lend their time, effort, and passion toward something they refused to unsee. They are revered because they had given up on something they held dear to accept the war waged against them.

Whether you sit it out, walk away, appease, or fight, who you are is measured against what you gave up and how major an inconvenience it was to you to give up your privilege. The Nehrus of the Congress Party were founding fathers only to the *nanands* metaphorically—those who belonged to the family of Hindu men. The Nehrus did not see Muslims and did not give up anything of value to protect the Muslims.

Not easy work at all.

Wars are so alluring because they simplify people by making chock blocks out of them, hence making them easy to shelve. Every tyrant looks at time and people the same way—as one lifetime. That is foolish.

To wage a just war, you must look at the invisible ones resting on dusty shelves. You look them in the eye and then suffer on their behalf by giving up something of value to you. Had Nehru done that, he'd have been one of the founding fathers with Jinnah. Jinnah was once hailed as the ambassador of Hindu-Muslim unity. You dig your heels in when you are defined only one part of your identity.

My ancestors shouldn't have been mob lynched in India, and I shouldn't have to make fear my home. My grandfather should have stepped into the *zanana* kitchen and asked the ladies to take turns cooking, and my dad should have just read more books and been less fearful of leaving home after home.

Dead dads, silenced women, and immigrants shot-at-sight always begin with anthems and end with someone trying to escape love.

We need to give an ode to the *bhabhis* and the *bahus* and the *founding mothers.*

We needed Muslim Feminism then and we need it now – men come and go.

Aisha Sarwari is the author of *Heart Tantrums* and *Brain Tumors,* published by Hurst and Penguin Books. Her memoir ranked number four in the Amazon gender category in 2023. She is an intersectional feminist and believes in the power of testimony to humanize the interior lives of women. She is the co-founder of Women's Advancement Hub, an NGO working to amplify Pakistani Women's narratives. She has been working for two decades in the field of Public Policy and Communications for government, NGOs, and corporate giants.

Instagram and X: @AishaFsarwari

Queuing For Clout

Adeel Hussain

In Pakistan, gaining entry into some private member clubs requires more than getting on a waitlist. Take, for instance, the Islamabad Club, where the by-laws cap its membership at ten thousand. A vast majority of these slots are withheld for government officials—that is, parliamentarians or senior officers stationed in Islamabad and embassy staff—which intensifies the scramble for the limited private membership slots. In hushed conversations, it is said that civilians, a somewhat derogatory term for citizens without any military background, can only gain entry with a presidential recommendation. Even with such a letter, the waitlist stretches well over six years. One might assume that a club established in the 1960s with funds from public coffers would uphold or champion democratic values. Instead, the club promotes itself with the promise of a 'royal experience', its principal sporting events revolving around polo and golf.

Another club, the Lahore Gymkhana, sprawls over 120 acres, roughly the size of the entire Lahore Fort complex, and has been situated on leafy Upper Mall since the early 1970s. Its premises are owned by the state and have been leased to the club for a nominal rent. Annual membership fees of the roughly six thousand permanent members go to the club and not the state. The fees are reasonable for government servants but, at roughly double of what you would pay at Soho House—a millennial addition to the Western club landscape—feel somewhat excessive for non-government workers. If six years on the waitlist gives you a fighting chance of admission in Islamabad, you would be lucky to be considered after two decades of waiting in Lahore. And yet, people wait. Some to partake in the sporting activities and the associational life of the club; others to signal their social status in line with the observation of Max Weber, an early sociologist, that a man who failed to "succeed in joining was no gentleman;" yet others, because they want access to the network of state employees to further their interests. More often than not, it is a mix of all three reasons.

There's something that distinguishes Pakistan's flagship clubs from their siblings in the Commonwealth world. Pakistan's clubs have grown in size after independence. Take Delhi's Gymkhana as a comparison. Situated just 250 miles south of Lahore, it was set up around the same era and with a parallel mission: to provide a sanctuary for stationed officers and recreate an ever-incomplete semblance of their homeland amidst what was perceived to be a hostile and foreign environment. The club's charter and lease agreement, inked during the British Raj, centered on promoting sports. However, instead of expanding in territory, the club has been repeatedly entangled in legal battles, defending its purpose, land use, and potential violations of its lease agreement. In a recent courtroom clash in front of an Indian appellate tribunal, the judges even denounced the Delhi Gymkhana for "perpetrating apartheid and shattering the most cherished Constitutional goal of securing social justice and equality of status and opportunity." Similar upheavals have beset the Colombo Gymkhana Club, Singapore's Tangline Club, Royal Bombay Yacht Club, and the Hong Kong Club.

As a whole, clubs in non-settler colonies are different from those dotted around London's St James's district, known colloquially as 'clubland'. They tend to have a lot more space. While in the mofussil, where Orwell, drawing on his experience in Burma, wryly described clubs as the "real seat of British power" despite often being just "dumpy one-storey wooden building[s]", clubs in urban centers have often secured prime locations through preferential land leases in upscale neighborhoods. The private fraternities in clubland were originally instituted to promote political ideas and lobby parliament, though they quickly turned into idle hang out spots for wealthy loungers, as popularized in PG Wodehouse's novels set in the Drones Club. In contrast, in the wider Empire there was little parliamentary representation to speak of, and clubs primarily served to institute disciplined leisure, very much in line with military practice. They were also much more open to families joining. This made them more akin to modern-day country clubs, though without the accompanying lower social prestige.

The Lahore Gymkhana is not colonial, but it is not noncolonial either. It occupies a liminal space between colonial and postcolonial identities. Its interior design eschews the quiet luxury of late colonial charm or any trace of Mughal grandeur, a faint echo of the latter still lingering in the Gymkhana's old premises that now house Quaid-e-Azam library. The clubhouse bares signs of neglected upkeep; the walls are hastily patched with thick paint; colonial-style rattan tables with their intricate weave are swollen by exposure to humidity and cleaning products, their glass plates, once epitomizing sophistication, now marred with scratches and stains; waiters sport clip-on bow ties; and the food is clubby. There is little that carried over from the regimented nature that defined colonial gymkhanas. Cultural events are few and far between. Unlike Delhi's India International Center, which has successfully become a hub of intellectual exchange with vibrant programming and a membership teeming with artists, writers and academics, Lahore's Gymkhana has not managed this leap. Its exclusivity is not a conduit to nurturing ideas, be they Whiggish or reactionary; it seems to have resigned itself to exist for the sake of exclusivity in leisure alone.

One could rightly argue that such exclusivity is justified. Civil servants, military personnel, the judiciary, and parliamentarians require a third space—something between work and home—

where they can unwind and eventually channel their rejuvenated energy back to state service. This need is echoed in Faisal Elahi's presidential order regarding the Islamabad Club, intended to be a "social and residential Club for the use, relaxation, convenience and entertainment of the officers of the Federal Government and the members of the diplomatic corps stationed in Islamabad." Since Islamabad was a planned city and primarily inhabited by federal government officials, there was no fear of detachment from the surrounding societal context. The management of the club, as Article 6 of the ordinance ensures, will always be "an officer of the Government."

Lahore Gymkhana is not run by direct government appointments. Here, members elect their own chairman, though less than a quarter of them typically bother to vote. Times are difficult. Younger Lahoris are less inclined to engage with the club, not least because of the stringent waitlist and membership criteria. It's partly because the Gymkhana's lackluster aesthetic does not lend itself well to social media and partly because the waitlist seems daunting. Mobile phone use and filming are discouraged, though even if their use was encouraged, images of club sandwiches on worn-out rattan tables would hardly go viral.

Recently, there have also been setbacks from the courts. Although the Lahore High Court has not threatened to withdraw the lease, as Indian courts have repeatedly insinuated, and it has acknowledged that the club was not performing any public duties, a judge recently ruled that the Gymkhana was indeed a "public body." There was no other way to classify it, given that the government's land had been provided nearly free of cost.

This ruling caused quite a stir within the club. During the next chairman elections, Salman Siddique, just appointed, emphasized the dire implications of being labeled a public body. He warned that this designation could mean that the club's leased land could "be taken away by a simple stroke of the pen." In a moment of self-reflection, he addressed the questions that many Lahoris have begun to ask: "Why are they [the Gymkhana members] enjoying this kind of facility?" To repair the damage, Siddique insisted that the club must do a better job of communicating to the wider public that it does not "take any money from the government."He underscored the club's value to society at large, describing it as "the biggest human resource perhaps congregated under one roof anywhere in the world—the best professionals, the best legal minds, the best chartered accountants, the best fiscal experts, the best doctors, the best specialists, the architects, the engineers, you name the professions—it is all here."

The belief that one's circle of peers includes the best in the world is a common assumption among elites. It's the reverse sentiment of Groucho Marx's famous quip about resigning from the Friars Club of Beverly Hills because he did not want to belong to any club that would accept him as a member. At my school, for instance, it seemed inevitable that our best tennis player would sign a huge sponsorship deal and go on to win Roland-Garros, though this never happened. In the case of the Gymkhana, however, such beliefs seem harder to sustain. Given the massive brain drain Pakistan has experienced over the last decade—particularly after the military's increased involvement in politics—maintaining this premise seems difficult, even in jest. No Gymkhana members would pick their club's *sehat ghar* (health center) over Aga Khan Hospital.

Yet, the Gymkhana seems to occupy a transcendental space in the broader subcontinental imagination. During the Indo-Pakistani war of 1965, JN Chaudhari, the chief of the Indian army staff, allegedly enticed his *jawans* with the promise that their blitz into Punjab would lead them to "drink a peg of whiskey at the Lahore Gymkhana" by dawn. Whether or not the quote is apocryphal, which it well might be, the inventor hoped to rock (or stoke) some shared sense of Pakistani national pride. It is somewhat misplaced, given they could have chosen one of the many religious sites that typically evokes stronger emotive responses than tennis pitches and golf courses. When I visited Lahore for my book launch in 2022, the

Q&A section was largely sidetracked by an audience member who recounted their experience of being waitlisted at the Gymkhana club. They suspected that democracy itself had become an exclusive club, reserved for a privileged few. Mr. Twemlow, in Dickens' *Our Mutual Friend*, who referred to the Commons as the "best club in London", would wholeheartedly agree.

Clubs in postcolonial countries often seek to evoke colonial nostalgia. They market themselves as time capsules, offering a select few urbanites the chance to experience the cushioned lives of the colonizers and indulge in formerly (and very much formally) taboo activities. You can book a sanitized version of colonialism through 'period rooms' and city tours, which are sometimes, without irony, called 'safaris'. The framing reinforces a sense of superiority and entitlement, allowing participants to momentarily cosplay as explorers. As such, the clubs perhaps double as microcosms of broader societal dynamics, where the past can be selectively romanticised and, to borrow a Marxian term, commodified. In this sense, nostalgia emerges as both comfort and cage.

Even after a thorough vetting of one's clubbable nature and an extended stint on the waitlist, the doors may still be closed if one is inappropriately dressed. Lounge suits are preferred, though Safari suits and bush shirts, quintessential colonial tailoring inventions, have always been perfectly acceptable. Meanwhile, London's clubland has eased its clothing recommendation largely to 'smart casual'. Dress sneakers, or 'relaxed styles of formal shoes', have been widely upgraded to the 'preferred' category, moving beyond being merely tolerated or outright banned.

Traditional and local clothing has faced significant challenges in postcolonial clubs. In 1991, Daudayal Joshi, a BJP member recently elected to the Lok Sabha, recounted his rejection from Delhi's Gymkhana Club in gripping detail during a parliamentary debate. He said, "As soon as I entered the main entrance gate, a Sikh named Jeet Singh rushed towards me. I told him humbly that I am an M.P. [...] He said "No" [...] a person wearing dhoti-kurta cannot enter this Gymkhana Club. Even after 40 years of independence, people clad in dhoti-kurta won't be permitted to enter such a Club. [...] if I had come in a suit or pants and bush-shirt, then alone I would have been allowed."

After a lively discussion debating the merits of lounge suits—and, for some inexplicable reason, bathing suits, as an alien import to Indian society—Saifuddin Choudhury ultimately proposed a unique solution. He suggested that "the suited-booted people [who run the club, should] be ordered to wear dhoti and kurta as penance for what they have done." Perhaps an idea worth pondering over.

Adeel Hussain teaches law at NYU Abu Dhabi. Prior to joining NYU, he worked at Leiden University and the Max Planck Institute for Comparative Public Law and International Law. Adeel is the author of *Law and Muslim Political Thought in Late Colonial North India* and *Revenge, Politics and Blasphemy in Pakistan*.

Website: https://adeel-hussain.com/

A Difficult Home

Awais Khan

When I think of home, Pakistan is the first thing that comes to mind. Home is Pakistan, and Pakistan is home. Being a fairly big country, Pakistan is home to a lot of people—more than 230 million, in fact. This country has birthed us, nurtured us, and in many ways, has made us who we are today. It has given us a lot, but also taken a lot from us. Being a Pakistani is a unique experience; and it is one that doesn't really leave you no matter where you go in the world. And just like in any family, things in Pakistan are rarely perfect.

I was five years old when an older cousin who doted on me took me aside and produced a beautiful, colourful lollipop from the UK. My five-year-old self gasped at the sight. Lahore in the early 90's wasn't a place where imported things were readily available. In retrospect, I have often wondered if imported sweets really were available in Lahore, just not to me. However, at the time, to see a lollipop from London was akin to seeing the Big Ben. Here was something that had travelled all the way from the United Kingdom and into my small, pudgy hands. I had no idea what London was, but even at age five, I knew it was something important. A place to be cherished.

'Don't tell your other cousins that I gave you this lollipop,' my cousin told me, rummaging inside her handbag (also from London) and producing a single piece of tissue paper. Handing it over, she added, 'You're my favourite, so this is just for you. Have it now and get rid of the wrapper.'

I greedily slurped on the lollipop, taking care to put the wrapper in my pocket. There was no way I was letting any part of its Britishness go to waste. Perhaps I didn't realise it then, but it was the first time I had been asked to hide something. Even though it was a small lollipop, I was complicit in hiding it and the knowledge of that gave me a sense of power. Having finished the lollipop, I skipped back to my cousins, content in the knowledge that only I was special enough to have tasted that cherry-flavoured sweet and not them.

I also realised that I was old enough to keep secrets. Growing up in Pakistan—this, in a way—became my first exposure to what I like to call 'existential censorship'.

Being a Pakistani is an endless tussle between who you want to be and who the society expects you to become. Being a Pakistani also means being conditioned to hate the very thing that makes you a Pakistani. Perhaps it was the colonial hangover, but the idea of English being a superior language was drilled into me from the start. I grew up actively avoiding Saraiki—my mother tongue—oscillating instead between Urdu and English. This bias only grew stronger as I entered school and noticed that anyone who spoke in Punjabi was made fun of and treated like an outsider. If, God forbid, their Punjabi accent bled into their English, they were as good as pariahs. I was already a very shy kid, and the hatred for Punjabi and Saraiki made me retreat even further into my shell. Surprisingly, the hate came from those who had grown up speaking these languages and who immediately reverted to speaking in Punjabi as soon as they exited the school's premises. However, if they saw someone else speaking it in school, that kid was branded as *paindu*. Although I am reasonably fluent in Saraiki today, I deeply regret not being as versed in the language as I am in Urdu and English. It pains me to see our regional languages dying all because of a misguided notion that English is somehow superior, that knowing how to speak this language sets you apart from everyone else.

Unfortunately, this issue isn't just prevalent in Pakistan, but also in India and Bangladesh, or indeed, any country that was colonised in the past. Slowly and deliberately, I began to hide my roots, pretending that I wasn't from a Saraiki-speaking household at all just so I could fit in with the rest of my classmates. It wasn't until many years later that I realised how damaging that self-censorship was, and how much of my identity was snatched away from me. As a child of parents from Dera Ismail Khan and Multan, Saraiki ran in my blood, but I was too afraid to acknowledge it. As a matter of fact, I was constantly terrified of mispronouncing an Urdu word. I still remember the day when I called a wallet 'batua' in Saraiki instead of the usual Urdu pronunciation of 'batwa'. It was months before some of my classmates finally forgave me for this blunder.

Today, much of that has changed. I am proud of my roots, and I try my best to speak in my mother tongue whenever I can, but I also keep returning to the same question: why was this self-censorship necessary in the first place?

I don't have the answer to that yet, although what I do know is that for me, the censorship didn't just stop at language. As years progressed, I became aware of another longing in me, one that I was absolutely sure would be quashed, were I ever to voice it.

I thought I might one day be a writer.

Growing up, I had been an avid reader. I was one of those rare kids who preferred books over toys. In those days, there was just one big bookshop in Lahore that stocked international literature and that was Book Gallery (Now Variety Books). There, in shelves full of *Enid Blyton, Hardy Boys* and *Nancy Drew*, I felt like I was home. Even then, reading was considered to be a useless activity by many families in Pakistan. In fact, most of my classmates made fun of the fact that I liked to read. I was a quiet kid with little to do with anyone for most of the year, but suddenly I would become popular when exam season started. My classmates started coming up to me to get a condensed version of the assigned class reader. I lost track of the number of times I helped them, but while helping them, I also realised that I liked telling stories, and that's where my journey to being a writer began.

As I entered my twenties, another realisation dawned upon me. In Pakistan, most people only respected you if you were a doctor, engineer, banker, or a civil service officer. Even being a businessman at a young age was unacceptable as it implied you were being propped up by your father. You simply *had* to be involved in one of the professions listed above to command any respect in society. As for being a writer, or even contemplating to be one ... well, that was akin to professional suicide. I have lost count of the number of times I was grilled about my decision to write alongside my involvement in the family business.

'How much money will you earn?'

'Are you mad?'

'You are such a gifted young man. Why waste your considerable talents on something so useless?'

'If you're such a big writer, why isn't your book out yet?'

It was the last question in particular that really irked me. Nobody understood the long and gruelling process of getting published traditionally. They had no idea how hard it is to secure an agent, and then, a publisher. I genuinely believe that they expected me to produce a book like a magician produces a rabbit out of a hat. After a while, I stopped explaining and began censoring. I started telling people what they wanted to hear: I had put my writing career on hold and was focusing on 'real life'. The joy this statement brought for some people is hard to describe. It was as if they felt vindicated that I had finally capitulated and conformed to their idea of what a young man ought to do. In short, they were happy to see me as another sheep in the melee.

In Pakistan, when things get tough or unbearable, it is censorship that comes in handy. Just censoring certain aspects of your life from others brings sharp relief. However, unbeknownst to most people, I was still working on my writing, desperately trying to strengthen/improve upon my debut novel in order to find an agent and get published. Having said that, I do feel that it would be unfair to blame the people of Pakistan for holding such a pessimistic view of writing and publishing. The fact is that there is a dismal publishing industry in Pakistan. Let alone paying advances, publishers sometimes don't even pay royalties here. In Pakistan, getting published is like ticking something off your bucket list, or simply engaging in a hobby. Nobody takes publishing seriously, least of all the publishers.

'We published your book. What more do you want? Just hold it and be happy.'

That's the standard reply from a lot of publishers except the few that do follow industry guidelines. Most of the time, authors are hoodwinked into signing the most outlandish contracts with vanity publishers, effectively ensuring that most of the money that is generated will go to the publisher despite them having already taken money from the author to 'publish' the work. Therefore, most Pakistani authors have to look to either India or the West to get published. Sadly, even India isn't as open to Pakistani authors as it used to be due to the recent trade ban in place between the countries that prohibits any books from crossing the border.

A lot of people ask me why I seem to bloom when I am in London. Why is there a spring in my step, and a smile on my face when I am there—when neither smile nor spring are things you see on me often enough in Pakistan. The answer is quite simple: freedom. In London, I don't have to pretend. I can finally be myself, and be around people who appreciate me for who I am and what I have achieved. I no longer have to avoid talking about writing or publishing in case I offend the 'true' professionals of Pakistan; in London, there are thousands of people who are writers too, others who are aspiring writers and who are going through the same journey that I am. Many people in London are still "figuring it out" and they are rarely judged for being in that liminal position. Most of all, nobody in London asks me intrusive questions about how much I earn from my writing or how much I should be earning. I've never really interrogated anyone about their salary or how much money they've got saved up, but I don't know what it is about being a writer that encourages people—even some fellow creatives—to ask probing questions, and even if I try to avoid answering those questions, I am met with a solid wall of outrage.

How dare I not divulge my secrets? How dare I not tell people how many millions I am hiding in my bank account? I honestly don't know what is worse: telling the truth, or censoring myself yet again? Sometimes, I do a mixture of both. Most of the time, I am met with vague nods, the faces only perking up at the mention of actual numbers.

As I navigate my thirties in Pakistan, I have come to realise that my relationship with this country and its people is very complicated. While it is true that I seem to blossom in other countries, it is also true that I find myself unable to abandon Pakistan. Deep down, I love my country despite all its faults. Like any relationship in the world, there are good days and bad days, but that doesn't mean that the relationship is not worth investing in. In spite of having to self-censor most of the time, I find myself missing Lahore when I am abroad. I miss the distinct seasons the city offers; I miss the vibrant culture, the general wariness for all things—especially writing, the food, and most of all, family. Pakistan is the one place where one can never truly be alone. There was a time not so long ago when I was going through a rough patch, and the one thing that stands out from that time is how accessible my friends and family were. Impromptu ice creams plans, excuses to come to my place for dinner, friends and family insisting on inviting me over for meals in a way only Pakistanis can, people checking up on me every minute of every day... all of it reassured me that I was safe, that I was cared for, and most importantly, that I mattered. Sometimes, it was just that one glance from a friend, a smile from a relative and life would automatically feel easier. It was also the smell of the monsoon rains, the changing seasons, the fleeting winters that reminded me that change was always around the corner, that change was the only constant in life. In the hustle and bustle of Lahore, from the dusty pavements of the walled city to the squeaky cleanliness of posh DHA, I somehow found myself again.

Pakistan is home and will always be home no matter where I go. It is the place that truly anchors me and like many Pakistanis, it is the only place that truly feels safe—a place nobody can ever take from you.

Awais Khan is a graduate of the University of Western Ontario and Durham University and has studied creative writing with Faber Academy in London. He is the award-winning author of *Someone Like Her* (Orenda Books; Simon & Schuster, 2023), *No Honour* (Orenda Books, 2021) and *In The Company Of Strangers* (Hera Books, 2022; Simon & Schuster, 2019) and the forthcoming *In the Shadows of Love* (Hera Books, 2024). He has been longlisted for the Short Story Dagger and shortlisted for the Dead Good Reader Awards in the UK. He has also been on the judging panel for the Cheshire Novel Prize (2022) and Gwyl Crime Cymru Novel Prize (2021). He runs the Writing Institute, Pakistan's largest institution devoted to creative writing and he regularly appears on television and radio with his most recent appearance being a full-length programme produced by Paul Waters for BBC's In the Studio.

He is represented by Annette Crossland.

Instagram: @awaiskhanauthor
Website: www.awaiskhanauthor.com

My Home

Ruby Haider

At the very outset, dear reader, let me apprise you of the fact that there are two highly unlikely—you may even say implausible—protagonists, that constitute the substance of my sense of self and of the space that represents my home.

Of these two, you shall be meeting one earlier in this account and the second as we conclude it. But before I do that I want you to understand the essentials that shape my biopic and the backdrop against which this has played out. My own story is a multi-hued tapestry of diverse stories that both individually and collectively give me an identity whilst shaping the topography of the entity that is my home.

Whilst it is not exactly in the league of the stuff that legends are made of, my story derives its plot lines from the lives and times of the people whose existence intertwined with mine as we charted out our divergent, yet converging, courses through life. From my earliest memory, my sense of belonging, in essence, was consolidated and enriched by the kaleidoscopic mix of stories that I heard from my elders. An early awareness of my own place, in the larger scheme of things, provided me a context that served to ground me.

In our family there were stories everywhere providing us, in our growing years, much food for thought. Quite literally, food. This then, dear reader, is the *Eureka* moment where I reveal to you without further ado the enabler of my earliest consciousness of self and of place. Please meet my aforementioned first protagonist: The Family Dining Table.

I can fathom disbelief in your eyes, dear reader. You look sceptical. And I don't blame you for it. The dining table? A protagonist? Most people would look at this particular household appointment as ordinary furniture, no more. However, for me, especially in retrospect, it was an altar of shared experiences at which I lived and relived the highs and lows of the lives of those whom I loved and who loved me right back. I consider myself fortunate to come from a lineage whose members held stories of events that had impacted their lives and times as a sacrosanct legacy. To be related and passed on to the next generation. Consequently, mealtimes provided the pause to our elders to share with us these personal anecdotal nuggets. The dining table, thus, was my first school. The conversation around it was an ongoing source of information and learning. Additionally, we were treated to a most enriching exchange of humour and poetry and wit and ideas. Being at that table gave me an awareness of where I was coming from which knowledge is, in my thinking, vital to be able to know where you are going.

I have known and lived in many homes in my growing up and formative years. This was due to the fact that my father was a government servant who was stationed to discharge his official duties in many small towns and cities in the Northern Areas of Pakistan. Consequently, I had a most nomadic childhood. Every eighteen months or so, Aba (as we called our father) would get his marching orders and the household would be plunged into a frenzy of packing in order to uproot and to move.

My father's post as the Cantonment Executive Officer entitled him and thereby us, his family, to live in huge colonial bungalows. These imposing houses, a legacy of the Raj, had large sprawling compounds with lush green gardens and staff quarters. My mother was a proud homemaker and a consummate hostess. Her aesthetics reflected in the varied appointments of our diverse homes. She loved flowers, and each morning the gardeners would bring her fresh blooms from our own gardens that she would arrange with the utmost gentle touch and care in an array of vases lined up daily, for her choosing, by the domestics. It amazes me to think how she managed to convert each of those large, unfamiliar and rather intimidating houses into the warm and welcoming space that became our home where we were happy and safe.

Not for too long. Soon enough the news of my father's transfer would arrive and the oft-repeated process of packing up to leave begun. Carpets and furniture and art and crockery and linen and bedding and clothes and toys and most importantly, since both my parents and us kids were avid readers, our books would be packed neatly in wooden crates in an orderly chronological-by-name order. Large tin boxes were then carried and piled high into the waiting trucks. We were a family of dog lovers too so any of our beloved four-footed friends who happened to be in residence at the time would board the trucks and sit sprawled across the loaded luggage. My parents being most benevolent and generous employers had a retinue of loyal domestics, some of whom moved with us. Once the trucks were ready and the baggage had been secured with thick ropes, Aba asked us to get seated in the family car, mostly a station wagon, that he would drive himself. He would then take the lead and the convoy of trucks, complete with our appointments and adornments and pets and domestics, would move slowly but surely behind him as we headed out to newer frontiers. I think now that the retinue that we presented must have made quite an intimidating spectacle... somewhat on the lines of the great Mughal on the move. It was, as the poet says, a sight to dream of, not to tell.

So a new home every two years. A room with a different view. A new school. And there lies the rub since my growing up years, though idyllic, were marred by the fact that I was a fairly overweight child. Each new school was a renewed torment. Children, by nature, are honest and generally prone to call a spade a spade. I remember nervously entering the gates of my new school clutching my father's hand tightly. Often jeering cries taunting me for my weight followed us. This dismal state of affairs would persist till I wrote that essay in class that the teacher had me read aloud. Only then would my classmates look differently at me, as if I was suddenly much more than just a fat girl. They wanted to be my friends. I had been heard and I belonged.

Because my mother, Amma, was intrinsically a homemaker, our home remained our safe and happy place, no matter what geography it was situated in. Our dining table offered us food for the palate and also for thought. Along with their other stories, we also heard about my parents' pre and post-Partition lives.

I was fascinated by the thought of my mother as a young girl growing up in their ancestral family home, along with her four sisters and one brother, in the far off city of Lucknow. *Aiwan e Ahmedi,* as their home was called, was named for Ahmedi Begum, the imperious lady of the house and also my maternal grand mother. Their home ever resounded with the laughter and chatter of the hordes of cousins, aunts and uncles who were regular visitors.

Her marriage to my father took Amma away to the far-away scenic tea estate of Shillong in Assam. Here, her life took a completely different turn to her previous more sheltered existence. Shillong was a most exciting microcosm of the British way of life. Aba was a member of the Shillong Club and played Bridge there regularly. My mother was quick to join him in his interests and became an avid card player, though her game was mostly Rummy. She entertained their friends beautifully at home and her table elicited high praise. Her genteel Lucknow upbringing had instilled in her a most refined culinary sense which stood her in good stead. Her lifelong mantra repeated to the diverse cooks in her service was to cook food on low heat. The flame, for her, determined the taste of food. The lower the flame, the slower the process of cooking, enabling a higher release of aromatic juices of the raw edibles thus ensuring a more stellar quality of the cooked meal. Amma firmly believed that the doors of a home must always be open to welcome and entertain. She honoured relationships with family and friends, and they cared for her deeply in return. Since we moved homes so often, my parents had a different set of friends in each of their port of call. But wherever they went and whoever they befriended, my mother's table drew attention and appreciation. For Amma, food was much more than mere sustenance. It was an art form. An essential component of building strong ties and cementing lifelong relationships.

My parents got married in February 1947 and in August of that year the cataclysmic Partition of the subcontinent took place. My father opted for Pakistan and soon the newly wed young couple found itself on a train to Lahore. They could have been headed for Mars as far as my mother knew. There is a heartwarming anecdote about how she stood hopelessly lost and terrified in the tumultuous crowd at the Lahore Railway Station. A shy 21-year-old girl from Lucknow in her gharara that swept the platform and with her long lustrous hair in a plait that snaked down her back. She was bewildered and hopelessly lost. Her husband, my father, had told her to mind their suitcases while he went to look for a porter to help them carry their bags. As the minutes ticked away she felt more and more alone in this strange new place.

She was so terrified that she started to sob softly. She told us later that in that traumatised moment, she saw her guardian angel's gentle smile and kindly eyes even before he touched her on the arm softly. His turbaned head identified him as a Sikh, and having sensed her nervousness, he invited her to sit with his family as they waited for their train to Delhi. Lahore had been their forefathers' home, but they were now sadly constrained to leave it and to migrate to Delhi. They were as confused and lost about their bearings as she was, he told her. Somewhat reassured, she relaxed and happily shared their tiffin. My mother never forgot their kindness and the wholesome taste of their home cooked meal.

I sometimes feel that my mother's first foray into a strange new homeland was rendered less traumatic as the familiarity of shared food bonded total strangers on that noisy and clamorous platform.

Consequently, in all our different homes food occupied a prime position. We shared our hopes, fears and dreams around the dining table.

Our nomadic life exposed us to different sets of people. But wherever we made our home, my parents were quick to make good friends. Our homes saw quite a traffic of visitors on almost a daily basis. Depending on the time of the visit, they were either entertained with snacks for Elevenses, afternoon lunch or dinner at night. Much bonhomie and good fellowship prevailed, inculcating in us, even as children, a deep respect for the value of congenial social interaction especially on the home front.

I think I carried some of my parents' hospitable DNA to the home that I made together with my husband, Naseer, when we were married. As a young couple just starting out in life, we had guests over for a meal or to stay with us fairly regularly. My husband loved having friends and family over, as did I, and our home frequently resounded to the sound of good cheer and laughter.

I have been blessed to have lived in a number of happy homes as a child and to have made mine, after marriage, a happy place too. My three children had their school friends over constantly, and then cousins who came from different climes to spend their summer holidays with us. When that happened, mattresses of all shapes and sizes were pulled out, and our bedrooms looked like the crowded platforms of the railway stations in Pakistan where passengers often sleep on makeshift beddings as they wait for their trains.

This state of affairs often reminded me of what I had heard, again on various family dining tables, as a child about family members trickling in from India to Pakistan during Partition. The home of my eldest maternal uncle and aunt in Karachi became the destination for these displaced people till they found their place in the scheme of things. Apparently, the stoves in their kitchen were never put off as enormous amounts of food had to be prepared each day, twice a day, for the multitude. But through it all my uncle and aunt remained ever welcoming and warm, sharing their space generously. Their home came to be known as Hamari Manzil or Our Destination which it was... not only for those to whom it belonged but for all those lost people who streamed into a new country to start their lives afresh in 1947.

For me, my mother and her sisters were my golden girls, moms, aunts, friends all rolled up in one. My maternal uncle, their much loved only brother, pursued a distinguished and honorable diplomatic career in foreign lands but after retirement made his home in Karachi. Which brings me to the matter of my home.

And more importantly to introduce you, dear reader, to the second protagonist of my biopic. The vital throbbing backdrop of my home. Please give a rousing hand to my crazy, compassionate, ever giving, no place for the weak hearted, home to the brave city: Karachi.

My city, Karachi, is a sprawling cosmopolitan metropolis that is home to people from all parts of Pakistan. Karachi has a beat of its own and pulsates with the energy of its diverse population. My kitchen is a microcosm of the colourful fabric of this city. There is representation in it from Bengal, Sindh, Punjab along with Bano who identifies herself as a Muhajir. Their politics and languages differ and often loud arguments can be heard from the direction of the kitchen. But the heat subsides soon enough and harmony prevails as cups of tea are passed around to be sipped in mutual camaraderie.

Then there are those others who are called upon in case of household emergencies such as leaking pipelines, electrical short circuits or pest control etc. All these worthies are an integral part of the enablers of my home and hearth. An intrepid work force, these men are products of the underbelly of this city. They exhibit a certain bravado with a somewhat sassy approach to life and to all the unpredictable stuff that it throws at us. No challenge is too big for them to tackle in order to ensure the smooth workings of my houshold.

Nothing is impossible for them. Even under the most dire circumstances they operate under the slogan: Ho jaey ga, baji. Beyfikr ho jaein. Literally: It shall be done, sister. Worry not. And I don't!

I love everything that's Karachi. Its hustle bustle, its chaotic traffic, the enterprising entrepreneurs of its roads with their merchandise rocking on rickety wooden carts. I love the roadside eateries and the cheeky urchins who plaster their noses to the window of my car looking for a penny or two. I love the flower sellers and the women who sell me dusters to clean my home. I love what the young man who came to fix the airconditoner in my home said to me after one look at my malfunctioning machine: Baji, yeh Karachi hai. Yehan cheez chalti naheen, galtee hai. Lost in translation but nevertheless he said: Sister, this is Karachi. Here stuff doesn't work; it rusts.

Whatever it's shortcomings, I love my city unconditionally. Karachi is home. Its my happy place. When I lost my husband after almost four decades of a happy marriage, which in and by itself is no mean achievement, my children wanted me to move out from the home that Naseer and I had made and shared. They felt that the memories of our times spent there together would be too painful for me.

I was then too dazed to put up any resistance. I promised them that I would look into the matter when I returned from my annual trip to New York. Six weeks later, I remember vividly landing at Karachi airport in the dead of the night and being driven home. I was apprehensive about entering my home all alone at that quiet hour. As Bano opened the door for me and I crossed the threshold, my home seemed to envelop me in its warm, familiar embrace. I knew then clearly that a house may be built of brick and mortar, but a home can only be made with love. With lasting relationships and all the laughter and tears that the homesteaders have shared together over time.

My home welcomed me on that dark night as I stood at its door to enter it and I knew in my heart then that this was where I belonged.

As I go on in life, I know that my home shall continue to be the stage where memories are made. Together with my family and friends, I shall celebrate life here. My home shall continue to bear witness to my own stories as I share these and pass them on to all those who care to listen.

Epilogue:

I am sitting propped up by pillows on my bed as I write this. It's a mellow afternoon and a soft breeze blows in gently from the open window of my bedroom. The dappled rays of the sun fall on my dressing table, dancing across the framed photographs of dearly beloved faces. Some no more with us.

I'm reminded of a black-and-white framed photograph of a young couple that travelled with us all across the country and found a place of honour in all the homes we lived in as children. The pretty young bride sits demurely with her heavily worked gharara spread around her in a semi-circle. Her handsome groom, in a white sharkskin formal long coat, stands proudly behind her. On the lower right-hand corner of the now faded photo is the photographer's name, along with the place and date of the image. The inscription reads: *C. Mull. Lucknow. February 6, 1947.* This then is the source. For me this is the beginning of that precious space that I would call my home.

Born into a family where a love of both Urdu and English literature abounded, **Ruby Haider** developed early a keen appreciation for the beauty of the oral and written tradition in these two languages. Poetry, drama, banter, wit and humour... Her growing-up years were shaped by a daily nourishing dose of these forms of creative expression.

Her Facebook page identifies her as: Dreamer. Writer. Idealist. She loves to write. The canvas of her writing is her own life and everyday experiences. Ordinary things move her deeply, and she writes about these. However, the growing constituency of her readership convinces her that there is a beauty about the ordinary that renders it extraordinary. You just have to look for it!

A Story Of State Apathy And Citizens' Resilience

Zebaish Raza Cheema

My journey of patriotism, over the course of time, has transformed from being an ignorant, blind patriot to a well-informed, constructive patriot. Patriotism is the feeling of love, devotion, and attachment to a person's country of birth, and it manifests itself in different forms throughout an individual's life. Blind patriotism equates to irrational, unthinking support for the government, while its practices do more harm than good for the people. Constructive patriotism promotes positive practices and critiques negative ones to curb them and create positive outcomes. The version of patriotism a person believes in at a given point is a product of the biased or unbiased information fed or imparted from different sources and the level of critical thinking that an individual is capable of. Blind patriotism excessively upholds the dominance of a country's leaders and institutions while constructive patriotism advances the supremacy of people. My version of patriotism has now shifted from being institution-centric to being people-centric.

My primary purpose for writing this piece is to underscore the stories of perseverance of my fellow Pakistanis while highlighting the bitter reality of political precariousness in the country. Political uncertainty in a democratic country arises when 5-year plans are seldomly executed in their entirety, with successive governments often discontinuing the former government's programmes without solid justifications and out of political rivalries. The focus then of the government is not on the cardinal job of people's development (which demands long-term, comprehensive planning) but on flashy and hollow short-term initiatives (which would get them re-elected in the next term). Interference of non-political and non-state actors also intensifies this uncertainty. Pakistan is generally considered a politically uncertain country where the agenda of people's development predominantly exists only on policy papers with little to no practicality. In such a politically precarious environment, people's perseverance-filled stories mostly die out before being fully blossomed.

As a kid, I used to feel everything was hunky-dory in Pakistan after watching and listening to the state news TV channel with my grandfather and father. However, the contrasting commentary on current affairs done side-by-side by my father and grandfather, while watching the cleansed version of the news, always put me in a fix. In the 1990s and early 2000s, there was an absence of social media and the presence of an overly sanitised, grossly misleading version of school textbooks and state media. As per what people were indoctrinated with through media, for me, the two biggest enemies of Pakistan were quite evidently India, for the state's security, and oddly enough, cotton bollworm (colloquially known as *American Sundi*), for the cotton producers. The 9 PM news on state television promulgated about the dangers of these two enemies quite consistently. But now, I feel the two biggest enemies of the country are its myopic, megalomanic rulers, and law-breaking citizens. Truth be told, the country's enemies are more inside than outside.

Growing up and not knowing any better, there was a time when I used to think of Pakistan's flag as being the tallest in the world. For me, the possibility of Pakistan having the tallest flag was synonymous with it advancing in every field in comparison to other countries. I remember, as a kid, stating this fact extremely confidently and with pride on a lunch table full of cousins from different age groups, whilst they all laughed at me for this absurdity. I must have overheard a discussion on TV or taken the lyrics of a patriotic song literally, leading me into this false belief of Pakistan being at the top of its game.

As an adult, with all the information with which I can create an informed perspective of patriotism, I would characterise my patriotic feelings as bittersweet as opposed to swelling with pride, the latter being the case as a child. The imbalance in civil-military and judicial relations has brought Pakistan down many times, internally in front of its people, and externally in front of the international community. The ruling junta not being able to find, or rather not wanting to find, a sweet spot where the interests of the country, its people, and the ruling elite are aligned, has dispirited the country's inhabitants who wish for its prosperity. In contrast, the resilience of my compatriots takes the edge off the incompetence of the rulers, who find a way, in the face of all the adversities, to weather the storms coming their way.

Pakistanis create their own ways out in situations where the institutions and systems do not support them. With Pakistan's current unemployment rate at 6.3 percent as per the Economic Survey of Pakistan (2023–24)[1], inflation at double-digits for the last couple of months, and constant exchange rate fluctuations, around 3 million people have shifted towards freelancing to make ends meet. There are countless other examples where Pakistanis stood up for themselves where the government should have given them a leg up. Where the rulers diminish the passion of my patriotism, in the same way, my fellow countrymen's courage-filled success stories restore my faith in the future of my country.

I am not, by any means, claiming that only my countrymen have talents of different sorts or have a distinguished ability to bounce

---

1   (2024). Pakistan ECONOMIC SURVEY 2023-24. In *www.finance.gov.pk*. Economic Adviser's Wing, Finance Division, Government of Pakistan. https://finance.gov.pk/survey/chapter_24/Economic_Survey_2023_24.pdf (p. xii)
The Pakistan Economic Survey 2023-24 states, "According to the Labour Force Survey (LFS) 2020-21, the unemployment rate is 6.3 percent."

back from challenging situations. People belonging to other nations definitely have these qualities as well. However, being resilient when the state and its institutions devise user-friendly, supportive, and uplifting structures and policies for its people is a different ballgame compared to people who have no choice other than being resilient because the state has insignificant interest in facilitating its citizens. The Pakistan Hockey Team qualified for the finals of the 2024 International Sultan Azlan Shah Cup solely on their own talent, without any help from the government or the Pakistan Hockey Federation. The irony is that hockey is Pakistan's national sport. The players carried the ball by taking part in international leagues and paved their way towards this tournament.

Speaking of hockey, Pakistan won its last Olympic gold medal in hockey in 1984. After 40 long years, the country won another. The quintessential resilience of the Pakistani nation reached its pinnacle when Arshad Nadeem, a 27-year-old javelin throw athlete from Mian Channu (a small city in Southern Punjab), won Pakistan's first individual gold medal on 8th August in the Paris Olympics 2024. It was not only a gold medal win for the country, but Arshad's legendary javelin throw at 92.97 meters created a new world record. Arshad is a construction worker's son with no major public or private sector support. He used to train with makeshift tools at home. Financially, only his family and neighbourhood supported him in this arduous journey, including arranging funds for him to buy an international-level javelin just 5 months before the Paris Olympics. On 8th August, the whole nation was awake, Googling the javelin throw's rules (as Pakistanis are a cricket-obsessed country) and praying for Arshad. Arshad hugging his coach and physician teary-eyed after winning was a sight for sore eyes. Arshad's countrymen's hearts swelled with pride when a Pakistani athlete stood on the Olympic podium after 40 years, becoming the reason Pakistan's national anthem played in front of the world.

Arshad had the will, so he created his way. But how many people in Pakistan would have the financial, physical, and mental capacities to opt for this sort of uphill battle to attain their goals? So, the next logical question becomes: why is *creating ways for personal passions and collective benefits'* often a tough row to hoe for an average Pakistani?

To offer some perspective, allow me to delineate the country's origin and the ensuing political ineffectiveness. Pakistan gained freedom from the British colonial powers in 1947 to exist as a democratic country, but it faced around thirty-four years of military dictatorship. The rest of the years are popularly regarded as hybrid rather than purely democratic. There are many reasons the Pakistan military wields such intimidating power over the country. The administrative structures of the Pakistani military were inherited from the British. British generals headed Pakistan's military until 1951. After that, the authority was transferred to the first native Pakistani military general, also the country's first military dictator. Pakistan also has complex, quarrelling neighbours in the east and northwest. The British pulled out of the subcontinent in 1947 in haste due to the economic difficulties caused by WWII. As a result not all stakeholders were involved in determining the crucial geographical demarcations involving the borders Pakistan shared with its eastern and northwestern neighbours. Pakistan and India have fought three wars in which the Pakistani military defended the country. The odds were in favour of going to war in 2019 too, but things calmed down before escalating to a menacing level.

On the political front, the leaders left with the humongous task of leading a country after the founders of the nascent state passed away had inadequate political training. The country's first constitution was passed in 1956, nine years after its creation. Our leaders lacked political vision and steadfastness. Moreover, they were controlled by their selfish desire to accumulate as much wealth and power as they could at the expense of the country's development. There were also periodic racial and provincial skirmishes where the politicians and bureaucracy of one province wanted to dominate the rest. In 1971, East Pakistan separated and formed a new country, Bangladesh, a result of the selfishness of politicians and the military's domineering involvement in the internal affairs of Pakistan since its inception. Pakistan turned seventy-seven years old on 14th August 2024. In all these years, not one elected and democratic government was able to complete its 5-year constitutional term. Pakistan is brimming with stories of resilience, but on account of its political and economic instability, those feats of courage never get the commercial and state-level recognition they deserve.

33-year-old Islamabad-based Faizan Sameer, a lone football warrior in a cricket-fanatic country, wants to hear the Pakistani National Anthem play in the Football World Cup. Faizan is the only Pakistani UEFA (the Union of European Football Associations) Academy Graduate with a distinction in Football Management. He has been involved with football for the last fifteen years, including serving as a football coach for a futsal team sponsored by the Pakistani real estate company Eighteen as a part of their CSR initiative. Faizan, as a coach, spearheaded his team's win in a couple of national tournaments, but this was not enough for him. He wanted his passion and expertise to help aspiring football players in Pakistan, so he took the self-funded course with the UEFA Academy equipping administrators, players, and specialists to further their careers in a range of football-related activities. The UEFA experience led him to create the Football Academy in Islamabad promoting grassroots-level football among youth, especially women. Primarily, the Football Academy is financially supporting itself. It is the first academy and club from Pakistan to get an invitation from a top European club, Borussia Dortmund to attend their renowned 12-day training in Germany as part of their youth development program.

Lyari, one of the oldest settlements in Karachi, is regarded as "Mini-Brazil." It is a famous saying that every Lyari child starts playing football from childhood. Football is in the blood of the people of Lyari. Before the Fall of Dhaka (1971), professional clubs in East Pakistan (now Bangladesh) used to train and hire footballers from Lyari. The majority of the national team's players at the time were from Lyari. After Bangladesh's creation, this number significantly reduced. The Pakistan Football Federation (PFF) has been in place since 1947, but it has not developed its structures and policies for passionate individuals like Faizan and football fanatics in Lyari, who all want Pakistan to make a mark in the football world. FIFA, football's governing body, has also suspended PFF two times in the last decade due to undue third-party interference.[2]

On the subject of sports, a Pakistani making the rounds in the global e-sports community is Arslan Siddique, widely known as Arslan Ash. Arslan is a 28-year-old, Lahore-based Fighting Games player. He is the 5-time winner of EVO (Evolution Championship Series), the biggest fighting game tournament in the world. He is a 4-time EVO champion of the Tekken 7 video game—a feat no other player in the world has ever accomplished—and a 1-time EVO winner of Tekken 8. With the EVO win in 2023, along with winning the EVO Japan and Tekken World Tour Finals titles in Tekken 7's final year, Arslan became the only triple-crown champion in the game's history.

After winning the finals of a tournament held in Karachi in 2012, Arslan was supposed to go to Korea, but the organisers misappropriated the funds. Arslan was robbed of his first rightful international gaming exposure and couldn't compete internationally till 2018 due to inadequate funds. Six years of his prime gaming life were wasted because the government did not recognise e-sports' future potential and Arslan's talents. He proved his mettle and started getting international sponsors, including his current sponsors, Twisted Minds—a Saudi Arabian e-sports organisation—and Red Bull e-sports. For someone who put Pakistan on the international e-sports stage, these sponsorships should have come from within the country.

Arslan single-handedly created the e-sports category in the Pakistan sports industry. He is an undisputed Tekken king and

<hr>

2   Wasim, U. (2024, May 12). FIFA'S FOUL ON PAKISTAN FOOTBALL. *Dawn*. https://www.dawn.com/news/1833021

belongs to a billion-dollar e-sports industry expected to grow by 7.10 percent in the next four years, concluding in a market volume of US$5.7 billion in 2028.[3] There are said to be innumerable talented, budding gamers in Pakistan. In spite of all this, Pakistan still does not have an esports federation to regularise the process and help gamers with visa issues. Interestingly, Arslan also got an offer from Japan to go and live there that he denied. He is running his own gaming company, Ashes Gaming, to provide a platform to upcoming gamers in Pakistan—he wants to give back to the community.

According to the World Bank, the poverty rate in Pakistan is expected to remain at 40 percent through FY 2024–FY 2026.[4] Public sector schooling has been in a shabby condition, with an abundance of ghost schools for many years now. Sadly, the state has taken no initiative to resolve this issue. In these conditions, most children from impoverished backgrounds, if and ever they attend schools, cannot have quality education, and the cycle of poverty continues. Shahzad Roy is an icon for Pakistani millennials like myself. He is a celebrated pop singer and, most notably, an education transformist. He founded Zindagi Trust, a charity-driven initiative started in 2003, aiming to reform government schools into model institutions for the government to replicate, delivering quality education with a comprehensive approach.

According to the Economic Survey of Pakistan (2023-24), the national literacy rate is 62.8 percent. The National Education Policy (2017) by the Ministry of Education, Pakistan, defines a literate person as somebody with the ability to read and write a simple paragraph with understanding in any language and can do basic mathematical calculations. By this definition, if the literacy rate is 62.8 percent, then it is exaggerated. This definition of a literate person today is simplistic and reeks of mediocrity, not even

---

3   Sahu, H. (2024, January 16). The Global Esports Market: A Booming Arena with Stellar Growth. *Medium.* https://medium.com/@hritikasahu/the-global-esports-market-a-booming-arena-with-stellar-growth-226baf7c6e6f

4   (2024, April 2). World Bank expects 40% poverty rate to persist in Pakistan through FY24–26. *Mettis Global.* https://mettisglobal.news/world-bank-expects-40-poverty-rate-to-persist-in-pakistan-through-fy24-26/

touching upon the importance of literature, science, and critical thinking and analysis. If the aim of literacy is only to read and write an uncomplicated paragraph and do straightforward mathematical calculations, then Pakistan will keep churning out individuals with little to no critical thinking skills, empathy, and innovation. It is possibly one of the reasons why Pakistan has only one Nobel Prize holder in its history.

Zindagi Trust adopted two Karachi-based government schools in 2007 and 2015. The Trust renovated the schools' infrastructure and environment to make them conducive to learning. They focused on improving school governance, developing teachers, and changing outdated teaching practices. The Trust blended academics with extracurriculars such as chess, arts, music, and sports. As a result of these reforms, students produced distinguishable academic results from before the schools' adoption. It seems that Shahzad Roy's vision is to first redefine literacy in Pakistan according to modern world standards and then make a blueprint to reach there.

Give a man a fish, and you feed him for a day. Teach a man to fish, and you feed him for a lifetime. Sehrish Khan, the founder of the charity-driven Fareezah School, Rawalpindi, is teaching the underprivileged people around her to fish. As per the Economic Survey of Pakistan (2023-24), there are 32 percent out-of-school children in the country due to financial constraints. Having observed this in her house help's children, Sehrish first admitted them to a private school, paying their fee. After a while, she noticed that, having gone to a school for the first time, that too a private one, they could not keep up with the classroom's environment and requirements. As a result, they started being absent habitually. Sehrish then decided to open her own charity-driven school in 2016 from her courtyard, with just three students. Slowly and gradually, she rented out a space and is now close to changing the lives of 240 students with the help of fifteen teachers and support staff. Fareezah School provides free education, books, and copies to students up until grade 4, ensuring academic foundations are up to par. They are then admitted to government schools with minimal fees so that they can continue their educational journey with confidence.

With few resources and minimal support that Shahzad Roy's Zindagi Trust and Sehrish Khan's Fareezah School currently have, it would take time to scale Zindagi Trust to reach more public schools and Fareezah School to reach more deserving children. These are just two examples, but there are countless other Pakistanis working in the education sector. If Pakistan's Ministry of Education can join hands with individuals like Shahzad and Sehrish, it is definitely possible to improve the country's educational standards in the coming years. However, the public-private partnerships (PPPs) in Pakistan present their own perils. To name a few, unstable governments, changing policies, excessive red tape, and rigid regulatory frameworks make PPPs unworkable in the long run.

Pakistan suffered one of the worst floods in its history in July and August of 2022. During those floods, one-third of the country was underwater, affecting 33 million people in the already vulnerable 90 districts of the provinces of Sindh and Balochistan. More than 1,700 people lost their lives. Having followed the news in those months during and after the floods, I can only remember the tangible relief work done by Hadiqa Kiani and, regrettably, not by the federal or any provincial government. Hadiqa is a popular singer and philanthropist. She, under the umbrella of her charity organization, Vaseela-e-Raah, constructed 370 houses, two mosques, two maternity centers, one school, and one grocery store in Tambo and Kundi villages of the district, Naseerabad, Balochistan, in a year and handed them over to their rightful owners. She used to update her social media pages regularly about the progress and completion of relief activities.

Since around March 2022, Pakistan has been in political turmoil. The sitting government was sent home through a vote of no-confidence by the opposition parties in April 2022, who later formed a coalition government. Later in July 2022, when the floods were wreaking havoc in Pakistan, by-elections were held in Punjab, the most populous province of the country, with no significant concern shown towards the flood relief by the new government or the opposition. The new coalition government launched the Prime Minister Flood Relief Fund, the efficacy of which is alarmingly unknown. There were serious allegations of embezzlement of donations against the government-created relief fund. If an individual like Hadiqa, with a newly formed charity, could produce practical relief results with limited resources in a district in Balochistan, the state could and should have done much more in the rest of the affected districts with its vast supply of resources.

Article 38 of the Constitution of Pakistan is about the promotion of the social and economic well-being of the people.[5] This article sheds light on the state's welfare responsibility towards its citizens by raising their standard of living, providing them with facilities of work and livelihood within the country's available resources, giving them social security, social insurance, and basic necessities of life such as food, clothing, housing, education, and medical relief, all while reducing income disparity among the country's individuals. Despite being stated in the country's constitution, Pakistan, in all its seventy-seven years of existence, remains a welfare state only in theory only and not in actuality. Nonetheless, as Pakistanis, we always see some light at the end of the tunnel, and now I turn to another inspiring story.

A UN survey revealed that Pakistan is home to about 4.6 million orphans. The majority of these orphans are under the age of seventeen. Sophiya Warraich, a psychologist and philanthropist, along with her husband, Mehboob Aslam Lilla (DIG Police), founded the Almarah Foundation (a primarily self-funded, registered NGO), in Lahore in 2021. They care for orphaned, homeless, and unattended children in nine orphanage houses called *Apna Ghar*, as if they were their own children.

The mutual sense of ownership between Sophiya and Mehboob

5	(1973). THE CONSTITUTION OF THE ISLAMIC REPUBLIC OF PAKISTAN. In *www.na.gov.pk*. National Assembly of Pakistan. https://na.gov.pk/uploads/documents/1549886415_632.pdf (pp. 19–20) and the children in *Apna Ghar* makes this initiative distinct. Sophiya, in an interview, shared her experience of visiting different orphanages before founding her own. Regardless of all the facilities in those shelter homes, she could feel an overarching sense of deprivation in the children's demeanours, something children with nurturing parents do not experience usually. She made it a point to strive against it while founding her own shelter home. Children housed in *Apna Ghar* call Mehboob "papa" and Sophiya "mama."*Apna Ghar* also has child psychologists who look after the children's emotional needs and mental health.

In a span of three years, more than 220 children in the orphanage have been on their way towards a shining future. This is exactly something that the Pakistani citizens expect of the state, but it has not up until now made any voluminous provisions to parent the 4.6 million vulnerable underage population. If Sophiya can make her vision to parent orphans a reality, so can the state with all the means and capital to make this happen.

Consider a person thrown into the ocean with no lifeguards around to help. If he knows how to swim, he can survive. If he is not a swimmer, no matter how much he tries, the mighty water will bog him down. The circumstances of the majority population of Pakistan are synonymous with the person who cannot swim and has no lifeguards to count on. However, Usman Riaz, a 33-year-old Karachi-based Pakistani musician, animator, and filmmaker, is a swimmer and a survivor. He made history creating the country's first-ever 2D hand-animated film, called *The Glassworker*. It was released in cinemas on 26th July 2024 and earned Rs.30 million in revenue, remarkable for a 2D hand-animated Pakistani film. *The Glassworker* has been shortlisted as Pakistan's official submission for the Oscars 2025 in the categories of International Feature Film and Best Animated Feature Film. It was selected as one of eleven films at the Countrechamp official competition and screened in the Annecy International Animation Film Festival (France), the world's most prestigious animated film festival. The makers also had the honour to have *The Glassworker* screened at the Cannes Film Festival (France), Guadalajara International Film Festival (Mexico), Shanghai International Film Festival (China), and the Hiroshima International Animation Festival (Japan).

Usman shared in an interview that he was studying on full scholarship at the Berklee College of Music, but dropped out after three years to lay the foundation of Mano Animation Studios in Pakistan after raising $116,000 from Kickstarter, a global crowdfunding platform. Selected at twenty-one, Usman is also the youngest-ever Ted Fellow. While speaking at a TEDx conference in Japan, he was invited to the esteemed Studio Ghibli. After perusing his animation portfolio, professionals at the studio advised him to institute an animation studio, which he would need to make Pakistan's first hand-animated feature film. Usman created *The Glassworker's* pilot after the crowdfunding campaign, which helped him onboard international producers. The film was a labour of love in its purest form, and it took Usman ten years for his dream to see the light of day without any help from institutions or the government.

Talking about the firsts in the country's film industry, the Pakistani science-fiction fantasy film and box office hit, *Umro Ayyar – A New Beginning,* was released in June 2024. Its impressive visual effects (VFX) were all done locally by Jubilant Studios, Pakistan's first-ever visual effects company. For Hollywood or Bollywood, with the number of resources they have, this probably means nothing. However, for Pakistan to not outsource the VFX of a sci-fi film and do it locally is a moment of extreme pride.

On a hopeful edge, individuals like Usman and companies like Jubilant Studios amaze the world with their talent, but on the flip side, Pakistan's entertainment and film industry is still not formally recognised as an industry by any government of Pakistan. There is no concept of royalties for artists and creatives. Every now and then, news about the government funding the film industry circulates. Creatives in the industry were and are still waiting for these claims to be actualised.

When pinpointing the outrageous shortcomings of the rulers in derailing Pakistan, it is only fair to elucidate where citizens, too, cross their constitutional and moral limits—which is equally, if not more, perilous for the country. In the presence of rules and regulations, if a mob burns alive a member of a minority community on mere allegations of blasphemy or destroys public property during protests, then those Pakistani citizens are as much traitors as any ruler who sells the country's stake for personal gains. Having said that, unlawful citizens breed because of a state's mismatched priorities regarding its citizens and a lack of accountability by the state. It is in the hands of the state to ensure the implementation of laws.

Pakistani rulers and their citizens share an oxymoronic relationship in that they are poles apart in their preferred directions instead of working as a team. Commonly, the direction rulers take is to do the bare minimum to get elected again instead of drafting and implementing state-beneficial and people-friendly policies, while responsible citizens want to see their country economically, socially, and politically on par with others besides having a sustainable quality of life. Regardless of Pakistan being a democratic country, elected public representatives play second fiddle to military establishments, thus having negligible free will to take on independent policymaking and execution. This leads to economic challenges and lopsided inter-institutional relationships, causing a tonne of other issues such as corruption and nepotism.

Myth or not, it is common knowledge in Pakistan that during the 1960s, Pakistan International Airlines (PIA) helped set up Emirates Airlines, and South Korea crafted its five-year plans with the assistance of Pakistan's planning authorities. Everyone can see where the Emirates and South Korea stand and where Pakistan does. The odds are high that the professionals who might have aided Emirates or South Korea were similar to the underappreciated and underutilised stories featured in this piece, who unfruitfully waited for their due potential to be substantiated but lost in the race to nepotism and corruption. To sustain success and progress, consistent policies and strong political structures are needed, devoid of cronyism and monetary dishonesty. With political inefficiency in place, people's well-intended and self-supporting initiatives for the country's progress largely remain short-term, unscalable, and unsustainable.

In recent times, if anybody had doubts about the general public's supremacy over the governments, Sri Lankans in 2022 and Bangladeshis in 2024 categorically cleared those doubts by dethroning sitting governments no longer serving their interests. History suggests that revolts do not take place overnight. Years of simmering oppressions and suppressions trigger a nation to take individual and combined steps to correct the transgressional governing systems. It is only sensible that governments sense the tide of revolts beforehand and transform their ways before getting outnumbered by the mighty public.

The stories I put under the spotlight here are a tiny reflection of Pakistanis, whose voices mostly get muffled under the weight of narratives of extremism and injustices. Some people in these stories saw the suffering of their fellow Pakistanis and tried to ameliorate them, while others pursued their burning passion to create history. The reason they continue to spend their physical, intellectual, and financial energies on them is because they believe in their resilience. In a country with a victim mentality like Pakistan, where the blame-shifting tactic is ubiquitously employed, from the top brass to the grassroots-level, to shun responsibility for personal misdoings, these individuals are voluntarily taking up responsibilities and providing practical solutions to the never-ending problems. These are some underrated, unsung heroes doing their best in unlevelled state-created playing fields.

In Pakistan, blind patriotism corresponds to the worshipping of institutions and some self-serving individuals revered as deities. But respect is earned, not commanded. It is the people who form a nation, elect the rulers through the power of votes, and pay taxes to fuel and finance the state machinery. So, the only logical route is to give the citizens the power to hold the public office holders, who defect in their duties, accountable for their state-crippling and self-seeking policies and actions irrespective of the institutions they belong to. Rather, such defectors usually remain untouched, free of scrutiny and penalty—opposite of what should happen. More often than not, the public office holders in Pakistan paint a picture of entitlement and elitism—their job should be public service though, not the other way around. On top of that, the provision of tax-funded public amenities such as education, healthcare, accommodation, and transportation are often advertised as favours done for the public. Whereas, to have rightful facilities like schools, hospitals, housing, and public transport are inherently the right of the citizens that they can command and not the favour that keeps them indebted to the authorities. Democracy is a government *of the people, by the people,* and *for the people.* Constructive patriotism is the way forward for Pakistan, where people are educated about their rights and responsibilities and can critique the state's policies and actions to bring about positive change.

Zebaish Raza Cheema (*who was named by a well-known Urdu author, Mustansar Hussain Tarar*) is a Rawalpindi-based aspiring writer. She feels, as an introvert, expressing herself through writing comes more naturally. She is a business graduate and an HR professional currently making a segue into full-time copywriting. She enjoys writing on social issues, with seven of her non-fiction pieces getting published in different publications, including Dawn, The Express Tribune, and The Nation. She has also won two writing competitions: first place in the article writing competition on "*International Week of the Disappeared,*" organised by the Defence of Human Rights and Public Service Trust, Pakistan, and third place in the essay contest on "*China-Pakistan Friendship in My Eyes,*" organised by the Chinese Embassy in Pakistan. Her journey as a writer is a blend of online writing courses and her self-learning about this skill over time.

Facebook: @zebaish.raza.cheema

Islamabad, Ugly City

Dur e Aziz Amna

In 1997, Pakistan turned 50, and I turned 5. That's the age psychologists peg as the starting point of memory—a child's memory, that is; it is hazier to pinpoint when a nation's memory begins. Sure enough, one of my first conscious recollections is of being out and about on the evening of the 14th of August, 1997. It was not something we would have typically done. My parents were serious people living in a sleepy residential colony near Rawalpindi's Ayub Park; going gallivanting to the capital on a night when the 'loafer awam' hit the streets would have been out of the question. Luckily, my uncle was visiting. He was the Platonic ideal of the mamu as imagined by a five-year-old—charming, playful, in love with fast cars. That evening, he wanted to drive his fast car on Constitution Avenue, and so we went—he, my siblings, and I. What I remember the most is the din of horns and pocket trumpets, our car gridlocked alongside hundreds of others. I remember the lights of Constitution Avenue. What I don't remember too much is the haloed buildings themselves, those shining monuments to nation and state that flank both sides of the avenue.

Islamabad, as many have observed before me, is a strange place. A manufactured city. An inorganic city. The area on the foothills of the Margalla was flagged as the new nation's brand-new capital in 1958, then handed over to the imagination of the Greeks. Constantinos

Doxiadis and his firm of architects designed the city, and it officially became the capital in 1967. Looking through the project description on the website dedicated to Doxiadis's work, one reads that the city was modeled as "A City of the Future." It is easy, in 2024, to read this with a world-weary roll of the eye. That tired city of dharnas and barricades, tear gas and sealed streets? But imagine: it is the '50s and the country is new, so new, a newborn with the lanugo and blood of childbirth still visible on its skin. What would you want for it but to be an emblem of the future? Jan-e-istaqbal, indeed.

I am interested in the beginnings of things, the headiness of the blank canvas. Yes, I have read enough postcolonial theory to know that the canvas was never blank, that the newly free states of colonial Asia and Africa were riddled with baggage. Still, imagine being the intellectual elite of such a newly minted country, tasked with making a new world. To get to work on a constitution, a government, a whole new city. To be standing by the window that overlooked the dawn of history.

In neighboring India, Nehru, too, wanted the new. In 1959, he aligned himself squarely with the modernist movement in architecture, saying, "The past was good when it was the present, but you cannot bring it forward when the world has changed." The aim was to eschew the provincial and the ethnic in favor of a secular modernity. Attempts at indigeneity—references to the Mughals, or Hindu nationalist symbols, or the heritage of princely states— threatened to divide the massive new country. The famous modernist architect Le Corbusier was tasked with designing Chandigarh, a city Nehru declared to be a symbol "of an India unfettered by the traditions of the past." Pakistan, famously, has almost never been secular, already declaring itself an Islamic Republic in 1956, and yet, it is clear in the design of Islamabad that the attempt, just like in Chandigarh, just like in the modernist architect Mazharul Islam's Dhaka, was at the new. No Mughal promenades here, unlike in Lahore, where one arrives and is immediately swept up by the city's easy beauty, the eyes feasting on the domes and minars, the colonial-era buildings on both sides of Mall Road. The last time we were there, it was early spring, when Lahore is at its finest, the sky clear and the trees in bloom, and my husband, Portuguese by descent and thus susceptible to a certain strain of orientalism, breathed a sigh and said, "Ah, now this is beauty." That's what we have been trained to think of as beautiful: classical, possibly European, certainly imperial. It is a far cry from Doxiadis's Islamabad, with its stark, white, federal buildings, its angular Supreme Court, the boxy cuts of the National Assembly. I argued with him that Islamabad's modernist architecture might be ugly, but it was intentionally ugly, which merited far more respect and dignity than the unintentional ugliness of, say, a replica of the Statue of Liberty in Bahria Town. He was unconvinced; hopefully, I can have more luck with the reader.

Part of it has to do with the way these buildings are used. The Shalimar Gardens, the Badshahi Masjid, and the fort in Lahore are accessible to ordinary citizens. In Islamabad, it is hard not to think of the imposing structures on Constitution Avenue as foreboding; the barbed wires, barricades, and gun-wielding guards are all intended to provoke that feeling. Why would the capital of a highly militarized state feel welcoming? *Mere mehboob kaheen aur mila kar mujhse*, wrote Sahir Ludhianvi, in his famous socialist takedown of the Taj Mahal as an emblem of imperial excesses, and not a suitable place for lovers to meet. There are certainly no lovers meeting on Constitution Avenue.

At the same time, from an architectural standpoint, Islamabad feels to me, in its unquestioning embrace of concrete and strict angles, in its impulse for the new, as deeply emblematic of modern South Asia. When I look at photos of Le Corbusier's Chandigarh or Mazharul's Dhaka, I feel a soft, gentle ache inside me. I recognize in them so many signs of Islamabad – modernist architecture, sometimes well-translated for the context, other times haphazard and out of place. These are the cities that were envisioned in the mottled dawn of Partition. They are true testaments to the post-colony, to that muddled oath of freedom and nationhood. The Mughals were great stylists; I'm not provocative or contrarian enough to suggest otherwise. But I look at the Badshahi Masjid and see easy, uncomplicated beauty, the way one sees a beautiful sunset over an ocean. When I see a modernist building flanked by the typical vegetation of South Asia—amaltas, shisham, kachnar—I see home.

Part of it is deeply personal—I grew up near Islamabad. More specifically, I grew up in Rawalpindi. About Pindi, the project description on Doxiadis's website says the following: "The existing town of Rawalpindi will perform the duties of a mother caring for her child, until the child is grown and becomes self-sufficient." Note, again, the themes of infancy and neonatality. Rawalpindi is not just Islamabad's less attractive cousin, as many visitors are wont to think. It is Dorian Gray's mirror, allowing and abetting Islamabad's beauty by providing necessary services and housing the millions of provincial migrants, like my parents, who arrive at the capital in search of livelihood.

But also, it feels to me that Pandit Nehru was right. *The past was good when it was the present*, he said. When we look at Mughal architecture and see it as origin, as our one, true heritage, we are pretending that a major encounter did not happen, that there was no fracture. We are gullibly imagining that there might be a way by which we reach into ourselves without going through Europe, when in fact, we have taken Europe and made it a subculture within ourselves, reimagining and superseding it.

In retrospect, so many of those dreams of early nationhood are dead. The utopic modernity that was going to lift everyone out of poverty and give them education and housing didn't pan out. It can feel like we are now in a different moment altogether, completely divorced from those early beginnings. But it is erroneous to think in that way. Pakistan has a problem of the archive—we are missing so much history and are trained often to be so deficient in history, that we're unable to see the connections that exist between the past and the present. We miss important continuities. Let me present one. In 1950, the average life expectancy in the country was 31; today it hovers around 67. There is a thread that connects those early moments of nationhood, of a state struggling to stand up on its feet, to today. We have so much further to go, and yet, in the constant din of news headlines that present everything as unprecedented, we forget how far we have come still. We forget, also, how young we are.

Whether we look back to early nationhood with nostalgia or with derision, it still feels important to consider the modernist monuments that were made in service of those dreams. It is time that we took the seriousness with which we treat pre-Partition buildings, whether they be Mughal forts or colonial-era rest houses, and train it towards the modernist architecture that is now an essential part of our history.

Dur e Aziz Amna is the author of American Fever, winner of the APALA and SABA Awards. Her work also appears in the New York Times, Aljazeera, the Financial Times, and in several anthologies. She is a graduate of Yale College and the Helen Zell Writers' Program.

Website: www.dureazizamna.com

Where Stars Are
Born Out Of Anarchy

Saba Karim Khan

It's approximately 8:55 PM, somewhere between Karachi and Abu Dhabi. I'm on an Etihad Airways flight on my way home; or perhaps I am returning from home? Karachi's signature, effervescent lights sparkle just as visibly at take-off as they do when landing—a familiar reminder of where it all began, and where some of it has recently, and quite abruptly, ended.

As the aircraft takes flight and the glow of the city's exterior begins to dim, I am hit hard by the realisation that this piece—demanding raw and visceral conjurations—will not be an easy one to write. I never intended to tell this story, but that was before the events that transpired, leaving me broken, empty, rudderless, battling that glint of desperation which often accompanies sudden tragedy.

On April 13th, 2024, a phone call at 3:35 AM knifed through the night all the way from Karachi to Abu Dhabi, breaking news that my mother had passed away peacefully in her sleep. More than a decade and a half ago, my father had thrust a similar surprise upon us, and so, when pieced together, the entire affair, sudden and irreversible, felt hard to rationalise. Sometime later, as I put pen to paper, it still feels imbalanced and undeserved, but then, I ask myself, is there really a good time for a parent to die?

Prior to any of this, I would have struggled to imagine a moment, or a series of moments, that could feel more devastating than the abrupt loss of our father. Twenty-five years old and still at college had felt too young to lose anyone, let alone a parent, and that memory, hauntingly real, still lingers. But despite being older now, the passing of a *second* parent—and that too with disquieting efficiency and almost clinical precision—is a different kettle of fish. Many of those she loved dearly were there in those final moments. There was no pain or prolonged suffering; she wasn't dependent on anyone, just as she had always wished for, and as my brother put it, no chapter of her life was left unfinished—except no one had been expecting anything remotely similar to happen, so this kind of shock severely stung.

For a while, life became a blur, even though I immediately returned to work in a desperate attempt to revert to some sort of routine and positive distraction. But in the initial days I was weighed down by a constant longing and load. Having lived in different countries, my mother and I primarily interacted via phone calls and WhatsApp messages, or her visits to us and ours to her. Photos and updates of every mundane occurrence in real time, especially of the children; endless conversations on the drive to and from work; recipes exchanged in the kitchen; tons of advice-seeking; and most of all, asking her to pray for something or the other—a book talk, some tiny ailment, a presentation at Yousaf's work, or gymnastics performances. The list was endless and she was invested in every bit of our lives.

A few weeks had to pass before I could muster up the courage to reopen the notes for this anthology that I had penned before my mother's passing. Amongst other stream-of-consciousness reflections, I could see how I had scribbled a bunch of intrusive thoughts when thinking about my complex relationship with Pakistan, untidy "what ifs" penciled all over:

"Fear#1: Yousaf's kidnapping—fear of being put on-the-run";

"Fear#2: And then I became a parent... exacerbating my fears of being on the inside and outside, at once";

"Fear#3: will my children speak or at least understand the language, will they spend afternoons with their grandparents?";

But then... this:

"Fear #4: will the phone ring in the middle of the night? Will I be infused with guilt, even if it's too late?"

As I reread these incoherent scrawlings, my mind wanders to the phone call about my mother's passing from some nights ago, and I am struck by several painful prospects: had I manifested something dreadful, or had there been lingering paranoia of some sort, or were we plain unlucky to lose both parents without warning? But among these frantic thoughts, one epiphany prevails: perhaps fear #4 is the identical fear that every child living far away has, about the phone flashing at an hour when it shouldn't, harbouring all sorts of potential news, the kind we don't want to receive. Like gypsies and nomads, we migrants, expats, overseas Pakistanis—call us what you will—spend our lives torn in two, staying awake in anticipation of news, and often times, in dread of it.

Pakistan, for me, was largely synonymous with my mother, who refused to live in any other country, with a stubbornness that we siblings often found frustrating. The echoes of the house help continuously interrupting our phone conversations, the dhobi requiring some weekly hisaab, the fragmented Wi-Fi connection forcing me to piece her words and make sense of them, her hurried instructions to Mona (who had been cooking with her for over three decades) to wrap up before the gas finishes, her incessant inquiring about what we wanted to eat the day we would land, and of course, her unmatchable expression upon the arrival of her children and grandchildren back "home."

For a long time, the place and the person had seemed difficult to disentangle. However, in the early hours of that obscure Saturday morning, much that I had taken for granted appeared to have altered. I was bereft of my best friend. I felt like a child whose toy had been snatched from them in front of their eyes, with no way of retrieving it. In such a scenario, this piece couldn't stay the same either, for as I sat down to write it, I felt my life reshuffle. The person who had been most invested in our lives, and in Pakistan, was no longer there. Most of all, my mind was now clouded by the question that, with Ammi gone, would Pakistan, too, become a different place for me, shoved into memory, a thing of the past?

———————

A Karachiite without a story is almost as rare or absurd as *Waiting for Godot* had felt, the very first time I read it. Perspective, on the other hand—be that about the country, about differing worldviews, or about kindness—appears to be less common.

Put another way, you'd struggle to meet a Karachiite who doesn't have a tale to tell.

This is *one* of mine.

I have a sharply etched memory from the first winter after I got married, January 30th perhaps. The evening breeze was nimble, a sedate storm rising in the dark skies. I was taking turns spreading saffron rice and exchanging jokes on the family WhatsApp group, preparing to set off for a theatrical premiere at Anwar Maqsood's house after Yousaf, my husband, returned from work.

The hours ticked by, sluggish at first, then painstakingly fast—faster still. I waited for him, lingered some more, then waited for news about him from somewhere, my mind fearing the worst; most days, Karachi was chock-full of news. Eventually, nightfall was upon us, a queer mix of fantasy and fear.

I kept thinking, maybe "no news" meant "good news", then peered out from the balcony. It was the same sooty spot where we'd clicked spur-of-the-moment photos that morning, staring at the garden beneath, which had been bustling with Sufi music and visitors, the night after our *nikkah*.

My mind wandered to the security guard downstairs, perched in his symmetrical cubby hole. He watched over our home through the glass windows of his grid quarter, a rifle slung over his slightly bent shoulder with what appeared to be nerve-wracking stoicism.

"Quick! Shut the gate", I'd hear the warning dribble off my husband's tongue every time our car swerved into the driveway. Most days, I'd smile, sometimes slyly, other times more daringly, mocking his excessive and relentless mistrust of our city. He was from Lahore, and I'd declared him "paranoid" at minimum—except, I would shortly be proven wrong.

Tonight, I exchanged niceties with the guard from my settled spot, a lop-sided grin, his tilted wave stoking the torched flame of a street lamp. I watched him soften my fear, reminding me that these, in fact, were extraordinary times; times filled with guns and bolts, where we must pass through metal detectors and be chaperoned by armed personnel everywhere.

Some more time had passed, and by now, I was running out of creative alibis that might rationalise Yousaf's disappearance. My husband was responsible to a fault; I could count on my fingers the instances he hadn't answered my phone calls since I'd first met him. This prolonged, unexplained departure appeared to signal something else, something more sinister. Moreover, this was Karachi—a city that never sleeps, but where staying awake often came at a price.

With few options left, in the misty glow of that brisk winter evening, I set off in our car, tracking the route from our home to my husband's workplace, each lane measured with inch-wise precision, my eyes in frantic search for a smashed vehicle, some rubble and smoke, or fiery ambulance sirens—I was becoming desperate for clues that might help stitch the story to a sensible climax. The streets stayed mute, and at first I couldn't understand why, until it finally dawned upon me that there had been no accident. This is what Karachiites would call a story, in some cases, of last words spoken.

My husband had been abducted.

Six armed men had stalled Yousaf's car, just one traffic signal before the road curved towards our home. A couple of them got in the car whilst the others followed on their motorbikes, forcing him to dodge his car through crammed lanes and sleepy check-posts, through sea-ports smelling of polluted waters and produce, until eventually they crossed the bridge to arrive at a scribbled signboard: "Welcome to Lyari."

I don't have any recollection of Lyari. At that time, it was an edgy, erratic hotbed, riddled with gangs, gunpowder, and granite, but also street rappers, footballers, valiant boxers—Karachi's "no-go", wild, wild West. Later, Yousaf told me that his entry into Lyari was marked by a rolling down of the windows and gunshots fired into the air, as the car roughly pulled up outside a seedy, vertical structure, its roof reaching into the clouds, walls spray-painted in colourful slang, and dimly lit beams of light cascading from one of the windows above.

At first, he resisted, attempted to rustle and barter outside, only to be slammed in the face by one of the doped ring men with the butt of his gun; when I saw him later, a dark, blinking bruise decorated his upper-left cheek. The young fellas shoved him up a flight of narrow, pitch-black stairs, leading to a six-by-six cell. Purposefully, the key turned in its lock, and he was left to marinate for a while.

Some time passed before they returned and led him into a bigger cell, filled with the smell of Lyari's angst, sweat and hashish. His abductors had risen in number, now close to a dozen overgrown boys, revolvers readied, bound together by a common mission. They wanted information, networks, ransom—reporting a successful outcome to the ringleader would mean larger commissions for the sicarios.

From here on, the story takes a biblical turn, a valiant, epic tale of stardust best saved for another time. Ultimately, he escaped, calling me to offer news. It was a story, fortunately, of survival.

But the story remained incomplete, as did the boys' mission; the gunmen hadn't got what they were looking for, and so they continued to plague and hunt. They put us "on the run", forcing us to switch cell phones, zip codes, house help, cities, and finally, even countries.

For nights after the incident, I would lie awake, replaying the horror of that evening in my head. The not knowing, then partially knowing, and finally the agony of fully knowing what had happened and processing the accompanying trauma. Gradually the bottom-line became clear: although Yousaf had returned home that night, for years after, we would remain "on the run."

What's worse, while I wasn't sure what it was that we were

running from, the irony that we might have been running away from a place called "home," wasn't entirely lost on me.

I'm gazing at a row of sleek, mostly black SUVs, silhouetted against a glittering skyline. Matching the mood is the flash and fancy of solid, neutral-coloured silk dresses, paired alongside elegant, expensive designer handbags—Dubai appears to be a hungry, expansive food and music festival that never comes to an end. My eyes hover to the opposite side of the salt and water creek, packed with humming souks and quaint, nippy dhows, carrying cargo and passengers across the waterway. Old Dubai doesn't boast the avant-gardism of the inland city, but the movement of jetties and people, amidst the rising incense of spices and musk, offers a striking vibe. When people say that the Middle East is only glam, that's far from accurate. There's variety here, still. And for better or worse, Abu Dhabi, where we live, isn't quite Dubai.

More than once, I have heard someone say to us: "You are temporary people here," which inevitably leaves me with the question of: "are we getting too comfortable?" Nearly a decade and two small children later, a closet of threatening "what ifs" still seems to define our lives, in this home away from home. Foremost, the fragility and agonising volatility of our jobs makes it seem as though we are hanging by a thread. What if we are suddenly asked to pack up and leave this place? Then there are the incessant enquiries of others: "But where are you really from?" Endless reminders of our brownness, that we haven't been admitted to a club reserved for those with white privilege, which brings to mind a story. A few years ago, 2014 to be precise, I was on a plane about to depart at the runway, moving countries to start life in Qatar, when a headhunter rang me. He was inviting me to a job interview at a global firm in Doha, which got me excited, but there was the caveat that I'd join at half the pay a "white" candidate would get, and as long as I came equipped with that information, things should be fine. Of course, passport privilege kicks in, and let's face it, we "desis" aren't exactly at the top of the ladder.

Back to the closet of burdens. The accusations of expatsplaining, a term I became acquainted with a few years ago—if I live away from Pakistan, am I still entitled to pledge patriotism? If I am an "expat" or "immigrant" and happen to support Imran Khan, does that make me delusional? Am I under the eternal effect of rose-tinted glasses? It doesn't end there; a few years ago, X (then Twitter) chatrooms were on fire with debates about why Pakistani authors inevitably write about mangoes, mosques, and the damp smell of the earth after monsoons. Was there a voyeuristic nostalgia that those living outside Pakistan were indulging in? As a storyteller, it felt forbidding, raising questions of who can speak about whom, who can write about "home."I wondered if I should play it safe and stop naming people and places in my stories, for fear of exoticizing, offending and expatsplaining.

Once we became parents, it meant entering a whole new arena of being on the inside and outside at once, with endless questions popping up: will our children speak Urdu, albeit with a twisted accent, or at least understand it? Would they create precious bonds with their grandparents, love and respect them wholeheartedly, listen to stories from them, just like we did when we were kids? Will they cherish community and human relationships, the way some in Pakistan still do, in a world that is rapidly becoming individualistic and isolating? Will there be shame about their parents' country of birth, given what they hear about it in the news and with TikTok becoming a vital source of information? Will they truly experience the art and poetry of Pakistan, or will it feel like some giant, exotic social experiment when they visit? Above all, will they grow up to question entitlement and privilege, forge familial attachments with the house help as we did, learn that hospitality and kindness are in fact ways of life? Is it even possible to develop empathy in a place that mirrors Narnia in so many ways? Will they subscribe to any of those values that our parents so painstakingly passed on to us and which no amount of monetary reward could teach or compensate for?

Don't get me wrong, I like my life here. In fact, I like it a lot, and we are certainly no victims, but these are questions, provocations and qualms that often keep me up at night.

I already told you I haven't met anyone from Karachi without a story.

Stories of violence. Of dead bodies dumped in sacks, left to soil in a garbage dump, only to be unearthed days later; of protestors storming into my father's university classroom and forcing him to abandon class, because how dare we try to reflect, question, debate, and educate; of five-year-olds mastering the act of deftly ducking under their desk during bomb-drill role-play at school, because a real blast could happen any day.

Then there are stories of how the city has gradually withered away. I've seen it every monsoon season in headlines showing statistics of pedestrians being electrocuted or tumbling into an open manhole. I've also witnessed each New Year's Eve waning with dreadful data from street-fire celebrations. "So many dead," the newspapers announce the next day.

Each story screams some irreparable fright, some inconsolable loss.

Karachi invokes a kind of *Sin City*, yet my divided self, straddling these two worlds of Karachi and not Karachi, struggles to think of a single night I have slept in the Gulf without the dread of a phone call piercing through the night. I have been haunted by the inability to touch those who matter most, the probability of news about someone's untimely departure, devastating regret for having left my kin in the first place—those have been my fears, which eventually came to be realised.

Yet I wish I could remember the place where I was born differently—a place filled with both dreamers and dark blood, those in violent pursuit of their dreams, protagonists unafraid of color. *A place where stars are born out of anarchy.* Every once in a while, we stumble upon these stars, who have stripped open the boxes that they were born into, to say, "You know what, I have always been taught to downsize my dreams so that they fit my reality, but this time, I'm going to outsize my reality, so that it fits my dreams."

There are young boys and girls producing hip-hop music from the narrow, poisoned alleys of Gizri and Lyari. I've filmed some of them, and in the process seen the world where they live and create soul-stirring rhythms. There are female mountain climbers and bikers, painters, sketch-artists and footballers, thriving in these so-called "slums." I remember a cycle-wala who would sit on a street-corner and fix cycles in Karachi's Clifton neighbourhood, well into his 70s or 80s, even when he barely had his vision left. Most times when we passed by him, he would be steeped in prayer. What could he possibly be grateful for, I wondered?

And then of course, there's the story of Arshad Nadeem, a javelin player and Pakistan's first athletic Olympic gold medalist, who defied all odds to create a new Olympic record and have his country's national anthem played at the Paris Olympics in 2024. Nadeem is from Mian Channu and had minimal access to resources and funding. Yet, "to strive, to seek, to find, and not to yield", as Tennyson put it in his famous poem, *Ulysses*—that seemed to be Nadeem's motto. He never gave in to the cynicism, but rather chose to swim against the tide.

These stars still exist amidst the anarchy but are barely spoken of anymore. Instead, Karachi feels like snapped smokescreens. The famous Clifton Beach, its liquid, silver sand, now a dark delusion; colourful buses teeming with toppling wayfarers, sparkling *mazaars* and music, swallowed by beggars; hawkers and hashish-smoking addicts peddling the business of religion and fear, all in the fight for food. Is it true what people say about Pakistan on television, in newspapers? All of it? Is it one of the most dangerous countries in the world?

It leaves me bewildered: our mother goes for a couple of tests and the hospital bill is PKR 50,000. I fear for my children's safety when we are out on the streets at night. Socially, too, I struggle to fit in, to relate to some parts of the pretentious, cliquish, cancel-culture. In that sense, not much seems to have changed since my school days; there's judgment abound but little acceptance. I find myself asking where I fit in within this elite capture. I no longer know where I fit even within the feminist debate, with so much copy-pasting from the West. I fear I might get cancelled if I were to express myself differently.

Most people are well-intentioned here, but grief and well-being, the most universal of emotions, are also massively misunderstood. "How are you" is frequently but loosely asked and hardly anyone waits for a full response. Instead, we are hit with "move on," "stay strong," "get it together for your husband and girls," "why can't you just cry?" Not only are these hollow and hurtful recommendations to hear, but practically speaking, such advice is tactless and misplaced. As a Pakistani girl, you are not licensed to make it about yourself, even when profound tragedy strikes—I learned this the hard way. I don't see myself forwarding these particular clichés about how to handle grief, on to our daughters. There will be several other moments when they'll be expected to take a back seat, play second-fiddle and prioritise someone else's well-being over their own. The loss of a parent should be an exception to glorifying such martyrdom and selflessness.

But here's the twist about Pakistan: I see glimmers of hope too, stuck between the crevices. I see people riding in bright-red public buses to attend literature festivals in Karachi; most of the sessions are jam-packed, and there's a definite storybook vibe. When I visit Mithi, I get treatment that feels kinder than five-star service. The salesmen at Liberty Books conscientiously recommend titles to me, works that they seem to be deeply familiar with. It feels organic, this human touch, some sense of community and humanity that still prevails.

The paradox is mind-boggling. This is a place where you can source marijuana and liquor, but where people plunge into the tendency to judge others for not being Muslim enough or modest enough; where membership at Sindh Club or entry into Karachi Grammar School or Aitchison College is akin to attaining membership to the white privilege club. Yet, the same folks drowning in privilege sometimes treat their house help in sub-human ways. I, on the other hand, feel strangely linked to my mother's house help. They are part of my grieving process, almost as if they strengthen my connection to my mother. I want to desperately cling on to them. All of this makes me wonder what might have been the outcome if Pakistan hadn't been our starting point. What part of my birthplace do I want to pass on to our daughters and which troubled edges do I shed? I think of these things often. I'm still on the run, and I'm part of the problem.

Most will say, Pakistan feels as if it is imploding. It probably is, and I am tired of hearing that it is resilient. It now craves kindness and kin. This place, called home, needs to get its house in order—though I wonder if it'll happen during our lifetime.

———————

A few weeks after the loss of our mother, I return to Pakistan for the second time. The trip is as crucial as it is painful, evoking a treasure trove of memories that we had cultivated with her over decades. Entering through the doorway where she always waited to welcome us, mustering up grit to step into her vacant but otherwise unchanged room, sifting and sorting through items meticulously organised, now left behind—every moment rippling with her absence in this all-too familiar space—it feels like repeated stabs of pain. But strangely, the reminders also tie us back to her in an impossibly intimate way. At night, the house help sleeps with us in my mother's room; we stay awake, listening to the stories they share about her from the days gone by and it lends quiet comfort.

My exit from Karachi is perhaps the toughest part. I tug and caress my mother's bed and her pillow, unable to stop myself, staring at her blank room for what feels like a long time—it's as if I don't want to leave, as if leaving might take me further away from her. It makes me realise how love and grief are so inextricably linked—you can't want one without making room for the other. Before exiting the house, I write in her memory book and end by saying, "Ammi—you taught us so much, except how to go on without you." It's like a moth to a flame, knowing that getting too close can end up burning you, but I make that choice, and I get burnt. And I wouldn't have had it any other way.

On the way to the airport, my brother stops at the graveyard so we can visit Ammi's grave. I take our two small girls with me there for the first time. The graveyard feels tranquil, with leafy florals and tinted lanterns hovering over some of the graves, making me wonder if a graveyard could, in fact, be beautiful and strangely poetic. I stare at the tombstone for a while, say a small prayer, and soak in the reminder that this is how it all ends. Soon afterwards, we leave.

As we drive past Karachi's buses and buildings, shops and street hawkers, they remind me of how far I have wandered from my life here, and how long I have been grappling with the yearning to neatly fit in somewhere. Perhaps such is the illusion of home. Some circuits of connection, between the past and now, ignite my mind—a slow-burning grasp, a restlessness kindled, of being inside and outside, both at once. I think of our mother, of her unrelenting will to stay in Pakistan, of how in her story, it had always been the protagonist.

Upon boarding the flight back to Abu Dhabi, I realise I am slowly drifting away, leaving so much that matters so far behind. I might hold much in memory, but the visceral link feels severed. Corridors where I could trace the sound of my mother's footsteps; echoes of the cupboards she cleaned as we spoke on the phone; the graveyard and its lit-up lanterns; her tombstone with her favourite lines inscribed on it, "Que sera sera, whatever will be, will be"—all left behind. I am a migrant, after all, and some might say, this is a choice I've made.

I think of the number of times I have taken this exact flight, passed by the same tourist shops at Jinnah International Airport, purchased last-minute snacks from a place that accepts only cash, noticed and lamented that this time the airport bookshop has shut down, and how less than two hours past this, I'm always in another setting.

By now, we are seated on the plane, listening to ambient airplane music, routine cabin crew instructions about frequent flyer programs and oxygen masks. A few passengers seem to be fidgeting with their luggage; a baby gets restless and shrieks, then suddenly stops. It becomes quiet inside, except for the air-conditioning that blows gently. A little later, I write to my husband: tough trip but had to be done. The flight is on time. We're about to take off. He will be there in Abu Dhabi, dutifully waiting to receive us as he always is.

As the aircraft launches into the sky, Karachi's expansive landscape escaping into oblivion, I discern a shift within me. I wonder what my thoughts look like and how I might feel remembering this moment some years from now. Will I carry my "before" and "after" into every day, every milestone, and every holiday from now on, as Liz Newman put it? "'Before' is full of memories, time spent with you and an ache that it wasn't enough that I needed more to hold on to. 'After' is full of memories that should have had you in them, potential moments now painful reminders of 'what could have been.'"

Will time make it better, I wonder, help me learn to live without my mother, wield her memories into some sort of meaning-making? Will I dream about her? Is death really nothing at all, except that she's slipped into the room next door? Will I be able to go on in her absence, even though she didn't teach me how?

It hits me then, and the disruptive shift starts to make sense. I realise that this time it does feel different, that this return is unlike every other time that I have left my hometown in the past. It's as if this time, I also leave a part of me behind—a part which, I suspect, will keep calling me back. Keep reminding me that this place, Pakistan, where both our parents now lay buried, is indeed a place where stars are born out of anarchy. I must not forget that, and if anything, make sure our girls know it too.

Saba Karim Khan is an author, award-winning filmmaker and educator, who read Social Anthropology at the University of Oxford and works at NYU Abu Dhabi. Khan's debut novel, *Skyfall,* was published by Bloomsbury and she is a contributor to the anthology, *Ways of Being: Creative Non-fiction by Pakistani Women.* She is a columnist for Khaleej Times and her writing, interviews and talks have appeared in The Guardian, BBC, The Independent, the Emirates Literature Festival, Lahore Literary Festival, NYUAD Institute, Gulf News, The National, Wasafiri, Huff Post, Verso, LUMS, Think Progress, DAWN, The Friday Times and Express Tribune. Khan's doc-film, *Concrete Dreams: Some Roads Lead Home,* produced by the Doha Film Institute (DFI), secured official selections and won awards at film festivals in NYC, Paris, Berlin, Toronto, USA, Sweden and India. Before joining the Academy, Khan worked as Country Marketing and Corporate Affairs Head at Citigroup. Born in Karachi, she now lives in Abu Dhabi with her husband and two daughters.

Website: www.sabakarimkhan.com
Instagram: @saba.karim.khan

Acknowledgements

A book, as we know, does not come into being by the author's pen (or laptop) landing directly on to the reader's page. If ever there was an example of co-creation, it is storytelling, especially when it comes to an anthology with multiple contributors. To mark the culmination of this incredibly demanding but equally rewarding craft, there are several collaborators and cheerleaders to thank.

The first time I spoke with someone about Home #itscomplicated was with Ella Hussain, then Publishing Manager at Liberty Books, on a fine, bright February afternoon, near the line of book stalls at the Karachi Literature Festival. Ella's instant reaction to my crazy idea about unpacking Pakistan through the voices of more than just "book writers" felt affirming—I had a clinching suspicion that a ripe creative partnership was brewing. Thereon, Ella has been an indispensable force in making this anthology possible. Even before any formal paperwork had been signed with Liberty, she laid her trust in my literary pursuits, lent her time and ready advice about curation and basically made things happen! We need many more enablers in the publishing world like her.

To my workplace, NYU Abu Dhabi, I will always remain grateful. This publication was made possible by the generous support of the NYU Abu Dhabi Grants for Publication Program.

Acknowledgements

Some years ago, my dear friend Khaula (who is my go-to person for creative recommendations), pointed me to Samya Arif, an illustrator, visual artist and designer. Collaborating with Samya on the cover for Home #itscomplicated has been a real high-point of this project and full of terrific creative surprises. Not only is she an artistic genius but her ability to capture what I had in mind for the cover with such nuance, wit and aplomb, makes her a rare talent. Her illustrations made my vision for this anthology come to life.

Kanishka Gupta, my literary agent, friend and creative mentor, has walked this whole journey with me. The efforts by him and his eagle-eyed editing team have been crucial in polishing and tightening this collection. As was the case with my novel, Skyfall, K's team has given us a far superior anthology by the time they were done.

The partnership with Liberty Books has been invaluable in getting Home #itscomplicated across the line. Thank you to the entire publishing crew there who took a chance on this book and backed it all the way.

Amber, dear friend, creative counterpart and now entrepreneurial ally, stuck with me through countless conversations about this anthology. She's had a front-row view to the "making of" Home #itscomplicated, offering generous advice about contributors, titles, and more. It fills me with joy that I could convince Amber to write for this collection herself and what a poignant piece she has done!

Shama and Mustafa, thank you for your unconditional support towards any creative craziness I subject you to and for being so genuinely invested in this anthology, as was evident to me in multiple marathon conversations we had about it over dinner. It offers much relief to think that I had two ready readers for Home #itscomplicated, even before it was out in the world!

Ian and Anuja, I owe you much for being such steadfast friends and allies, for making such a big deal of Skyfall (and actually reading it!), which really spurred me to get started on the next book and above all, for rising to the occasion so generously when I needed you both during this particularly challenging last year.

In all my creative discussions (including about the book) with John O'Brien at NYU Abu Dhabi, he has always been most magnanimous in offering his time to listen. In fact, he was one of the first people I showed the cover to when it was finalised. At times that felt rough, isolating and unprecedented, John offered a real sense of community at work to help me realise this journey, reminding me that storytelling is an indispensable part of my purpose and identity.

The myth of women having it all is just that: a myth. If it wasn't for our house-help Fatima and Ayaz, who are family, and their relentless love and support, I doubt I could pursue purpose. By stepping up for our children and home needs, they have offered me the bandwidth to embark upon other missions alongside childcare. In their absence, I'd struggle to keep all these different balls in the air.

Chris, dear friend and cheerleader throughout this long and tough process, just thanking you will hardly suffice. More so than ever since my mother passed away, I have constantly relied on Chris's time with a mixed bag of needs: seeking him out for validations, as a sounding board and sharing every implausible project idea along the way, only to complain about being too scattered later on. Chris has listened and unconditionally shown up. In some very dark hours, his unstinting spirit and sincerity helped me to keep coming up for air, all the time despite his own insane schedule.

My siblings, Gohar and Farrukh, and their children and spouses, Omar and Amina, are now, even more than before, indispensable to my being and spirit. Just knowing of their presence is a source of solace and has helped me in remaining afloat with this anthology, among other things. I fall short of words to express my gratitude for how much they have stepped in after Ammi's passing.

Yousaf and our girls, Mahnoor and Mashal – gosh, I cannot imagine life without the three of you. Despite being so young, our daughters, their intuition and humour, have been vital to my sanity and survival whilst putting this collection together. As for Yousaf, I admire how comfortable he is in skin, which I see every time he so generously celebrates whatever I attempt to do. He never dissuades me from reaching for the stars.

Ultimately, I owe infinite gratitude to each and every contributor to this anthology. Without your willingness to share your stories, intimacies and vulnerabilities, Home #itscomplicated, could not have reached into the reader's hands. I shall always be indebted to you for joining me on this journey to open a window into Pakistan, which more often than not, remains deliberately shut.

I hope, hereon, the needle begins to move.

9 786277 626495